**Barbara Winton** was born in 1953, the daughter of Nicholas and Grete Winton.

Barbara shared Nicky's deep humanity, stubbornness, and determination to do the right thing, often in the face of difficulty and resistance.

She was passionate about preserving his story, and became a fervent campaigner, continuing his work to support child refugees.

As well as a campaigner and author, Barbara was a complementary therapist, amateur gardener, nature lover, and loving wife and mother. Her husband Steve and children Laurence and Holly continue the Sir Nicholas Winton Memorial Trust, created by Barbara, to ensure Nicky's story continues to inspire others to do good.

Photo courtesy of Monni Must

# One Life

*The True Story of Sir Nicholas Winton*

## BARBARA WINTON

ROBINSON

ROBINSON

First published in Great Britain in 2014 as *If It's Not Impossible* by Troubadour Publishing Limited

This edition published in Great Britain in 2024 as *One Life* by Robinson

1 3 5 7 9 10 8 6 4 2

A CIP catalogue record for this book
is available from the British Library.

ISBN: 978-1-47214-866-7

Typeset in Sabon by Hewer Text UK Ltd, Edinburgh
Printed and bound in Great Britain by Clays Ltd, Elcograf S.p.A.

Papers used by Robinson are from well-managed forests and other responsible sources.

MIX
Paper from
responsible sources
FSC® C104740

Robinson
An imprint of
Little, Brown Book Group
Carmelite House
50 Victoria Embankment
London EC4Y 0DZ

An Hachette UK Company
www.hachette.co.uk

www.littlebrown.co.uk

*To my father – of course – and to my mother,*
*who looked after us with love and devotion.*

*Finally, to all those who give of themselves*
*unreservedly to help others in need, without*
*any thought of reward or recognition.*

Barbara Winton (1953–2022)

## *Notes*

Phrases and passages written in italics are taken verbatim from Nicholas Winton's diaries, notes and letters.

This book is written using British English terms and spellings. I hope American readers will be tolerant of the disparity.

# Contents

# Preface

I have discovered things from reading this book that I never knew about my own family, as well as rediscovering episodes long forgotten. I had questions myself about certain incidents in my past and I have found the answers here. It's strange to realise that Barbara knows more about my life now than I do.

Having a daughter write my biography may mean that it is not unbiased, but you would have to read it to find out!

*Nicky Winton*

Nicholas Winton
*October 2013, Maidenhead*

# Foreword

*by Dr Stephen D. Smith, Executive Director, USC Shoah Foundation, UNESCO Chair on Genocide Education*

There are some people that just stand out in history. Sir Nicholas Winton is one of them. Maybe it is place, time or circumstances that brings out the best in people, but one thing for certain is that it takes character, leadership and resolve to make decisions and act upon them. It was almost twenty years ago that I first met Nicholas. At the time I was just starting on my own journey of learning about the Holocaust. I was struck by his mild manner, his sense of pragmatism, his ability to stand back and see the whole picture. I suspected he was always like that. Just recently I sat with him again as a part of an interview for the USC Shoah Foundation. I asked what his life lesson was: 'Standard ethics and compromise, that's what we all have to learn to make the world a better place.'

I am so pleased that Barbara Winton has taken the monumental task of documenting Nicky's life, not least because the man himself is too modest and dismissive of his own achievements to see the relevance of his actions. And he is very clear that documenting history for the sake of it achieves nothing. He is a man of action and a man still very much in the present. But this book is necessary and important, because of the example he sets for others to follow. This book is a stimulating reminder of the good, not only present in Nicky, but in all of us. The story of his noble work is a true testament to the seemingly ordinary deeds each of us can do that make a slow turn towards heroism. Nicky's wish for his biography is exemplary; that it would not detail his deeds for their own sake, but rather would inspire others to pursue similar action, a reminder that we are all capable of effecting great change, if we will it. Barbara Winton reminds us, through the way she intricately unfolds his life, that there was not a singular morning upon which Nicky woke up and decided to forever alter 6,000 lives. Instead, he made a commitment to help each survivor one at a time and ultimately did his part in defending Czechoslovakian children from mass atrocity. At USC Shoah Foundation – The Institute for Visual History and Education, we have 52,000 audio-visual recordings of life stories from survivors and rescuers. We employ these testimonies in classrooms and museums around the world in the hopes of educating the next generation and preventing genocide. As the executive director, it is an honour that we can work alongside people like Nicky. Many testimonies in the archive attest to his timely actions, some of which appear in *Survivors of the Holocaust*, an Emmy award-winning documentary produced by the Institute. We preserve their stories after the fact, just as his scrapbook has done for so many – the scrapbook, in fact, that led to the discovery of Nicky's 'children' is the catalyst responsible for this biography. This in itself is a testament to the importance of keeping memory alive. Nicky does not like to be thought of as a hero, but in his actions, and through the thousands of people alive today who are descendants of the children he saved, he is a hero of the highest order. Valour does not only come through fire in the heat of battle, but high ethical standards in times when hatred and violence threaten the lives of innocents. The story in these pages is not one that inspires observation; it is one that demands action. A man who engineered an international child-transport system changed countless lives and had a ripple effect that will be felt for years to come. It gives us the hope necessary to continue fighting for the good. It is, indeed, a reminder that we can all – regardless of our past or present – make an impactful difference.

Thanks to this wonderful history, I feel I know Nicky even better. Thanks to his guidance, I will go about my work in preventing violent conflict armed with his lifelong observation that conflict can always be solved through 'standard ethics and compromise'.

Stephen D. Smith, *February 2014*

# *Introduction*

There are around 6,000 people in the world today who owe their lives to Nicholas Winton. They are the descendants of a group of refugee children rescued by him from the Nazi threat in 1939. Some of them know of his existence and the part he played in their history, many others do not. It was a short event in his life – nine months, in 1939 – but a critical one for those whose lives were saved, when he became embroiled in a race against time to rescue endangered children from the onslaught of the Nazi invaders in Czechoslovakia.

For him, that intervention was over in a flash and other adventures supplanted it. Only much later did this episode re-emerge in his life, bringing him visitors from all over the world, anxious to learn his story.

This short episode has come to define him in many eyes, though not in his. The only reason this story came to public attention fifty years later was due to the foresight of a fellow volunteer on the enterprise – a Mr W. M. Loewinsohn. At the end of the rescue operation, when war broke out and no further trains could be arranged, he compiled a scrapbook containing much of the material and correspondence related to their work, and presented it to my father as a memento of all they had accomplished.

This scrapbook has been the catalyst for the propulsion of Nicholas Winton into the public domain since 1988, when it was first brought into the media spotlight.

Many newspaper articles have since been written about this story. These tell of how my father cancelled a skiing holiday in the winter of 1938 to answer the call of a friend to fly to Prague and see what was happening there. This was after the Nazi annexation of the Czech Sudetenland in October 1938, which led to the influx of Czech Sudeten refugees into central Czechoslovakia. Seeing the plight of the refugees for himself, he set about finding a way to evacuate endangered children to the UK and, over the next nine months, managed to rescue 669 children from what was, for most of the rest of their families, the fate of internment and murder in concentration camps.

The articles have titled him 'The British Schindler', called him a hero and asked questions about why he had the foresight and the moral urge to conduct such a rescue when many others did nothing. They asked why he kept the story secret for fifty years, suggesting it was his modesty that prevented him from mentioning his actions, even to his own wife and family. He has been awarded medals and honours because of it, some sixty to seventy years after the event.

He is presented as a brave altruist who put himself in harm's way to single-handedly save a generation of Czech Jewish children. This story is not true – well, it is true but not entirely. A myth has developed since 1988, which has become the truth as well as the defining episode of his life to many people.

My father himself would not agree with many of these descriptions, and neither would his family and friends. What they would probably agree on is that the actions for which he has become known and honoured were characteristic of him and have been replicated, though admittedly not so dramatically, at other times throughout his life, and that his character and views helped to make him the right man in the right place to have maximum impact when it was needed.

My attempt to catalogue his whole life has been for several reasons: firstly, by examining his early life, to be able to understand his motivation to act in 1939, as well as his capability to achieve the outcome of getting 669 children out of occupied Czechoslovakia and into safe hands in the UK; secondly, to disentangle the real person from the myth of the one-dimensional 'hero' figure, and to point out where truth diverges from myth in the rescue story. Thus, by scrutinising his character throughout his life, I hope to demonstrate to those who feel great acts need a larger-than-life or 'special' personality to undertake them, that really it's possible for anyone who feels strongly about an injustice or a need to make a difference themselves.

My father's wish for his biography, having agreed to me writing it, is that it should not promote hero worship or the urge for a continual revisiting of history, but, if anything, that it might inspire people to recognise that they too can act ethically in the world and make a positive difference to the lives of others in whatever area they feel strongly about – whether it be international crises or nearer to home, in their own community.

He is not that interested if reading his story about the rescue of the children causes people to think, 'What a hero. I could never do anything like that. It's much too difficult and, anyway, heroes like that were only needed in remote history when we were at war. Now let me get on with my life.' But he will be a happy man if reading it inspires people to think, 'Well, things are not right in the world now. I can make a difference in my own way and I am going to do it.'

I'm starting this biography at the point where my father's rescue story became public in 1988. My parents, Nicholas (known to all as Nicky), aged seventy-eight, and Grete, aged sixty-eight, were very happily married and lived in a sunny open-plan house they had had built in the 1950s. They were retired but both had many interests and activities and were always on the go. My brother, Nicholas (known as Nick), aged thirty-six, lived in London, and ran a busy graphics company. Barbara – that's me – aged thirty-four, lived with my soon-to-be husband Stephen in Herefordshire where we had just rebuilt an old timber-framed farmhouse and were settling down to rural life.

My parents were visiting us in February 1988, having recently learned with great joy that they were to become grandparents at long last, and were mucking in to help get the house sorted. During that visit, my father was phoned by someone at the BBC; they had tracked him down somehow. What happened next turned my father's life from an ordinary personal story into an extraordinary public one.

# 1

## *That's Life!*

### *1988*

Nothing was the same again for my father after 27 February 1988. His search for a home for an old scrapbook of his, documenting the transportation of over 600 children from Czechoslovakia to Britain in 1939, had led him to the BBC studios of *That's Life!*, a popular Sunday-night show. The programme was going to highlight the story that night, and the producers had asked Nicky to come along to check the accuracy of the script and watch the item from among the studio audience. My parents had been given so little preparation for what was to come that Grete, thinking it might be rather dull, decided to stay at home. She could always watch it on TV and see it as clearly as he did from the audience. They really had no idea of what was in store.

You may remember *That's Life!*, a live weekly programme hosted by Esther Rantzen, covering consumer-type issues with humorous interludes, which regularly gained huge audiences of over eighteen million. Rantzen had got hold of the scrapbook through Dr Elisabeth Maxwell, a historian researching the history of her husband, a Czech Jew, and preparing a conference on the Holocaust for that summer, 'Remembering for the Future', to be held in Oxford in July 1988. And so, for the first time, this story fell right into the hands of someone really interested and knowledgeable.

She, in turn, had been shown it by my father who had, for some time, been trying to find someone who might find the historical details interesting. Dr Maxwell was fascinated by the original documents and letters compiled in the scrapbook, and, in particular, the list at the back, comprising the names of all the rescued children, along with the names and addresses of those who had agreed to foster them in Britain in 1939.

Her Czech-Jewish husband happened to be Robert Maxwell, then owner of Mirror Group Newspapers, and so a long article on the subject of the children's rescue, titled 'The Lost Children', was splashed across three pages of the *Sunday Mirror* the same day as *That's Life!* featured the story. The article described how these endangered children had been saved by Nicholas Winton, who had organised trains to bring them to Britain and foster families to look after them. It asked where all these children, now adults, were today.

What happened that evening in the TV studio was a producer's delight – an ambush of an unsuspecting innocent. My father had been placed in the front row of the audience as the programme began. Esther Rantzen produced the scrapbook and explained its contents, telling the story about the evacuation of endangered, mainly Jewish, children from Czechoslovakia just before the outbreak of war, including the facts that nearly all of their families left behind were murdered by the Nazis and that the rescued children had never known how they had come to be saved. She flicked through the book, pointing out various letters and details, until she finally came to the list of all the rescued children, their names and the addresses of where they'd been sent taped into the back. Picking out one name on the list, Vera Diamant, she addressed a woman in the audience, introduced her as the Vera on the list and told her she was sitting next to the man who had saved her life.

It was a wonderful moment, one that Vera (now Vera Gissing) later frequently recalled, saying how much fulfilment it had brought her to meet her saviour at last. For my father, it was wonderful too, but also an unexpected emotional shock for which he had been totally unprepared. Normally an emotionally restrained man, he could not hold back tears when Vera threw her arms around him and said, 'Thank you, thank you', all in front of the audience and cameras. The programme shows him trying to discreetly wipe away tears from behind his thick-lens glasses and force his face to remain calm. For the second 'child' introduced that night, Milena Grenfell-Baines, sitting on his other side, he managed to remain more composed, though still looking poleaxed by the shock of their – and his – emotions.

The programme makers were delighted, of course, to have produced such an emotional and intense TV moment – one that had so nearly been thwarted before the show began. Nicky had seen in the audience someone he knew, Rudi Wessely, and had asked Vera to move so Rudi could have her seat. Vera, having been placed there and forbidden to move by the show's producers, had refused and so their first encounter had not been so joyous. Esther Rantzen later admitted that the moment she introduced them was the only time

Vera Gissing meeting Nicky on *That's Life!*, February 1988

on TV when she had burst into tears and had to stop to recover. Her view was that 'If you get real positive emotions on TV, it reaches right into viewers' homes and hearts, and this did.' And if Nicky and Grete had been warned, then it would not have happened so spontaneously. 'Sometimes as a producer you don't ask the family.'

It took a long time for my parents to forgive Esther for this emotional shock and it became a sparring joke over the years between them whenever they met her. They were media virgins then, but, in the years that followed, they became more used to the tricks used by the media to get a good picture or response for the cameras.

So when Nicky was invited back to *That's Life!* for the following Sunday's show on 6 March, Grete accompanied him, to give him support for whatever was in store. She had been watching at home, horrified, when he had been ambushed, knowing how stressful such an unexpected and personal encounter would be, and all in the public gaze. Though this time they had an inkling of what might occur, they were still amazed when, after Esther had reminded viewers of the story, and had asked if any people in the audience who'd been rescued by Nicholas Winton could stand up, they saw about five rows of people getting to their feet.

It was a very dramatic moment for all concerned and one that has since been shown many times when the Czech children's rescue story has been depicted.

It turned out that Dr Maxwell, brilliantly, had thought to write to all the addresses in the list of the original foster parents of the children, found in the back of the scrapbook, to discover if they still housed people who had knowledge of the fostered children from 1939. The first *Mirror* article had also made an appeal to 'any of the young escapers' to get in touch. Amazingly, as she described later, she got positive replies from over 200 of the addresses.

This had allowed the *Sunday Mirror* and *That's Life!* to contact people who knew they had come from Czechoslovakia on a train and been taken in by a foster family in 1939, but had no idea of how it had been organised. Some believed that it was the same organisation that had arranged the much larger German children's transport (known as the Kindertransport), which had rescued almost 10,000 endangered German and Austrian children before the war. Some of those contacted became the audience for the second *That's Life!*. They were middle-aged men and women who had, just days before, discovered an essential piece in the jigsaw of their early life.

So how was it that this brief but dramatic TV experience changed Nicky's life? Well, it was the moment when the story of the rescued children was made public; the moment that these 'children' – by now adults in their late fifties and sixties – began to discover how their escape from Czechoslovakia had been organised, and that man

The rescued 'children' stand up on *That's Life!*.
Nicky and Grete are seated front right.

was one of those responsible. Not only that, but he had documents, letters and photos, all miraculously intact from that time.

It was hard for Nicky and Grete to get to grips with what was happening. These 'children', now adults, began to call, write, and appear at on their doorstep, asking questions, wanting to see the documents, bringing their own treasured documents kept from that time to show him, and to look at the list of rescued children taped in the back of the scrapbook to check if their names were there.

Their emotions, long suppressed since childhood, were released when they came face to face with Nicky, realised that he personally had helped to save them, and that he was the only link that many of them had to their past – their families left behind in Czechoslovakia and nearly all murdered by the Nazis.

No one up to that point, looking at the scrapbook, had fully understood the emotions involved in the story. It had seemed a fascinating piece of old history, but, to this group of people, it was a vital link to their past and it seemed to rekindle long-repressed emotions from childhood – not just related to them leaving their families, but to being sent away by their parents and being that family's only survivor. Many had not thought about their past for some time until they'd been reminded by the *Sunday Mirror* and *That's Life!* or by a letter arriving from Elisabeth Maxwell. Others had continued to wonder about it, but had been unable to discover any details about how they had come to arrive in the UK and ended up where they did.

Someone Nicky already knew, who'd been through the escape operation, was Rudi Wessely, who had nearly inadvertently sabotaged the first *That's Life!* show; he'd been in the audience that day because he was also a rescued child from Czechoslovakia. He and Nicky had met in 1983 through their mutual work for Abbeyfield, a charity offering supported housing for the elderly. They had discovered their link when, during a break in a meeting, Nicky had asked Rudi what his accent was, and Rudi had told him his story as far as he knew it. Nicky, replying that he'd had something to do with the Czech Kindertransport, had offered to check his list of rescued children to see if Rudi's name was there, and he'd phoned him the same evening to confirm it. However, at the time, both Rudi and Nicky were more interested in talking about Abbeyfield than the past that linked them.

Nicky, no doubt, had given Rudi's details to Elisabeth Maxwell as the only person he had ever met since the war who'd been on one of his transports. Over the years since, there have been regular letters, phone calls and visits to my parents (and then, since my mother's death in 1999, to my father alone) from those 'children' who had discovered their story and wanted to have it confirmed by looking at Nicky's list of names.

Now, with email, enquiries come that way too. Some make contact, are satisfied and that's it. Others remain in touch, become friends and visit on occasion or come regularly to chat, laugh, go out for meals, like a normal extended family. Because one thing that has happened is that Nicky has, for many, become an honorary father to those who lost their own father in that terrible time.

When the enquires began, my mother once again became the secretary she had been when she first met Nicky, but now on his behalf. She kept tabs on who phoned, wrote, visited, and could remind Nicky about them when they next made contact. She was brilliant at recalling stories, the ups and downs of lives lived, while also being the hostess who provided meals, teas, drinks for whoever came. Nicky was long used to inviting whoever he met wherever he had been to come back home for a meal, provided by Grete, and he continued to do this with his new-found 'children'. This was all in addition to their ongoing busy life.

But that was not to be the end of it. The network of 'children' who passed on to each other the story of their rescuer extended to other countries, including Czechoslovakia, Israel, the USA,

Canada, New Zealand and Hungary. Initially, it was all low-key – individuals discovering previously unknown parts of their history and wanting to talk, to ask questions, to help to fill the gaps in their memory.

For most of us, our early memory has holes, but often these are filled by family stories and photos – there are people we can ask. For the child refugees, the gaps had remained all their lives until the chance finally arrived to find a few answers: How had they got to Britain? What had happened to their families that had caused them to send their children 'Into the Arms of Strangers'?* Nicky was, for many, a link back to the families that they had lost.

This diverse group of people, from all over the world – now quite elderly themselves – call themselves Nicky's 'children', and so do my brother and I, despite being younger than them all. Not only do these rescued 'children' appear but also their own children and grandchildren too, sometimes with their parent, but sometimes having only discovered the story after their parent, the rescued 'child', has died.

An abiding theme in most initial visits is the family – not just those who did not escape, but even more so those who came to be born after, who gave meaning to the lives of those who had lost everything that was most precious. Pictures are produced of their children, grandchildren, husbands, wives, to demonstrate to Nicky that new lives were made, which were rich, worthwhile and meaningful. Questions are asked; some he can answer and some he can't. How did they come to be selected? Did he meet their parents? They hope his memory or the scrapbook can provide the facts so long missing for them. The pages of the scrapbook provide many helpful details of their rescue, and as they peruse it, the story of how Nicky and his colleagues carried out their rescue is revealed.

* The title of a 2001 Oscar-winning documentary about the whole Kindertransport movement.

Over the first few months after the initial publicity, the story of how Nicholas Winton had organised the rescue of 669 children from Czechoslovakia spread through the community of ex-refugees. Many had kept in contact through a network of links, from their school days at the Czech school in Wales during the war or through other survivor organisations. (There were ex-refugees, of course, who were not part of this loose network. They had forged new lives and didn't want to be reminded of such a painful part of their history.)

By the time of the conference 'Remembering for the Future', organised by Dr Maxwell for July 1988, over 150 people from all over the world had identified their names on the list in the scrapbook. The conference, primarily a scholarly event, commenced with a meeting of survivors, many of whom were from the Czech rescue. Dr Maxwell invited Nicky to attend the pre-conference meeting to enable the 'children' to meet their rescuer and offer thanks for what he had done for them fifty years before.

As many wanted to give thanks more tangibly, contributions were collected by Dr Maxwell, who purchased a gold ring inscribed with the words 'Save One Life – Save the World', a quotation from the Jewish Talmud, which was given to him there. The money raised had so much exceeded the cost of the ring that the rest was donated to Nicky's current charitable enterprise, an Abbeyfield extra-care home for the elderly, to purchase a piano for the residents.

Others met him the following year at the International Reunion of the Kindertransport, a fiftieth anniversary meeting organised by Bertha Leverton, a child refugee who came to Britain on the much larger officially organised Kindertransport from Germany and Austria in 1938 and 1939.

However, his first major trip abroad was to Israel in May 1989, to donate his scrapbook to Yad Vashem in Jerusalem. Yad Vashem describes itself as the world centre for documentation, research, education and commemoration of the Holocaust and, through the auspices of Dr Maxwell, they had agreed to give the scrapbook a home. At last Nicky had found people and an organisation who were more than just dispassionately interested in his scrapbook. For the 'children', it was an important part of their story, and for Yad Vashem, an invaluable historical document, which shone light and hope into a dark corner of Holocaust history.

# 2

## *The Kindertransport Scrapbook*
### *1938–39*

The scrapbook's pages are full of pictures, documents, letters, photos – all relating to nine months' frantic activity by a small group of dedicated volunteers, drawn together by an impulse to help and do what they could, especially when they discovered that there was no one else doing very much.

The initial pages show brochures of Czechoslovakia – pictures of Prague and young people dancing in their national costumes. These pictures seem incongruous – a striking contrast to what features next and a reminder of what was lost for so many.

On the next page is a map – startling in its clarity – headed '*Ein Volk, Ein Reich, Ein Führer! Gross Deutschland 1938–48*', and showing the countries of Europe Hitler intended to annex, with dates, starting with Austria (1938), Czechoslovakia (1938), Hungary (1939), Poland (1939), Yugoslavia (1940) and so on, right through Europe, Russia and Turkey. If anyone had doubted Hitler's intentions, they were laid out here for all to see in black and white. Nicky had come across it while in Prague in January 1939.

Then, a short letter dated 22 December 1938 stating that 600 children now in Czechoslovakia were in urgent danger and needed help from the Committee for German Jewry, and asking for equal treatment for them to that which the German and Austrian child refugees were receiving. It was signed Schmolka, Steiner, Blake

– three volunteers already struggling to help those fleeing Germany and the Czech Sudetenland to escape the Nazis.

The rescue of children from the Nazi threat in Germany, Austria and Czechoslovakia before the Second World War is known as the Kindertransport (Kinder being 'children' in German). Around 10,000 children were rescued from Austria and Germany by a group of Jewish and Christian agencies, which formed the Movement for the Care of Children from Germany, later known as the Refugee Children's Movement. Many determined humanitarian people were involved in this undertaking, but its remit did not extend to Czechoslovakia.

The 22 December letter in the scrapbook marks the beginning of Nicky's involvement, for the Blake on the letter was Martin Blake, a close friend of Nicky and a teacher at Westminster School. Around the time of that letter, Nicky received a fateful phone call from Martin. Nicky and Martin had been planning a Christmas skiing trip to Switzerland, which was, in fact, a Westminster School trip for pupils, with Martin in charge and Nicky as an accompanying adult. This he had done before in previous years and much enjoyed. So when Martin phoned and said he was not going, that he had gone instead to Prague and Nicky should follow to see what he was up to, Nicky was intrigued. He had his two weeks off work booked, and with a spirit of adventure and his close friend summoning him, he had no hesitation in changing his holiday destination.

Nicky and Martin were both intensely political, Martin having introduced him to his friends in the Labour Party, and they spent much of their time together talking politics, especially the growing threat from Germany. He was already very aware of the dangerous and violent atmosphere permeating Europe and the threat Hitler and his party posed to peace.

In 1933, Hitler had become Chancellor, the political leader in Germany, and had begun to put into effect his programme for strengthening the German state and restricting the rights of Jews, communists and political opponents through violence, intimidation and loss of employment and other rights. From that date, Nicky had seen first-hand relatives and family friends fleeing Germany, leaving everything behind in a state of fear and desperation. He knew that Hitler had plans for expansion, having read and discussed *Mein Kampf*, Hitler's autobiographical manifesto. Many others, in particular politicians and those attacked in print by Hitler, had read the book but had not taken it seriously.

It was hard to take seriously the hatred-filled manifesto in the 1920s, but by the time Nicky and his friends were reading it after Hitler came to power, his intentions seemed all too possible. They saw that these plans had already begun to be acted on in 1938, firstly by annexing Austria in March and subsuming it into greater Germany. Then, after 29 September and the infamous Munich Agreement signed by Britain, France, Italy and Germany – which gave the Sudetenland to Germany in return for an end to Hitler's territorial ambition – the German army marched into, and occupied, the Czech Sudeten borderlands.

Sudetenland was the region bordering Germany and Austria inside Czechoslovakia. It was home to around three million ethnic Germans, over twenty per cent of the total Czech population, living alongside ethnic Czechs, Slovaks and Hungarians. After the Munich Agreement, Germany immediately annexed the Sudetenland, leading to a flood of refugees into the centre of Czechoslovakia, made up of those groups that Hitler had already targeted in Germany. As well as Jews, this included political opponents, including communists and social democrats, and intellectuals, Roma and other minorities. Camps were set up around Prague, the capital, for the enormous influx of displaced people.

With Kristallnacht in November 1938, when a series of attacks occurred against Jews and Jewish businesses across Germany and Austria, and regular tales of violence and intimidation against

Jews, communists and others who resisted Hitler, Nicky was well aware of what was happening inside the borders of Czechoslovakia.

Nicky arrived in Prague on New Year's Eve and went straight to Martin's hotel, the Grand Hotel Šroubek on Wenceslas Square, the wide boulevard in the centre of Prague, extending from the National Museum down to the entrance to the narrow streets of the old town. The hotel was a beautiful though slightly gloomy place, which still exists today (as the Hotel Europa), completely unchanged in its faded glory, with every fitting – lights, stair rails, plaster work – an example of the Art Nouveau style that infused Prague at the time. He did not have much time to appreciate his surroundings, however. Martin quickly brought him up to speed on the political situation and the refugee problem as they made the ten-minute walk to the British Committee for Refugees from Czechoslovakia (BCRC) office at Voršilská 2, a small side street off Narodni, the busy street on which the National Theatre stood. There he was introduced to Doreen Warriner, the powerhouse running the BCRC operation.

Map of Europe detailing Hitler's expansion plans

Warriner was an amazing woman who deserves her own biography, though she does have a chapter in William Chadwick's *The Rescue of the Prague Refugees*, and she wrote her own memoir of the time, *Winter in Prague*. Doreen had followed her own impulse to help back in October 1938. She had been working as an assistant lecturer in economics at University College London and was about to go to the USA to finish a Rockefeller scholarship. Having experience in Czechoslovakia and a love for the people, she set off for Prague instead, with a bit of donated money and a vague urge to help in the wake of the exodus of refugees from Sudetenland. Having sized up the situation on arrival, she had offered her services to the BCRC. She was a forceful, idealistic woman and, with a small group of helpers, was attempting to organise the safe transit to Britain of those adults most at risk from the Nazis. Many had fled from Germany into Czechoslovakia and others from the Sudetenland once it had been over-run, bringing their families but little else.

German agents were already in Prague, trying to find and take into custody those on Hitler's wanted list: his political enemies, particularly leaders of the Sudeten Social Democratic Party, communists and other Sudeten anti-Nazi activists. Warriner's task was to help these men and their families escape through Poland to Britain.

She was staying at the Alcron, a grand Art Deco-styled hotel a couple of hundred yards down a side road off Wenceslas Square and visible from the Šroubek. The centre of Prague being relatively compact, both the office on Voršilská and the later one on Rubešova, behind Wilson railway station, were within a five- to ten-minute walk of both hotels.

A first letter in the scrapbook from Nicky to his mother, Barbara, is undated, but describes, despite all the turmoil, a few hours spent seeing the sights and taking photos – one of his ongoing hobbies. But it also recounts that later the same day he was already helping out in the office where Warriner's secretary Bill Barazetti, himself a refugee, was trying to give assistance to desperate displaced families asking for help to emigrate, for money to buy food and for places to stay. This was followed by helping out at another office used by what Nicky termed 'the Kindercommittee' further away across the city, which seemed to be supported by the Lord Mayor's Fund in London, where they handed out paltry sums of money to desperate mothers to buy food for their families. Here also were pleading mothers asking about sending their children to Britain.

A note Nicky wrote at the time, which was put into the scrapbook, shows the intense emotions swirling around the office as he witnessed the terrible dilemma the parents faced for survival; how, if they could not be helped, then perhaps their children could, by being sent away to safety in a foreign land. However, this was not something these organisations could help with.

No sooner had he done two hours' work there than he was off again, late for another engagement already booked. The intense pace of activity may have protected him from the paralysis seeing such despair can produce, but he was deeply affected by the suffering he witnessed and keen to be of help.

Warriner lost no time in sizing Nicky up as potential assistance in her mission. Seeing that he was interested, she promptly got him involved in what was going on at her office. Fairly quickly, Nicky realised that there were many child refugees alongside the children of those who Doreen was smuggling away who did not have anyone concentrating on their future. He suggested that he could focus on them. Unable to do more herself, she encouraged him to take on the task and he set about it immediately. Doreen was a whirlwind of activity; with little time to teach Nicky the ropes, and with no time for them to get to know each other, their conversations were limited to practical matters.

It's hard to know at what exact point Nicky decided that he was going to throw himself into the task of attempting to get endangered children out of Czechoslovakia and into Britain, but his early letters to his mother already showed that he had crossed the line between offering some local short-term assistance and a commitment to something much bigger.

Another letter to his mother, sent a day or two after the first, suggested that his decision was made; his 'work' was just beginning and 'Miss Warriner has already asked me to be Secretary of a Children's Committee for Czechoslovakia which I suggested should be formed. It will mean a lot of work'. His initial holiday from work was only two weeks – hardly a fraction of the time necessary to start such an undertaking, though he did manage to get approval for an extra week when he realised how much had to be done.

He asked for his mother's help, writing: 'I have another job which may be difficult. Could you go to the Immigration section of the Home Office and find out what guarantees are needed to bring a child into the country?' He rattled off a list of questions for her to find answers to in order for him to discover the possibility of getting started. Would the British government allow children in? If so, under what conditions?

His method of co-opting his mother to his chosen task – that this was a job that needed to be done now and she was the one to do it – became a familiar method throughout his life when engaged in charitable activities. He had made HIS decision, there was a worthy job to do, so surely anyone who could help, would. He had no doubt that she would agree and, of course, she did. He was aware of the difficulties, indeed Doreen had pointed them out to him, but at this point the motto he later lived by first came into action: 'If something is not impossible, then there must be a way to do it.'

On 10 January, he was writing to the BCRC back home, asking them to be of assistance. The next day he wrote to Martin Blake, newly returned to London, giving vent to his dissatisfaction at the slow pace in the BCRC London office. Other frustrations involved getting a working list of endangered children that he could use. There were a number of refugee organisations already at work in Prague, each dealing with their particular interest group and each looking for help to get their charges to safety. The five committees that were in contact with Nicky and the BCRC for assistance with their lists were aiding Jews, Catholics, communists, Austrians and Germans, and political writers. Each group wanted Nicky to use their list as his only priority and before long it became clear to him that negotiations would take time and lead nowhere. He decided to take control, telephoning each committee and informing them he had a list from another group and would be using that unless they sent theirs immediately, which he would then integrate. This strategy worked and he had his five lists for compiling into one the next day.

There is no evidence in his letters of any hesitation about getting stuck in or worry that he was not up to the task or that those already running organisations would not take him seriously, despite, after all, him just having turned up and being in no way official. The flimsiness of his role was obviously not apparent, as the committees and parents who wanted to get their children out dealt with him without query. He seemed to give everyone the impression that he was competent and was doing a specific job. Once it became known amongst endangered groups that someone was concentrating on rescuing children, he was besieged in his hotel from early in the morning until late at night by parents coming to beg for help to get their little ones to Britain. Some had relatives already in the UK who could sponsor them, but most had no such assistance.

He spent much time dealing with such requests, taking names, photos and details to add to his growing lists. This was all done in German as he had no Czech. He quickly learned one sentence in Czech to say to visitors, 'I am British, but I cannot speak Czech', so they did not just walk away quickly when he spoke to them in German, the language of their oppressors.

However, his lack of Czech led to a discomfiting incident. He wrote in his notes on 11 January, 'Well, after a hard day's work . . . I thought I would go for a little walk. On the main street I got into a crowd of young Czech youths who were walking along, shouting. I did not know what it was about but any excitement was good enough for me, so I walked along with them. Not being able to understand the lingo, I could naturally not join in the shouting, but at least I helped to swell their ranks. After a little while a great number of police arrived and dispersed the procession. When at last I found myself standing next to another unoffensive-looking man I asked him what it had all been about. He told me it was an anti-Jewish procession and the shouting was anti-Jewish slogans. I suppose therefore that I must confess to having taken part in an anti-Jewish demonstration.'

He mentioned to Doreen, one day when they ate a quick snack together, that he had a feeling he was being followed. Doreen confirmed that not only he but all of them were being kept an eye on by German agents, as their work involved people in whom the Nazis were interested. However, Nicky did not feel anxious or intimidated by this; he felt that he himself was not in any danger and whenever he saw that a likely agent was listening in to his conversations, he had no compunction in telling them in his best German to 'piss off', which they invariably did. After all, there was nominally a Czech government in Prague and the German invasion had at that time reached no further than the Sudeten borderlands.

On 12 January, a flight set off to London with twenty children on board. This had been funded by the Barbican Mission, an organisation whose purpose was to convert Jews to Christianity. Nonetheless desperate parents had agreed to this and were sending their children to the Barbican's residential home in England. Nicky's involvement was purely logistical so he went to the airport to see it off, along with a cohort of journalists and cameras. This is where the well-used photo of Nicky holding a young boy in his arms was taken. The boy, named Hansi Beck, sadly died later of an inner ear infection. An article in the *New York Times* the following day mentioned the Barbican flight, saying: 'The children will be brought up in London homes and in the Barbican Mission until they are eighteen years old, when, after training as artisans, they will be sent to British colonies and dominions. The youngest passenger today was three and a half and the oldest eleven.' No suggestion was made in the paper of the children's eventual return to their previous homes.

In his letter to Martin, Nicky also mentions going to a party where he heard about a woman who worked for the Swedish Red Cross and was looking to take thirty children to Sweden. He arranged to meet her for lunch with Doreen in tow, but while beginning to talk to her about his plans, he received a swift kick under the table from Doreen, which stopped his flow. She was suspicious of the girl and her instincts were good, as on checking she discovered the girl was spying for the Germans.

However, as she was indeed working for the Red Cross and did have funding and homes for children in Sweden, Nicky pressed on with the arrangement – his only with her – and on 16 or 17 January, a further thirty children were flown off to Sweden.

Warriner suggested Nicky should go out to visit one of the refugee camps that had sprung up around the capital to see what was happening there. During a harsh middle-European winter, these were sheltering those who had fled from the Sudetenland when the German troops had arrived. He was to accompany the well-known Independent UK MP Eleanor Rathbone, who had been campaigning in the UK to help refugees in Czechoslovakia and had come to see for herself how things were.

Before the Barbican Mission flight. L–R: Hansi Beck and his parents, Peter Niethammer and mother Annerle, Ilse Stein, unknown girl (Courtesy P. Needham)

Rathbone was a forceful, eccentric woman who, early in the 1930s, had recognised the threat from Hitler and joined the British Non-Sectarian Anti-Nazi Council. In 1936, she began to warn about a Nazi threat to Czechoslovakia and was outraged by the Munich Agreement, making a nuisance of herself in Parliament. Nicky's role that day was to guide her round the local refugee camps and make sure she got back safely without leaving any belongings behind, a noted habit of hers. Nicky was in awe of her, her forceful manner and lack of airs or vanity, saying, '. . . she never dressed; she just covered herself'.

Accompanying him also to the camp was a businessman he had met on the plane from England who had been intending to try and sell motorcycles to the Czechs. Nicky had suggested to him that business might not be good under current conditions and that, if this was so, he could come and see what Nicky was doing. It had proved to be the case so he'd turned up, interested to see what Nicky was up to.

As an aside, this man, who Nicky knew as Mr Hales, was in fact Sir Harold Hales, until 1935 a British MP. He had mentioned that he had sponsored a trophy for the Blue Riband, an award for the fastest transatlantic ship, though failed to mention his parliamentary career or knighthood.

Journalists reported that official figures gave the number of 250,000 refugees in Czechoslovakia, including not only Jews but also democratic Germans who had fled their country, communists and Sudeten democrats as well as many ordinary Czechs. The conditions in the camps were terrible, with very basic shelter and food, freezing cold, with young children and families without possessions. To find a situation such as this in a relatively prosperous central European country must have been truly shocking. For Nicky and his colleagues, this was not 'a quarrel in a far-away country between people of whom we know nothing', as trumpeted by Neville Chamberlain. Nicky's parents and whole family came from Bavaria, which he had visited, just a stone's throw from the Czech border. It was a totally familiar culture, especially as most Czechs spoke some German, in which Nicky was fluent.

As they were touring the camp, Nicky lost his businessman and went back to search for him, finding him in a tent, sobbing, overcome by the tragedy of what he was seeing. Not a surprising response perhaps, seeing the atrocious conditions the young children and their families were forced to endure, but Nicky's upbringing had taught him not to show emotion or to despair. He knew that to achieve anything he would need to remain focused, and he steeled himself against his emotional reaction.

Another letter to his mother on the same day thanks her for the information he requested and mentions his social activities are now all about making useful contacts: 'Those evenings I *bummel* (German for stroll or wander), I try only to do so with people who may be of some use to me in this work.' He goes on: 'As far as I can see, my work re: children is only just starting. I shall very likely have to carry on in London. If this is so, I shall try to make HQ at 20 Willow [Road – Nicky's home]. If I can possibly avoid it I don't want to work anywhere near any of the existing committees. From experience this end, they can only retard the work. I may therefore need someone practically the whole time I am at work at Willow. Any offers?'

Having quickly discovered how slowly bureaucratic committees can progress, he was determined that working outside them would facilitate his aims. His temperament and sense of urgency also led him to want to be in charge; he was too impatient for the niceties of organisational protocols. Another decision that his mother would be a useful person to have on his team led to him making an early play for her assistance.

\*     \*     \*

At some point during his stay, another two Englishmen turned up, sent by the boys' prep school they taught at, to find and bring back two refugee boys to be looked after by the school. These men were Trevor Chadwick and Geoff Phelps. Trevor taught Latin primarily at Forres in Swanage, founded by Trevor's father and now run by his uncle. Having collected two boys, and also a girl that his mother had sponsored, they left, but Trevor was back again immediately. He had seen the situation and wanted to help. His focus being children, he attached himself to Nicky and they worked together building a list of children over the next few days until Nicky finally had to return home to work. Trevor followed soon after, but had offered to return to carry on the job if Nicky managed to get all the permits and guarantors needed for the rescue to really take off.

He sped home on 21 January and was immediately back at his stock exchange job. However, his mind remained on his 'unofficial' job and how to get permission to bring in the children and find homes for them. Doreen Warriner had sent a letter to Margaret Layton, Honorary Secretary at the BCRC, commending Nicky to her as someone to be put in charge of a children's section, saying, 'He is ideal for the job. He has enormous energy, businessmen methods, knows the situation perfectly here . . . all he needs now is authority to go ahead. It is an opportunity for the committee to get the services of a really first-class organiser . . . Winton will get things through, if you will give him status as Secretary of a children's section.'

Obviously overwhelmed with her own work, and desperate for the London end to get moving, she was hoping the BCRC would let Nicky get on with it, but with their backing.

Nicky soon discovered that support would be slow and on their terms, though. A month after his return and initial visit to the BCRC offices, he received a letter from Miss Layton telling him that the Children's Movement bringing out German refugee

Doreen Warriner (1904–72)
(Courtesy H. Warriner)

Trevor Chadwick (1907–79)
(Courtesy C. Chadwick)

children was unlikely to help them with theirs. Also having heard from a colleague that Nicky was intending to apply separately for Home Office permits for children, she was warning him against it 'as the Home Office is always antagonised by a multiplication of applications'.

However, Nicky had not been sitting waiting for the BCRC to give him permission to start working. He had already produced reports for newspapers about the desperate situation for Czech refugee children, written to various organisations involved in refugee assistance and made his own advances to the Home Office. He did all this not, apparently, as an independent person, but using the title of Secretary of the Children's Section of the BCRC, the role that Warriner had hoped he would officially receive.

He had decided he couldn't wait for official recognition, the endless meetings and discussions that might eventually lead to this appointment, so having obtained some BCRC headed paper he just added his name and the title, 'Secretary, Children's Section' to it and his home address, got a ream printed and set to work.

It was indeed another three months before official recognition came; on 24 May, a letter arrived from Miss Layton stating that Nicky had been officially made Secretary of the Children's Section of the BCRC. It was a belated acceptance of the fact; by that date, four transports had already arrived bringing refugee children from Prague to Liverpool Street station in London where Nicky met them and organised their collection by foster parents.

During February Nicky had obtained the requirements of the Home Office for bringing in unaccompanied children, and though conditions were given, they were not insurmountable; a separate application was needed for each child containing a medical certificate, a £50 guarantee to pay for their eventual return, plus a foster parent or guarantor to look after the child until they were seventeen or were able to return home. This completed application would lead to an entry permit being issued. £50 is the rough equivalent to £2,500 today, so a not-insignificant sum and out of reach of many individuals, but the guarantee could be found through supportive organisations and donations.

Having got permission from the Home Office, Nicky must have informed Trevor Chadwick who returned promptly to Prague to make good his promise to manage that end of the process. He, at some point too, seemed to become 'official', though when is not recorded; probably like Nicky it was long after he was actually doing the job. However, he was obviously in Prague again by the beginning of March, as a telegram of congratulation was sent to Nicky jointly by him and Warriner, though for what is not known. The first Home Office permits? The first placing of a group of children? Whatever it was, the first transport left Prague on 14 March (over the next six months, another seven would follow).

The following day, Hitler broke his agreement and invaded the rest of the Czech lands. The office in Prague was now working under Nazi rule and needed their permission for children to leave. It seems from Doreen's and Trevor's own notes that the first transport was of twenty children and by plane, not by train. However, after the German occupation, all further transports were by train, leaving from Wilson station in central Prague with German soldiers in attendance on the platform.

Chadwick had to let parents know when homes had been found and make sure the permits were in place and the trains paid for. He had to negotiate with the occupying German command for exit permits for the children, which were given mostly without difficulty, though names were scrutinised for any which matched those they particularly sought. Accompanying adults on the trains were expected to return, but it appears that some endangered women escaped this way. One for certain that I know of, a Jewish lady named Grete Reichl, was helped to get a place by an American lady, Henrietta Eisenberger, living in Prague, who also accompanied at least one of the trains, but who returned to help further.

Trevor wrote a letter in 1966 to one of his 'children' who had discovered his then address in Norway. 'Except for letters from my mother mentioning a Jewish girl whom she "took", this is my first contact with one of "my" children from Czechoslovakia.' He goes on to talk about how he got things done with the Germans in Prague in 1939: 'They gave me an unpleasant time at first and I remember putting on the screaming table-thumping act – always reliable with those louts – and demanding an interview with the Kriminalrat (I remember my deep delight in the word Kriminalrat) . . . Ironically he made things easier for me, after my blow-up, than did our Home Office.'

This was Kriminalrat Bömelburg, head of the Gestapo in Prague. To Trevor he seemed: 'an elderly, smiling gentleman, far from sinister, who eventually proved to be a great help, sometimes unwittingly. He was really interested in my project and his only Nazi-ish remark was a polite query why England wanted so many Jewish children. He happily gave his stamp to the first train transport, even though I had included half a dozen "adult" leaders on it. I went to the station accompanied by a Gestapo clerk, and all the children were there, with labels prepared by my helpers tied round their necks. The train took them off, cheering, through Germany to the Hook of Holland, a hundred or more.

'Soon Bömelburg sent for me. He said people were throwing dust in my eyes. It was now absolutely forbidden for any adult to leave the country without a special Ausreisebewilligung and the "leaders" of my transport had really escaped illegally. I expressed my deepest sorrow and grovelled. I was a blue-eyed boy again and thereafter he agreed to stamp my lists of children for transport without delay. I sealed my friendship with him by "confessing" after the second transport that I had discovered one child was not Jewish. (There were several Aryans in all transports.) He praised my honesty and begged me to be careful, because of course the Nazis would look after "Aryan" children.'

Trevor's somewhat devil-may-care character, plus his ability to be forceful or conciliatory as necessary, seemed to make him ideal for the role he had taken on. He was like a kind uncle to the children, who felt safe with him, while also able to appear honourable and compliant to the Germans who held the fate of 'his' children in their hands, even while he was breaking their rules. Without a Gestapo stamp on an exit permit, there was no chance of leaving. At the same time, he cut corners and worked all hours to get as many children as he could on the lists he sent to Nicky and then onto the trains they organised.

However, despite the relatively amenable German attitude, unpredictable interference could occur at any time, and the level of tension in the Prague office was ratcheted up as the hoops they needed to jump through and suspicion of their activities increased over the months. Sometimes the Home Office permits needed to enter the UK were slow in coming, meaning that a train was ready but not the entry papers. At those times Trevor managed to find a printer to forge the entry documents for the Germans to stamp so the train could leave. Then once at the British border these fakes would be swapped for the tardy but valid Home Office permits. They sailed very close to the wind, but waiting was not an option. Nicky's and Trevor's impatience with the relaxed Home Office was palpable.

Over time, Nicky collected a few volunteer helpers in addition to his mother. One was Barbara Willis, the friend and soon-to-be wife of Martin Blake, who was already working for a Christian refugee association. A later one was the mysterious Mr Loewinsohn who seemed to be organising the documentation and final reports towards the end of the project, and perceptively put together the scrapbook which he gave to Nicky.

Barbara even produced a list of the BCRC local societies around the country, which provided a launch pad for his search for guarantors and foster families. He would get home from his day job at the stock exchange around 4 p.m. and set to work sending out press releases and pleading letters for guarantee funding, and producing little cards with photos of children on to send out to prospective foster parents.

Nicky had discovered that many who felt moved to take in a child had preferences for who they took, though they may not be able to articulate them well. This led to much delay in correspondence back and forth, so the cards were a way of pre-empting this. When a person said they would like a girl of about ten years old, Nicky would send a card with six photos of girls around that age, and a choice would be made. No time was given to the fairness or commercial feel of the process. It was quick, and getting as many children placed as soon as possible was his main concern. The scrapbook holds some of these cards showing up to eight pictures of children, topped with tracing paper on which their names, dates of birth and religion were written, with those found foster homes marked 'Placed'. They remain a stark depiction of the lottery involved in who came and who did not and how many were never able to make the journey to safety.

Other pages of the scrapbook are filled with the letterheads of organisations with whom he was in correspondence in the hope of finding homes and financial guarantors: the YMCA, Boy Scouts International, the Salvation Army, Trades Union Congress, The Woodcraft Folk (who sponsored around twenty children), numerous church organisations, Jewish organisations and refugee organisations.

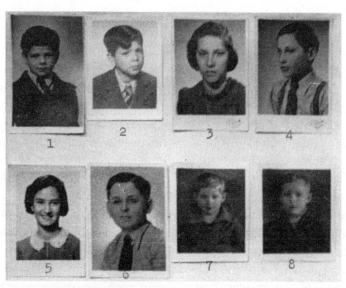

A photo card sent to prospective foster parents

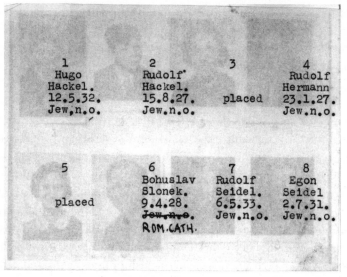

| 1 | 2 | 3 | 4 |
|---|---|---|---|
| Hugo Hackel. 12.5.32. Jew,n.o. | Rudolf Hackel. 15.8.27. Jew,n.o. | placed | Rudolf Hermann 23.1.27. Jew,n.o. |

| 5 | 6 | 7 | 8 |
|---|---|---|---|
| placed | Bohuslav Slonek. 9.4.28. ~~Jew,n.o.~~ ROM.CATH. | Rudolf Seidel. 6.5.33. Jew,n.o. | Egon Seidel 2.7.31. Jew,n.o. |

Cover of same photo card with child details

With the invasion of the Czech lands, the urgency Nicky felt increased and he was soon writing imploring letters to be published in various papers and journals asking people to come forward to take or sponsor children.

On 4 May he wrote a letter to a newspaper with a plea to readers' consciences: 'Dear Sir, Tales of violence and war, Treaties made and broken, concentration camps and social ostracism have become so commonplace in the daily papers that the average person has completely lost his normal moral standard. A few years ago the publication of a story about a number of refugees without nationality or home who were starving in No Man's Land, not being allowed admission by one country but being expelled by the other, would most certainly at the very least have made people stop and think. Now they are too inured to such tragedies even to consider how they might be able to mitigate such suffering. They are content to consider themselves as individuals without responsibility for what is going on in the world today. They hope it will all come right in the end but, in the meantime, they can do nothing.

'The more conscientious, perhaps, dream the platitude that, if the individual were perfect, all would be perfect, and go home resolved to lead good lives. But there is a difference between passive goodness and active goodness which is, in my opinion, the giving of one's time and energy in the alleviation of pain and suffering. It entails going out, finding and helping those in suffering and danger and not merely leading an exemplary life, in the purely passive way of doing no wrong. And they can help to an enormous extent.

'In Bohemia and Slovakia today, there are thousands of children, some homeless and starving, mostly without nationality, but they certainly all have one thing in common: there is no future for them if they are forced to remain where they are . . . Those who left the Sudetenland after Munich are in the worst plight. Without homes, jobs, nationality or permits to reside in the country, they wander hither and thither getting charity where they can and only hoping they will not be found by the police and sent back to Germany where, at the best, a concentration camp awaits them. They are mostly middle-class people, doctors, teachers, journalists, civil servants, whose only crime has been their outspoken defence of democracy. Surely we owe a debt to these people who have lost all for those ideals, which we are now striving to maintain . . .'

He goes on to ask people to foster or sponsor or donate money towards the sponsorship of the refugee children and ends: 'Help to save the children of this courageous and desperately unfortunate people whose self-sacrifice has been our gain.'

These pleas and articles written by Nicky and others, such as the Reverend Rosalind Lee of the Unitarian Church, brought in hundreds of offers of help through the spring and summer. However, they had thousands on their list and only hundreds coming into Britain. In the hope of getting a much larger number out, Nicky resorted to writing to America: to the President of the American Jewish Congress, the Governor of New York, the Senator for New York and even the President of the USA himself. The replies he got to all these, included in the scrapbook, were much the same: a bill was going through the Senate to allow more refugees into the USA and nothing could be done until it was enacted, which was hoped to be soon; the recipient was unable to help, but had passed the letter on to others more involved in the field etc. etc. But it was all too late; no bill was passed in time to take in any children.

Articles put into a magazine, *The Picture Post*, with photos of some of the children drew big responses. A packed letters page torn from the magazine and put into the scrapbook is full of heart-felt notes from people offering homes to some of the pictured children. However, not everyone was happy with Nicky's business-like methods of obtaining homes for the mostly Jewish children. One day some rabbis arrived at Willow Road to complain to him about

Jewish children going to Christian homes, or even worse, to the Barbican Mission home. Nicky, in calmer moments, understood their concerns, but just then, with the urgency at its peak, he was not conciliatory. He told them forcefully that he would not stop placing children wherever he could, and if they preferred a dead Jewish child to a converted one, that was their problem.

He had, however, in a February report, commented, 'It may not be generally known that although Munich is four months back, only twenty-five children ... have been brought out of Czechoslovakia. These were brought out under conditions which are not even acceptable to a large section of the British public, in so far that an undertaking had to be given, if they were Jewish, that they should be baptised.' He was therefore not unaware of the religious sensitivities involved. Some of the endangered children in Slovakia were from orthodox Jewish families who would only allow them to leave if orthodox hostels in Britain would admit them. This agreement was not easily forthcoming, and meant these children could not escape. Children whose parents allowed them to be fostered by whoever would accept them were placed by Nicky wherever he could find a home, only providing that foster carers were screened by a member of the BCRC group in their area.

In the scrapbook is a newspaper article from the *New Statesman* dated 10 June: 'I have seldom seen a more moving sight than the arrival of 130 Czech children at a Liverpool Street platform last Friday. They have been coming over in batches; this was a large contingent. One of them was less than three years old, the eldest must have been about fifteen. Policemen kept a gangway for the crocodile which was led off to a gymnasium ... and curtained down the middle. The children sat on benches on one side of the curtain, the parents were on the other. As each name was called out, the child went through an opening in the curtain and was welcomed by its new parents on the other side.'

Nicky and his mother went to Liverpool Street station to meet each arrival and assist with the formal handing over of the children to their foster families. It did not always go smoothly. Some foster parents did not arrive on time and on occasion they did not appear at all, and individual children had stories to tell my father, fifty or so years later when they met, about what had happened to them that day. But overall it worked and the children went off to their new lives.

Further into the scrapbook there are letters from parents thanking him for his help, letters from rescued children also thanking him, or to his mother, Barbara, thanking her. There were also letters to Trevor Chadwick and Nicholas Winton from HICEM in Bratislava, the Jewish emigration organisation that had offices in many cities. HICEM was co-ordinating the details of endangered children in Slovakia and repeatedly urging them to deal with the most desperate cases.

Chadwick organised five transports leaving Prague up until June 1939. Then things began to hot up there for him and he felt his presence was beginning to endanger the operation due to other activities he was engaged in. These were not specifically described by him but could have been related to assisting wanted adults. Reluctantly he asked for a replacement and returned home, probably in early June, obviously disappointed to have to leave with so much yet to do. The list he had prepared had 5,000 names of children whose parents were desperate to send them abroad, and he felt that so few had thus far been sent.

What happened at the Prague end of the operation gets a bit hazy after this. Warriner and her two assistants, Christine Maxwell and Margaret Dougan, had already left back in April after her illegal transports of adults had come to Nazi attention and they were in danger of arrest and had to make quick exits. Against enormous odds, Warriner and her team had helped get out many thousands of refugees, including hundreds of Sudeten socialists and other anti-Nazi activists, along with their wives and children. She had been helped by R. J. Stopford – a British official at the Embassy – who had managed to be enormously supportive of her illegal activities while appearing to remain above suspicion as a government representative. Stopford left with the British Legation in May. Beatrice Wellington – another independent helper working like Warriner on behalf of the endangered adults – also left, though later in August, having continued the dangerous work of smuggling adults out as long as she could, at no small risk to her own safety.

The BCRC, having done its major work and running out of funds, was replaced by the Czech Refugee Trust Fund in July 1939 under British government control, and a civil servant called Creighton was sent to Prague in place of Chadwick. He was not there long and seems to have been followed by a Mrs A. E. Guthrie, as a letterhead with her name as Honorary Secretary, British Committee for Refugee Children, Prague, is in the scrapbook, alongside Chadwick's and Creighton's. Whoever was in charge there, the system set up by Nicky and Trevor continued through the summer into August with three more trains, the largest being on 1 July when 241 children came at once. A seventh transport left on 20 July with seventy-six children and the eighth on 2 August with sixty-eight children on board.

The ninth transport was prepared for 1 September with 250 children ready to leave, the largest number yet. Events that Nicky and his colleagues had long expected and dreaded unfolded to stop them in their tracks. The train was cancelled hours before it was due to depart, as that day, fatefully, Germany invaded Poland and all borders were closed. Two days later Britain declared war on Germany. It was a bitter blow for Nicky and his team. It is thought that nearly all the children due to leave that day ended up in concentration camps.

Judith Keller, her brother Zoltan and mother.

Judith Keller, who escaped on the July train aged six years old, turned up fifty years later to meet Nicky on the second *That's Life!* programme, having been told about it by her foster parents who had seen the first programme on TV and realised she was one of the children being sought. Her nine-year-old brother Zoltan had been due to follow her on the 1 September train. Along with her parents, he did not survive the war. There were others who'd had the same devastating experience.

However, we know of one, Ruth Steckelmacher, now Federmann, due to leave on 1 September, who escaped and made her way to Palestine. Some of her pictures and a letter recommending her are in Nicky's scrapbook and she identified them when she met Nicky in Israel fifty years later. Hers is the only testimony I know of about what happened that day. She told of receiving an early call from her aunt to say the train would not be leaving but of making the trip anyway with her mother by taxi to Wilson station where they were turned away at the entrance by German soldiers. It seems that all those children who had not already been warned the train was cancelled, and who arrived at the station, were sent away, back to their homes or lodgings. How many others found alternative routes to safety is not known but Nicky's overriding sense then and later was of great disappointment and sorrow. One day earlier and they might have got through.

One of the lodgings the children returned to was an apartment owned by Ruza Erhmannová, Ruth Federmann's aunt, and loaned to the BCRC for the particular use of unaccompanied children. She was born in Vienna but moved to Prague on marrying and bought two apartments there to turn into a kindergarten. In late December 1938 or early January 1939, seeing the danger approaching, she'd offered Warriner a deal. In return for Doreen's help to get her own two children to England, she would loan the BCRC one apartment as a hostel for children from outside Prague who needed somewhere to stay while awaiting their train's departure. Before long the apartment was hosting hundreds of children, as well as a few adults, who had arrived in Prague to take their place on one of the trains Nicky and Trevor were organising. Ruza's children were not forgotten by Warriner and were added at the last minute to a transport though never put on the official list. They were not the only ones unlisted in the chaos of the fast-paced operation.

After the 1 September train was cancelled, over forty children due to leave on that transport returned to Ruza's apartment. These names are listed in a document found in the archives of the Theresienstadt ghetto, set up just outside Prague by the Nazis to house Jews as a holding station en route to concentration camps. The papers reveal not only that around the beginning of September these children stayed with 'Erhmannová', but also, with the gruesome bureaucracy the Nazis became known for, the places they went on to and the dates. Mostly it was Auschwitz.

Others due to leave on that fateful train must have returned to different lodgings or homes. A final letter in the scrapbook from Mrs Guthrie, dated 2 September 1939, concerns the fate of the children remaining in Prague who were due to leave on the cancelled train and who now needed to be looked after or returned home. It seems the authorities were closing down her committee. However, that was the last missive from the Prague end, with no further information about these children, who they were or what happened to them.

With war now declared and Nicky's part in the rescue over, there was no more he could do for the remaining children. His thoughts turned elsewhere, and he left the aftercare and wrapping up of the operation to others. His mother, Barbara, charged with managing any ongoing matters, dealt with problems arising for the children if their foster families could no longer keep them or if other issues arose, and she continued to do this throughout the war. She befriended some of the older children and kept in touch with them, some for many years. One of these, Susanne Medas, remembers her as a 'tall and stately lady; she wore an elegant outfit and had a fox-fur round her shoulders . . . She was completely in charge, and that impressed me.'

Indeed on one occasion at Liverpool Street station, the ortho-dox Jews who came to collect some children refused to take their luggage as it was the Sabbath, a day of rest, when they believed that any form of work was forbidden, even carrying cases. Barbara insisted that they should pick up the luggage, berating them with the words, 'My son has worked day and night and done everything possible to save these children and you say that you can't break the Jewish law. What sort of nonsense is that?' They buckled under her uncompromising order, meekly signed for the children and took them away with their luggage. She could be fierce and impos-ing when necessary. It's likely that she found this task, which Nicky had asked her to take on, to be a truly satisfying one. She had been a housewife and mother since marrying at seventeen and her intense intellect and strength of character had not been fulfilled in that role. She rose to the challenge wholeheartedly.

Judith's identity document, issued by UK government – front

Judith's identity document – back

**MOVEMENT FOR THE CARE OF CHILDREN FROM GERMANY, Ltd.**

BRITISH INTER-AID COMMITTEE

Telephone : MUSeum 2900 Ext. 61.

Room 61,

BLOOMSBURY HOUSE,

BLOOMSBURY STREET,

C Z E C H  S E C T I O N.

LONDON, W.C.1.

PLEASE QUOTE

Report "B".

2nd October, 1939.

STATEMENT OF CHILDREN BROUGHT OVER UP TO THE
1st SEPTEMBER 1939, SHOWING OUR COMMITMENTS
FOR RE-EMIGRATION GUARANTEES.

Transports from Prague.

|  |  |  |  |
|---|---|---|---|
| 1st | 14th March, 1939 | 20 | |
| 2nd | 19th April, 1939 | 36 | |
| 3rd | 29th April, 1939 | 29 | |
| 4th | 13th May, 1939 | 61 | |
| 5th | 2nd June, 1939 | 123 | |
| 6th | 1st July, 1939 | 241 | |
| 7th | 20th July, 1939 | 76 | |
| 8th | 2nd August, 1939 | 68 | |
| Various transports from Vienna etc. | | 15 | |
| | Total | 669 | |

Specification of obligations:-

Before re-emigration deposit required .............. 20

of which - Boys under 12 ...... 5
Girls under 12 ...... 13
Girls over 12 ...... 2

Re-emigration deposits, etc:-

Cheque and cash deposits ..... 63
Securities ..................... 1
Bank Guarantees .............. 50
Personal guarantees ........... 134
Other Committees .......... 116
Movement ..................... 28
Czech Trust Fund ............. 22
Children's Section ........... 177       591

Children who travelled on own visum .................... 58

TOTAL 669

Report 'B' – transports from Prague

On the last pages of the scrapbook are a series of reports summarising the entire enterprise. These list the numbers of children brought out on each of the eight transports, the costs and guarantees paid to date, the ages and gender of the children and their religion. It is interesting to see the breakdown of religious affiliations as it demonstrates that although the majority were Jewish, not all were. In fact the list reads: 'Jewish 561, Unitarian 52, Roman Catholic 34, without confession 17, 664 (total)'.

Finally there is the complete list of names of the children brought out between March and August 1939, their destinations and financial guarantors. It was this list that Dr Maxwell used to make contact with some of the children in 1988. However, any list of the 250 children destined for the final train that never left, which would have existed in Prague, has never been found.

The scrapbook put together by Mr Loewinsohn must have been handed to Nicky around the end of that year. By then Nicky was already busily engaged in war work and looking forward, not back. It was only his urge to keep records that kept the scrapbook intact, along with some old diaries and letters, through his various moves over the next fifty years.

There the Kindertransport story ends. The chronicle of how Nicholas Winton became the person that was ready, able and willing to undertake such a task follows.

# 3

## A Formative Heritage

### 1989

The Israel visit of 1989 was more than just an opportunity for my parents to deliver the scrapbook to Yad Vashem. It was also a chance for Israeli 'children' to meet Nicky and Grete and have that chat: about their names on the list, the families left behind and the lives made since.

Hugo Marom, one of those 'children', who was now a successful airport designer and alumnus of the Israeli air force, hosted a lunch for Nicky and Grete and other Israelis who had discovered they had been on one of the 1939 trains. Meeting these warm, welcoming people and their families was the highlight of the trip and Nicky did his best to answer the questions they put to him about that time. The story, written up in the *Jerusalem Post*, led others in Israel who had made the same original journey but were not on the grapevine of Czech refugees to discover the news and make contact.

Sometime later that year, Hugo wrote to Nicky saying he wanted to put him forward for recognition by Israel as a Righteous Gentile. Nicky was startled; it was not something he felt appropriate. He and Grete had seen the Avenue of Righteous Gentiles at Yad Vashem with its trees and plaques in honour of those non-Jews who had risked their lives to save Jews during the Holocaust.

He knew this did not apply to him and so he replied to Hugo quickly to let him know, 'I can't possibly accept. My contribution was far too modest and my life was never in danger. Besides, Mother and my paternal grandparents were German Jews. My parents were baptised; I was baptised and later confirmed; I've never practised any religion. In fact, I am agnostic. I certainly didn't consider myself Jewish, but since meeting you children and going to Yad Vashem, I sometimes wonder what I really am, but I suppose, in the eyes of Yad Vashem I am a Jew . . .'

Though the letter prevented Hugo taking this further, he still wanted Nicky to receive recognition for his part in the rescue and so started a campaign that led to a letter of thanks from the then President of Israel, Ezer Weizman, which Nicky received in 1994. Much of the interest in Nicky's involvement in the Kindertransport developed around the question of 'Why did he do it?'; why did he feel the impulse to help when so many did not? What motivated him and what knowledge did he have that led him to act urgently when the British and US governments thought that there was no hurry? After all, it was pointed out that he was a well-paid, cosmopolitan young man enjoying a good lifestyle in the heart of London, with many friends and interests to fill his time. From a cursory examination of his life until then, he had shown no signs of altruism or intense idealism or the kind of hardship that would cause empathy with the suffering of others.

This view is superficial, however. A detailed look at his family history, upbringing, schooling and early adulthood does shed light on his motivation and actions. Along with his natural character, his background and early life moulded him and prepared him to act at just the time it was needed. There is much to examine, not least the Jewish family background and the conscious suppression by his parents of their Jewishness while integrating their family into British life just as the First World War was taking place.

So, on starting to look at my father's early life, I began with his family history. Having never been a convert to genealogy, or even family anecdotes, it was all new to me. On telling me some stories, a second cousin commented, 'Surely you know all this stuff!' I didn't, but the more I learnt, the more hooked I became. Sure, my father and his contemporaries were interesting, but his parents' generation were fascinating – and complex! How I wish now I had met them all but I only ever knew my grandmother, Barbara (who I am named after), her brother Emil and his wife Kate. That generation really deserve a whole book to themselves but I have only room for a flavour. This then was the stock from which my father grew and these characters the people who influenced his early years. What follows in this chapter, before I look more deeply at Nicky's early school years in the next, is a look at the family surrounding him. Through this it can be seen how, as a result, he would have already been aware of the political climate in Germany.

My father, Nicholas George Wertheim (now Winton), was born over one hundred years ago on 19 May 1909, the second of three children. His grandparents on his father's side, Nicholaus and Charlotte Wertheim (née Kahn), both German-born, had come to Britain in the late 1860s, a part of that wave of German-Jewish immigrants at the time. They started off in Manchester, but around five or so years later bought Stonecroft, at 5 Cleve Road in West Hampstead, North London, which would be the family home until the 1930s. Nicholaus was the director of a bank and in the 1870s was sent to Moscow to represent the bank there. While there he also held the position of American Honorary Consul, despite being a British citizen.

Nicholaus and Charlotte had four children: William, known as Bruno (b. 1877), then Alexander, known as Sasha (b. 1879), Rudolf, Nicky's father (b. 1881) and Hannah, though Hannah's birth date is not recorded and there is scant trace of her life in family records. The 1901 census shows the family ensconced at Stonecroft and the inhabitants listed as: Nicholaus aged sixty-four, now anglicised to

Nicholas, his profession given as a merchant banker; his wife Charlotte aged fifty-four; and two sons, Alexander aged twenty-one, a farmer's assistant, and Rudolf aged nineteen, a bankers' clerk, both recorded as born in Russia. The two other children are not on the census, so obviously were living elsewhere at the time. Bruno seems to have been in Germany, as it was common for young men going into finance to learn the business in other countries. Also in the house were three servants: a housemaid, a parlourmaid and a cook.

The following ten years saw seismic changes at Stonecroft, as the next census of 1911 revealed. By then both Nicholaus and Charlotte were gone, having died within a few months of each other in 1905. Rudolf was married and his brother Alexander was no longer there. It seems that Nicky's father, Rudolf, had gone to Germany in 1907 at the age of twenty-six to find a wife, and returned with Babette Wertheimer who was nineteen, nicknamed Babi.

Their first child, Charlotte (Lottie), was born in 1908 when Babette was twenty, Nicholas (Nicky) was born when she was twenty-one and Robert (Bobby), the youngest, when she was twenty-six. Babette was from a prosperous, respected and highly intelligent family who had lived in Nürnberg for some generations. With similar surnames, it seems that both their families may have originated from Wertheim, a town not far from Nürnberg and it is likely they were introduced by extended family or friends in the area.

Rudolf appeared to be the one out of the four children to inherit the house. It was a large rather than grand house, now divided into nine flats, but at that time it housed his family and four servants. The 1911 census states that these were a cook, a parlourmaid, a housemaid and a nurse to help with the babies. Nicky's memories of his early childhood are sketchy and fragmentary. The cook would receive her daily instructions for meals from Babette, who herself did not enter the kitchen; it was the cook's domain. At mealtimes a piece of meat would be put on the table with its accompaniments, the family would take a helping and whatever was left would be taken away and not seen again – probably eaten by the servants, but not obviously used in further meals. This was a time before refrigeration, so fresh food was bought almost daily, and eaten straight away. There were regular shopping trips and similarly frequent food deliveries which arrived by horse and cart, including ice – a huge block which would get chunks cut off for the larder – as well as milk and other perishables. One particular incident Nicky remembers was of straw being put down on the road outside a nearby house where someone was ailing, to muffle the noise of the hooves to allow them quiet.

He was five when the First World War started and has memories of the family decamping down to the cellar at night, wrapped in blankets. Bombs were falling nearby from the German Zeppelins, sent to destroy railway lines in North London. These memories are of excitement rather than fear, so his parents obviously managed to keep their anxiety under control. After the war he had trips to the Whitestone pond in Hampstead to sail his toy boats, and later he and his friends would cycle around Hampstead as well as going swimming in the ponds on the Heath and ice skating in nearby Cricklewood.

Their home life in London resembled that of many upper-middle-class British families of the time, with the difference of being Jewish and having a name which set them apart. Their Jewishness did not seem to shape them strongly except that it informed many of their social connections. Jewish immigrants had moved into the Hampstead area over the previous fifty years and many in their social group had obviously German-Jewish names. Rudolf and Babette didn't appear to give much importance to their religious heritage; for example, they didn't attend synagogue or use any obviously Jewish religious rituals at home. In fact their pragmatism regarding this was to have their children baptised, so as to fit into British life more easily, rather than as a sign of their own Christian conversion. Babette also anglicised her name to Barbara by which she was generally known (and which I will call her from here on). This Jewish social group impacted on Nicky's later self-assurance; he was part of it but also not part. Non-Jews considered him Jewish with his German-Jewish name, but Jews considered him gentile due to his Christian upbringing and ignorance of their religious customs.

Rudolf and Barbara Wertheim circa 1920

Nicholaus and Charlotte Wertheim circa 1875

Their Germanness was most obvious in their private family life in that they mostly spoke German at home up until the First World War. After war was declared, Rudolf came home one day and said, 'We will not speak German at home anymore.' So, despite speaking German until the age of five, Nicky gradually forgot it to the degree that, in his late teens when he spent time in Germany, it took a bit of time for him to become fluent again.

Rudolf started his career in banking, listed as a bankers' clerk in the 1901 census then a bank manager in 1911, but after the war he began a business importing Czech glass. The company continued for some time but did not seem to be that successful as money was tight in the family, and in the early '30s during the general recession, it went bust. Despite his relatively poor success in business, it did not seem to prevent the family enjoying an outwardly

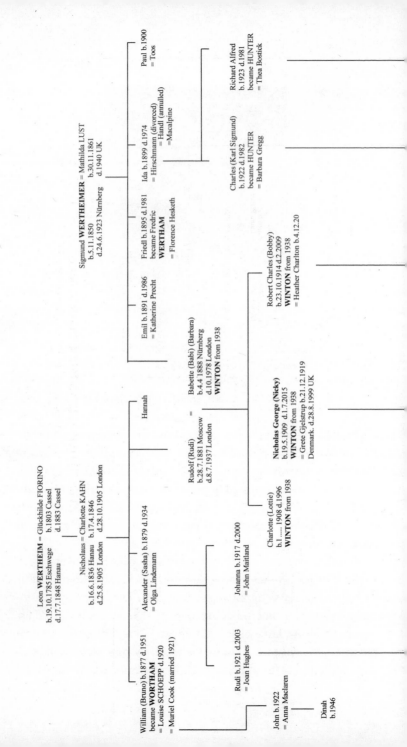

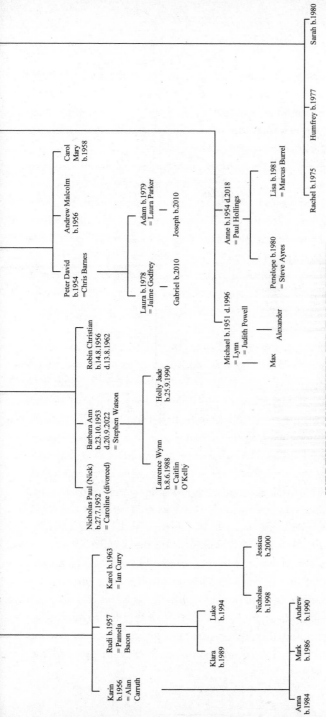

**WERTHEIM/WERTHEIMER FAMILY TREE**
(some family names changed to Wortham or Winton)

well-to-do lifestyle. He obviously put on a good front whatever the actual circumstances became. This front was maintained towards his children through a catalogue of material and emotional disasters that beset him and, to them, he was always a kind and supportive, though frequently absent, father.

The 1914–18 war was one of those stressful times for him. Though having relatives still in Germany, Rudolf was a British citizen and wanted to join up. He was refused permission to join a regular regiment due to his German background and Russian birth, despite producing his certificates of naturalisation. It was a source of huge exasperation to him. Nevertheless he served his country in the home-based Pioneer Corps. By the end of the war, his health had suffered to such a degree that he never truly recovered, leading eventually to his early death at the age of fifty-six.

But what of Rudolf's siblings? Bruno, the eldest, had left the family home by the age of twenty-four and there is scant record of his early life in family records. What there is shows him becoming an accountant and marrying in 1921, aged forty-four, to Muriel, fifteen years his junior, with whom he had a son, John. The family settled in Maidenhead by the Thames, where his brother Rudolf and nephew Nicholas (Nicky) used to occasionally visit. It seems, however, that events in his early adult life caused problems which reverberated through his wider family and which only came to light with some recent intense detective work. It is likely this had a huge and traumatic effect on the Wertheims, both during and after the First World War, and so I will mention the details.

This story involved an early marriage. His first wife, Louise, leaves no trace in the family archives; no photos or information relating to her survive and her very existence was hidden. Research in the last few years at the National Archives has led to her discovery and the reason for this erasure. Louise, or Lizzie as she was known, was from a German family named Schoepp, and met

Bruno in Berlin in 1901, marrying him the following year. By 1913 they had formally separated, though without divorcing, as that would have been a truly scandalous undertaking at that time, and Bruno gave her a yearly income of £518, worth about £23,000 today. She had grown accustomed to a rather nice way of life with Bruno, and after their separation was left with what she considered only a relatively small allowance each year. The following year Bruno became bankrupt, the years of high living finally taking their toll, but she continued to receive her allowance even after that from the Official Receiver.

However, while in Amsterdam in 1914 and running out of money to maintain her lifestyle, she was recruited by German Intelligence, being pro-German and attracted perhaps by the intrigue of being a spy and the chance to move in more glamorous circles again. The following year, she and her accomplice, Breeckow, were arrested, and charged with espionage and treason. At their trial, Breeckow persuaded the jury that Lizzie had acted under his influence and while he was sentenced to death, she received ten years in prison. However, once in prison her mental state declined and she ended her days in Broadmoor, dying in 1920 of tuberculosis. Records show that Bruno attended her funeral. A year later he remarried and went on to have a more settled life thereafter.

It is hard to imagine a worse situation for a naturalised German family trying to integrate into British life during the First World War than for a story such as this to be linked to them, however obscurely. It is a tribute to their success in keeping the link hidden that no one from my father's generation seemed aware of the story, though inevitable that Nicky's parents and their siblings must have known Lizzie during her marriage to Bruno and followed the trial in 1915. Rudolf and Barbara both had difficulties in the war without this addition. Anti-German feeling was intense, worse even than during the Second World War, and Barbara was stigmatised socially, refused access to her bridge club and snubbed by many friends, while Rudolf had been refused entry to the regular army. A relative, even an ex-one, convicted of spying must have been shocking and terrifying for them. It seems possible that having their children baptised into the Church of England in 1916 was a further attempt to distance themselves from all things German, as was anglicising their name to Wortham for the war's duration. Whatever the circumstances, it seems certain that the story was never mentioned to my father or his siblings and buried away in their parents' memories. Bruno himself changed his name at some point to Wortham, possibly to also escape this connection, but that is not known. Wortham remained his family's name until the present day.

Rudolf's other brother Alexander is another mystery. He was listed in the 1901 census, aged twenty-one, as living at Stonecroft with his parents and brother Rudolf. His occupation of farmer's assistant seems not exactly in keeping with the other men in the house, both Nicholas, his father, and Rudolf, his younger brother, being bankers. By the 1911 census, Alexander is recorded as being on the Isle of Man and married to Olga (née Lindemann) but disappears from any family records.

Our recent discovery of him came about through the wonders of the internet, with two of his grandchildren making contact having learnt about Nicky and discovering the link. Even they do not know his story and how he came to be buried in a churchyard in Hereford where I discovered his grave – my great-uncle buried just a few miles from where I have lived for twenty-five years! With the name and location discovered, I found a letter in Nicky's papers, which Alexander wrote to Rudolf in 1931 mostly complaining about having recently broken his leg, but also intriguingly asking 'whether there is a small keepsake for me from dear Hanni's estate?' and ending 'Your very affectionate brother Alex', which shows there was some ongoing contact between them.

Could Hanni be Hannah, the fourth sibling who leaves even less of a trace, just a name, no date of birth, death or record of existence? Apart from this possible mention, the only other trace of her was found in the testimony of Lizzie Wertheim during her trial, when she states she stayed with Bruno's sister in Hampstead after their separation. Who else could it be? So perhaps Hannah married and lived near her family but her life remains a mystery.

And now to Nicky's mother's family who were no less intriguing and influential than his father's, in fact even more so. Here again their stories were, if not exactly hidden, then at least not really discussed by our family. As mentioned, Babette/Barbara came from an intellectual German-Jewish family called Wertheimer living in Nürnberg, a large beautiful Bavarian city, which had been home to a Jewish population for at least 700 years. The family were well integrated into German society, her father Sigmund being a successful businessman, at one time head of the city council and a reserve officer in the army. Her mother, Matilda Lust, was eleven years younger than Sigmund, one of five children, also from Jewish stock. It seems likely that the families knew each other, as not only did Matilda marry Sigmund but Matilda's sister Frieda married Sigmund's brother Adolf.

Adolf and Frieda (Nicky's great-uncle and aunt) left Germany first for Britain then Australia, along the way changing their name to Winter, perhaps during the First World War. Nicky's diaries of the mid-1920s make occasional mention of visits to Uncle Adolf and Aunt Frieda in London, so they were still in London then. They had three children; the middle one, Ella, became a writer and, after marrying Lincoln Steffens, a well-known American political journalist, became active in the movement fighting for the rights of agricultural labourers in California. They were friends with the writers John Steinbeck and Henry Miller and philosopher/anthropologist Joseph Campbell. After

Steffens' death, she married Donald Ogden Stewart, an American playwright and screenwriter. After he was blacklisted during the McCarthy anti-communist purge, they emigrated back to London. She only died in 1980 and yet was not involved in any family get-togethers. Sadly I had never heard of her until recently when I came across her autobiography, *And Not To Yield*, in my father's bookcase.

But back to Nicky's maternal grandparents, Sigmund and Matilda. They had five children, Barbara being the oldest, born in 1888, then Emil, Frederic, Ida and Paul. It's hard now to imagine what it was like to be a woman growing up at the end of the nineteenth century – the expectations placed on them of making a good marriage and the limitations for work and independence. In Germany, a woman's role was summed up by the three Ks: Kinder (children), Kirche (church) and Küche (kitchen).They were not allowed to vote until 1919, though that was nine years before British universal suffrage.

However, Sigmund and Matilda had rather progressive views for the time, as their two girls were not held back from following academic possibilities. Barbara was one of the first girls in Germany to take the *Abitur*, similar to the International Baccalaureate today. Despite this high achievement, she married aged nineteen and came to London rather than continue on to university.

From her home in London, bringing up three children, playing bridge and attending cultural events, she witnessed her much younger sister, Ida, forging a brilliant medical career. All five siblings were extremely intellectual and bright; the life of the intellect was valued highly in the Wertheimer family. Talking to Nicky about his mother, his feeling was that Barbara, having foregone a career for marriage, had been most likely left frustrated and envious of Ida and her life, with a dissatisfaction in her own circumstances that never passed.

Ida was born in 1899, eleven years after Barbara, and so was only ten years older than Nicky. She was a determined and forceful character like her elder sister but more so, and against the odds enrolled at the University at Erlangen to study medicine in 1918. Her studies continued from 1918 to 1925, stopping temporarily in 1921 to marry a Mr Hirschmann, with whom she had two sons, Karl (Charles), born in 1922, and Richard, born in 1923, but even these interruptions did not stop her completing her doctorate.

Marriage was not to stop her career, but there must have been problems as it was not long before they divorced. She next had a relationship with, though no evidence of marrying, a Mr Bing who was the director of the largest toy factory in Nürnberg. Nicky remembers, while doing his bank training in Germany in 1929, being invited to visit the factory and to select any toy he wanted as a present. He chose a large, beautifully made metal clockwork ship, not the most practical gift to take home.

Ida must have been a determined and formidable woman to have overcome all the obstacles she met. In 1933, having been practising as a doctor in Berlin, she fled Germany for Britain and quickly married Frederic Handl, a friend of Barbara and Rudolf. This marriage was not a love affair, rather a favour. Being desperate to escape from Germany and the increasing anti-Jewish atmosphere, she had persuaded Handl, originally Austrian but now with British citizenship, to help by marrying her in order to obtain British citizenship. Frederic Handl was close to Barbara and it seems that this was a favour to her, on the understanding that when Ida was established with her own papers, they would divorce or have the marriage annulled. Frederic Handl had been widowed many years before and had brought up his two daughters himself.

One daughter was Irene Handl, born in 1901, who looked after her father until 1937 when she started on her very successful acting career. She appeared in films and TV sitcoms alongside actors such as Peter Sellers, Tony Hancock and Eric Sykes. Irene – or Dolly as she was known at home – remained a close friend of Barbara for many years.

Ida had been well off in Germany but had to leave all her possessions behind. She and her children anglicised their name to Hunter on arriving in the UK, Hirsch being 'deer' in German, and wanting no doubt to keep the initial letter. In the late '30s she undertook further training in psychiatry, which became her specialty for the rest of her life.

Ida visited Nicky and his parents frequently in the early days, but in later life Nicky never saw her and, though she lived to 1974, I never heard her mentioned during my childhood or teens. Nicky remembers that there was tension in the relationship between Barbara and her sister, and his loyalty to his mother kept them apart.

Family group circa 1933. L–R standing: Nicky, Ida, Rudolf, Barbara, Frederic Handl, seated: Lottie, Richard Hunter

It is quite likely that the envy Barbara felt for the career that Ida had developed, while her role remained as housewife and mother, was aggravated further by more personal issues. It seems that having received UK citizenship through her marriage, Ida was reluctant to then annul it, despite having agreed in advance, and for some time remained married to Mr Handl. As Mr Handl was Barbara's close friend and later her lover, she may well have been incensed by Ida's reluctance to let him go and even jealous that an intimate relationship may have been really happening.

During the Second World War, Ida moved to Lancashire for her work and, at some point, the marriage was indeed annulled so that Ida could marry George Macalpine, a son of the local building dynasty, and a much older man. When he died some years later, she returned to London.

She had encouraged both her sons to become doctors, despite Charles wanting to study mathematics at which he excelled. Ida dominated her sons, and they grew up damaged by her refusal to let them live the lives they may rather have chosen. When Charles decided to marry she thought it would distract him from his intellectual calling and refused to go to the wedding, thereafter turning her full attention onto her youngest son, Richard. Living and working together in an open-plan flat, lined top to bottom with books, they researched the history of psychiatry and interesting case histories. These were turned into books, two of which became well known and influential: *Three Hundred Years of Psychiatry, 1535–1860*, and the book which brought her fame and controversy, *George III and the Mad-Business*, which postulated that George III had porphyria, an inherited physical condition which caused mental symptoms. This book inspired Alan Bennett to write his play on the subject, which was later made into the film, *The Madness of King George*. Indeed, Ida was portrayed as a character in the play.

Nicky did not see Ida after he moved to Maidenhead in 1950. Their lives, so closely interwoven for a short while, separated for good. She lived in London but was totally engrossed in her work and did not welcome family interaction. Her life and Richard's involved reading, more reading and cataloguing her collection. Both she and Richard smoked furiously and both died from lung cancer. She did not always behave well towards others and was always concerned about money, and it is likely that the trials and injustices she suffered in Germany before escaping had a profound influence on her and the way she related to others. How much her life and character influenced Nicky is hard to know, but he certainly admired her plain-talking and her strength of character.

Friedl Wertheimer was the third child of Sigmund and Matilda, born seven years after Barbara in 1895. He visited England frequently, possibly to stay with his newly married sister, and found himself caught there when the First World War was declared. He was briefly interned but obviously not considered a threat as he was paroled to commence medical study at King's College London.

After the end of the war he returned to Germany to finish his medical degree at the University of Erlangen, contemporaneously with his sister Ida. He specialised in psychiatry, studying in clinics throughout Europe and bringing him into contact with Freud and other notable trailblazers in the field.

In 1922, he changed his name to Fredric Wertham and emigrated to the USA, joining the psychiatric clinic at Johns Hopkins University in Baltimore and applying for citizenship. There he met his future wife, Florence Hesketh, an artist, who collaborated with him on his first book, *The Brain as an Organ*, a study on neuropathology.

He went on to found pioneering clinics, one in Harlem offering psychiatric treatment for the poor African-American immigrants living there. His fame and notoriety came with his study into the effects of comics on juvenile violence, called *Seduction of the*

*Innocent*. He spent the rest of his life researching violence, writing up case histories of several tragic murders as well as campaigning to censor violent images from comics. He believed that some comics were mass-conditioning children to 'confuse violence with strength, sadism with sex, racial prejudice with patriotism, crime with heroism'. He did not spare television either, considering that the violent images in programmes could affect behaviour. It is interesting to see that this discussion still goes on today, without any clear resolution. He believed that violence was not innate in humans, but the result of social conditioning and arising from social and economic injustice, racial bias, authoritarianism and mass exploitation of fear and hate. He therefore believed that violence could be reduced by changing society.

He was obviously a focused, sharply intelligent and idealistic man who spent his working life in clinics, universities and Senate hearing rooms, as well as courtrooms. It doesn't appear that he made trips to visit his family in Britain and there is no evidence of much contact at all. Nicky and Grete did meet his wife in New York during their honeymoon in 1950, but he was too busy to see them and there were no other opportunities. He died in 1981 aged eighty-six.

Fredric Wertham

Barbara's two other brothers were Emil, second eldest, and Paul, the baby of the family, born in 1900. Emil came to Britain sometime before the 1939 war and lived initially in Manchester, having set up a plastics factory there. He married a German girl from Bamberg, near to Nürnberg, called Kate, who was Catholic, which caused some waves in both families, but they lived happily together until he died in the 1980s.

They were very much part of the family group and were often visitors to our family home in Maidenhead. I remember him as a very well-dressed, elegant but warm great-uncle who loved horse riding. The only advice he ever gave me was to 'count your blessings', which I have never forgotten. Kate was even more well dressed and elegant, and was definitely the star of the family with her immaculate make-up and designer dresses.

Paul, the youngest sibling, remained in Germany, living in Hamburg at the time that Nicky did his bank training there, later moving to Rotterdam where he worked in the leather trade. During the war, when the Germans invaded, he was hidden for years by a Dutch family, surviving to later marry the daughter, known as Toos. He died having developed an ear infection during a trip to South America for his business soon after. He certainly looked after Nicky like a kindly uncle in Hamburg for the months Nicky was there and took his role seriously, lecturing Nicky when he partied too hard about his responsibilities and the need to tone it down a bit. However, his light-hearted side meant they had fun together too and he helped Nicky develop a healthy balance between leisure and work, which never left him. Perhaps Nicky's sharp sense of humour and love of laughter came from this young uncle.

Nicky's early life was very family orientated, with much of his time spent with close and extended family. This reliance on family support has stayed with him, and throughout his life he remained regularly in touch with his siblings and their families and often urged his own children and grandchildren to remember the value of family ties. Many of his character traits, views and aptitudes can be seen in his parents, uncles and aunts, though others seem very much his own.

What seems clear, however, is that though there was an emotional closeness, there were also aspects of life in his parents' generation that remained private and were never discussed with the children. This capacity to keep different sides of a life separated was inherited by my father and appears through his own life as a recurring theme. Other qualities and skills that he developed as he grew up came from his school experience, which was another major influence on his worldview and behaviour.

# 4

## *School Days*

### *1989*

In June 1989, Nicky met more of his 'children' at an event in London: the International Reunion of the Kindertransport, organised by Bertha Leverton, one of the 10,000 German children brought to Britain who wanted to mark the fiftieth anniversary of their rescue with a get-together.

Over 1,000 grown-up *Kinder* turned up – a huge number but still only a fraction of those who'd come from Czechoslovakia on the trains Nicky and his colleagues had organised. For those Czechs who attended, it was an opportunity to meet a pivotal person from that time who might be able to answer some of their long-held questions.

The same happened the following summer at a reunion of the alumni from the Czech school in Britain, where many of those who came on the trains were educated during the war. Yet more of his 'children' turned up, and Nicky and Grete heard new stories with interest and often delight from those who had gone on to have successful and fulfilling lives despite the appalling adversity they had suffered so young.

The school had been established by the Czech government-in-exile for refugee children in Great Britain during the war. It had several homes but its final location from 1943 onwards was at the Abernant Lake Hotel in Llanwrtyd Wells in Wales. It closed at the end of the war, when most students returned to Czechoslovakia.

The school held about 140 pupils, many Jewish, but others were Roman Catholic, Protestant or without religious affiliation. About one third of the pupils had come on the Czech transports organised by Nicky, though others had fled to Britain with their parents. The pupils at the boarding school became a close-knit bunch, having gone through so much together and becoming like a big new family. This was a very different schooling to the one my father had gone through and which no doubt moulded them, as his did him.

## *1916–26*

Nicky had started prep school at the age of seven, right in the middle of the First World War in 1916, at University College School in Frognal, Hampstead, a brisk walking distance from home. He had not, like many other middle-class boys, been sent away to school to learn to be independent at an early age, though the war and his family's situation during it may have played their part in that. His memories of that time are few but, despite his German ancestry during the virulently anti-German mood of the First World War, he does not remember being especially unhappy or bullied.

It may be that it wasn't his nature to notice any slights, as his parents certainly suffered from being of German descent at the time. His mother's ostracism by her British-born friends for the duration meant that her social life was reduced to the family's German-Jewish friends in the neighbourhood, who were likely to have been in a similar position. Changing their surname to Wortham for the war's duration perhaps also provided some shielding at school. Nicky made one life-long friend there: Stanley Murdoch, who would influence the next major step in his life.

Despite his close attachment to his parents, in 1923, aged fourteen, he badgered them to send him to Stowe, a new public school that had just opened that year. This was solely due to the fact that his best friend, Stanley, had told him that's where he was going and where Stanley went, Nicky wanted to follow.

Stanley lived across Cleve Road from Nicky, so not only were they at the same school but they also spent much of their free time together. Stanley would come over in the evenings and they would spend hours making crystal sets (early radios), involving winding wire round tubes to make the device for tuning in, and a fine wire, known as a cat's whisker, to touch the crystal at exactly the right place with the right pressure to get any reception. There was a real sense of achievement if they ever got it tuned in to a programme. While they were fiddling around with their crystal sets, Rudolf bought a wireless, the height of new technology at the time. It was full of valves, each as big as a light bulb, and the whole thing was the size of a cupboard. It was considered a marvel by the whole family, though being very expensive and delicate only Rudolf was allowed to touch it.

Nicky felt that the Murdochs were perhaps uncomfortable with his parents, and he was initially less frequently invited over to Stanley's house. Later this changed and he would go across, especially on Christmas Eve, and play poker. Mrs Murdoch had been one of the Gaiety Girls in her youth but was now 'one of the fattest ladies I'd ever met', according to Nicky. As Gaiety Girls – who formed the chorus line in musical comedies at the Gaiety Theatre in the Strand – would have been slim and athletic, she had obviously ballooned after marrying and having children. One memory of his, which demonstrates his affection for Mrs Murdoch, involved their family poker games. She would say while playing, 'Children, I've got a wonderful hand, don't bet,' not as a bluff, as some might, but to warn them she was about to win.

Stanley's father, James, had a musical instrument business in Oxford Street, which was run by Gerald, Stanley's brother, after his father died during the Second World War. Stanley, in adult life, worked in the same field, running Harrods' piano department. James invited Nicky and Stanley to his premises one day to listen to 'the best reproduced sound ever made'. On arrival, they entered a long room containing a gramophone with a huge 30-foot-long trumpet attached, an enormously exaggerated version of the usual gramophones used for playing 78 rpm records at that time.

Stanley was a larger-than-life, outgoing, cheerful character, though his Victorian upbringing, like Nicky's, meant that feelings were kept internalised. Their life-long friendship seemed to be based on the ease they had together, a shared sense of humour and lots of fun. They did not engage much in deep discussions or cultural activities particularly, and their political views were diametrically opposed, but this did not stop their brotherly love built from years of shared history. Indeed their closeness increased when they shared a flat for some years after leaving home in their early twenties, and only slightly diminished when Stanley married and moved out.

Anyway, back to Stowe. Nicky's parents were obviously happy to oblige their eldest son's wishes and contacted J. F. Roxburgh, the founder and headmaster of Stowe. Nicky was accepted, though what the criteria were for admission are not known. He was in the founding year, along with ninety-nine other boys of around thirteen years old, entering in the second term in September 1923 and joining Grenville House.

There were a few in his time there who stood out. One was David Niven, who went on to become a famous Hollywood actor and writer, who had been expelled from his prep school and was therefore unable to attend Eton as had been expected. Nicky remembered him once arriving at school with an 'aunt' whom he showed around, his reputation as a ladies' man starting early! This story is recounted by Niven in his autobiography, *The Moon's a Balloon*, describing the woman concerned as a prostitute aged seventeen, who he had met when aged fifteen. He had fallen in love with her and visited her in London often, also bringing her to Stowe on one or two occasions, and introducing her to JF, as the headmaster was known. Niven wrote in glowing terms about Stowe: 'Stowe must be the most beautiful school in England.' He quoted a speech JF had given in the first term, when he said that 'every boy who goes out from Stowe will know beauty when he sees it for the rest of his life'.

Another pupil Nicky remembered was Geoffrey de Havilland Junior, the son of the aircraft pioneer, also Geoffrey de Havilland. Nicky remembers him arriving at school in an aeroplane, landing on a playing field – this in the early 1920s when flying was in its infancy. Geoffrey Jnr went on to become chief test pilot for De Havilland planes and carried out the maiden flights of both the de Havilland Mosquito and the de Havilland Vampire. He died in 1946 while carrying out high speed tests in a new plane, which crashed over the Thames Estuary.

Stowe suited Nicky. JF was very keen to bring out the best from every pupil and they were given a fair amount of freedom to follow their interests. JF's comment that he wanted to turn out young men who would be 'acceptable at a dance and invaluable in a shipwreck' suggested not only good manners but also resourcefulness, moral courage and an ability to put the needs of others first. This emphasis at Stowe certainly imbued Nicky with these qualities. Niven admitted to worshipping JF, as I think did Nicky, for his charisma and the atmosphere he created at the school. The boys wanted to earn his respect and live up to his high moral standards. JF had broken with the tradition of formal dress of top hats and formal clothes, which the other public schools demanded. The pupils wore grey flannel suits in the week and blue on Sundays. According to the current headmaster, Dr Anthony Wallersteiner, JF wanted to create a 'place where the individual enthusiasms and interests of a particular boy were catered for. So if you had a slightly maverick, eccentric boy who was good at Latin and Greek but absolutely useless at games – and therefore probably bullied mercilessly at most of the late-Victorian public schools – he would fit in fine at Stowe. Roxburgh believed that it didn't really matter what you were good at – it didn't really matter what your interests were – so long as you were interested in something. And it was the duty of the school to bring out that particular enthusiasm and gift.'

Stowe School

Niven also described his genius: 'The first to notice some special interest being shown by a boy, Roxburgh nurtured it, fostered it and made the boy feel a little bit special because of it.'

Though Nicky was fairly short (about 5'6" when adult) with a German surname, not gregarious or especially good at sports, with quiet hobbies such as stamp collecting and photography, he didn't come in for the kind of bullying rife at other public schools, only an element of teasing due to his name. He didn't seem to make many friends either, but there is no mention of great unhappiness or trauma in the diaries he kept. So it does seem true that the atmosphere JF created there suited boys like him as much as the more robust types.

Nicky did have remarkable freedom to carry out his hobbies at Stowe, the most bizarre being his keeping of pigeons. His diaries of the time list his pigeon purchases, dates, expenditure, even the cost of the wood he bought to make their cages. He seemed to spend large amounts of free time building the cages, which then remained at Stowe housing the pigeons even throughout the holidays. He would go for a walk or a run with a friend and release a pigeon or two at a distance, so they could fly home to the school. Carpentry classes also featured regularly, though mostly with pigeon-related end results. Niven also mentions the pet keeping which went on, and how it gradually got out of hand as boys kept more and more exotic animals. 'Monkeys, bears, hyenas and skunks filled the cages. Finally, the school zoo was shut down for reasons of noise and smell.' Set against this, Nicky's pigeon exploits seem fairly tame.

He even tried horse riding as the school had its own stables. Riding through the woods one day, he was hit by a low-level branch and pulled off, ending up dangling in the tree. He was not so keen after that, only riding a few times again, and later in life, when I was in my horsey phase and attending the local riding school, he did not seem particularly interested.

Nicky recorded a year and a half of the three years he was at Stowe in his diaries, from January 1925 until April 1926. There were lots of mentions of fencing, which he took up in his second year in order to avoid playing cricket. Fencing was newly offered in 1925; they were looking for volunteers, he had decided he hated cricket and it was his way out. However, he soon became hooked due to a natural aptitude and, before long, was taking part in fencing matches against other schools and even universities.

His fencing tutor was Felix Gravé who came once a week to teach the boys at Stowe. Gravé taught in a fencing club in

London, as well as at Oxford University, and a few years later became the first president of the British Academy of Fencing Masters, as well as writing a classic tome on the subject: *Fencing Comprehensive*. Gravé had taught Rudolf in London and seemed pleased to take Nicky on, telling him after his first lesson, 'I will make a good fencer out of you.' He was obviously a talented teacher as, before long, the Stowe team were winning most of their matches against other public schools, as well as beating much older students from universities including Oxford and Cambridge. Nicky continued to fence at a competitive level for many years and always joined a club wherever he happened to be living. While doing his banking training in Germany in 1929, he was asked to join the team in his Hamburg club for a match against Copenhagen.

On his return to London in 1931, he rejoined Gravé's club, Salle Bertrand, the same club that the founder of the British Union of Fascists, Oswald Mosley, attended. They even had an occasional bout together. However, no politics was talked and Nicky has no memory of him there other than for an occasional bout. By the mid '30s, Nicky was becoming seriously interested in left-wing politics and to imagine him fighting against Mosley but never mentioning politics seems bizarre. I think that this is another sign of his ability to separate completely different areas of his life. Politics was kept separate from sport.

The competitive fencing continued with matches all over the country through the 1930s, as the medals in his cupboard demonstrate. During that time, he trained to be part of the British team of fencers for the 1940 Olympic Games. Due to the outbreak of war in Europe the games were suspended and not restarted until 1948, by which time Nicky was living in Paris and no longer a candidate. However, he continued to fence wherever he was: in Paris in 1947–48 and going to competitions around France, and again in New York during his honeymoon in the USA in 1950.

Fencing was obviously a major pleasure in his early life and
brought him a confidence that he did not gain from his more solitary pursuits. Nicky felt that his success at fencing while at Stowe
gave him respect from his fellow pupils and reduced any teasing
which might otherwise have come his way.

Unbeaten Fencing team 1926, Nicky
(NG Wertheim) seated far right

His diaries of 1925 and 1926 had pages at the back for letters
received and sent, and these were meticulously filled in with dates
and names. Letters were obviously a lifeline to his family and
home life, and visits from his parents to Stowe were also listed
with exclamation marks. His friends were sparse at Stowe, with
his diary entries listing the same few names when mentioning
walks, fencing or outings. Nicky says now that his German-Jewish

name and background may have had a deterrent effect on friendships, though at the time he was not aware of particularly overt anti-Semitic or xenophobic behaviour. He seemed to look up to one of his friends, a fencing compatriot surnamed De Amodio, and noted with pleasure when he was made captain of the fencing squad. He also liked and respected several teachers, and particularly JF who he kept in touch with sporadically for some time after leaving Stowe.

Also at the back of his diary was a space for listing books he had read. Whether the number listed in 1925 was representative of his normal reading habits is uncertain, but catalogued under 'Books Read' that year were forty-four titles, including such authors as H. G. Wells, Kipling, Dumas, Hugo, Conan Doyle and Rider Haggard. Against *The Three Musketeers* (Dumas) he remarked, 'Extremely exciting', but against *The Man in the Iron Mask* (Dumas again) it was, 'Passes the time'. His reading seemed to stay with the classics throughout his life, rather than extend too far into modern authors, and his taste could not be said to be adventurous.

Academically he did not shine, except in maths. His diary entries list his position in class on an almost weekly basis with self-admonitions to do better. He was obviously keen to do well and took seriously any criticisms from his teachers. However, maths was his forte, often coming top of the class. He frequently finished his maths classwork early, so that at one time, his teacher, Mr Heckstall-Smith, suggested an extra puzzle for him to work on – to solve how to trisect an angle. After a couple of days his teacher asked how he was getting on, and on receiving a negative reply encouraged him to keep working on it. After spending quite some weeks working on this, covering multiple sheets of paper with his calculations, he eventually admitted defeat, whereupon 'Heckie' remarked, 'Well, it's not surprising; no one else has ever done it either.'

Apart from being a brilliant mathematician, writing a well-known book on the subject, 'Heckie' was also a larger-than-life character. Nicky tells of how he built a boat in his school study, which on completion was so large they had to remove a window and part of the outer wall to get it out onto the lake. How could a boy not admire someone like that? After JF, Heckstall-Smith had the greatest influence on Nicky and some months after leaving Stowe, he notes in his diary that while visiting Petticoat Lane market he 'bought a Cartesian diver for Heckie', so they obviously remained in contact.

Nicky attended the school's chapel regularly and after a while began to consider confirmation, the initiation into full membership of the Christian community, which an adult makes after childhood baptism. He considered it a very serious decision, and agreed with his housemaster, Mr Clarke, to spend a year maturing before making the final decision. Regular preparatory classes continued until March 1925 when he finally committed himself to become a full Christian. His parents and brother Bobby came to Stowe to witness his confirmation by either the Archbishop of Canterbury or the Bishop of London. Nicky only remembers that it was someone hugely important. It was a momentous occasion marked by Nicky being given a leather-bound copy of the *Book of Common Prayer* by JF, inscribed, 'To NG Wertheim, on being confirmed at Stowe March 21 1925 from JF Roxburgh', as well as a small bible from his father.

Thereafter he began attending communion and continued his weekly chapel attendances. He took it all most seriously and continued to believe in God until his late twenties, when discussions with his socialist friends and hearing of Nazi atrocities in the pre-war years began to plant seeds of doubt. However, his final loss of faith came at the start of the Second World War when he learned that both the British and German priests were blessing their troops before going into battle. This knowledge made him finally feel that there could be no God, as how could the same God be on both sides? His doubt has never left him and for the rest of his life he has remained agnostic.

All the boys had to attend the OTC (Officer Training Corps) at the school (more frequently now known as the Army Cadet Force). This was not a favourite; lots of marching about in uniform, often in the rain, with occasional longer training camps at other locations. He recorded each session in his diary and before his first camp outing, noted, 'I don't know what it will be like, I am dreading it.' In the event, it was not as bad as he had expected with some quite exciting episodes including a 'ripping tank demonstration'. Eventually he noted, 'I don't think camp is so bad as I thought.'

Mr Clarke, Nicky's housemaster

Another area to feature regularly through his school diaries was his health; he had frequent low-level illnesses, mostly colds or other infections, which he diligently recorded, including his visits to the doctor or school sick bay. He did not make up illness to escape class or sport, but seemed to be anxious when he was ill

– maybe something he had picked up from his parents. It was only a few years after the Spanish flu pandemic, which spread across the world, decimating populations. In the UK alone it was estimated that 250,000 died, with the illness accelerating rapidly from sniffles to death. Not surprising, then, that a child getting a cold brought huge anxiety to his parents, and thus to him.

He was lucky to be very healthy, with no major medical problems through his life until very old age. His early anxiety about his own simple complaints did not transfer onto worrying about family or friends who were ill with more serious maladies. He would never want to know exactly what was wrong with a friend or relative, concerned only that they were unwell and expecting their full and speedy recovery. That had been his own experience of his mild illnesses after all and perhaps he wanted to keep that old anxiety at bay by not giving it his full attention. He left the giving of emotional support to others who were more understanding.

After a year or so, Nicky had settled in at Stowe and seemed to be enjoying school more generally. He noted in late 1925, aged sixteen, that he 'was Captain of a (rugby) side for the first time. I scored a try. In work I am not doing badly. My pigeons are getting on very well. So am I.' However, he continued to look forward with excitement to the holidays, and obviously loved spending time with his parents, going shopping with his mother, helping out his father in his office, and even going along to watch them play bridge at their friends', not something you would imagine many sixteen-year-old boys enjoying.

His time at Stowe came to an end in July 1926, aged seventeen. His School Certificate, the public exam which all pupils took at that age, showed he had passed the Oxford and Cambridge Schools Examination Board exams in English, Elementary Mathematics and Physics, though he did not do well enough to matriculate to attend university. As the subjects studied also included History,

Geography, Latin, French, German and Chemistry, his aptitude for study had obviously continued to be a struggle. He did eventually matriculate after leaving Stowe by taking extra classes in the evenings, but his father was not keen that he go on to university. Family finances were under strain by then and it was decided that his eldest son would go into banking as he had done. Nicky did not resist, even if it were possible. He seemed content to follow the path his father had decided on for him for the next chapter of his life.

Stowe had given Nicky much more than an academic education. He had been influenced by the charismatic and honourable characters in authority, and been given space to make his own choices and decide what he enjoyed and was good at. Attributes Nicky had developed there of independence, determination and following his own instincts, based on the moral ethos of social responsibility, were to influence his future decisions and directions.

# 5

## *From Youth to Adulthood*
### *1991*

In 1991, Nicky and Grete made their first trip to Prague at the invitation of the Jewish community there who wanted to thank Nicky for his pre-war work. Quite a number of the children who had come to Britain on the trains of 1939 had returned to live permanently in Czechoslovakia, and some had now been alerted to the story of their rescue and wanted to meet Nicky. To make the visit even more significant, they were invited to stay at the hotel where Nicky had lodged in January 1939. Now called the Hotel Europa, then the Grand Hotel Šroubek, it was wonderfully situated on Wenceslas Square right in the heart of the beautiful medieval city, relatively untouched by wartime bombs.

The visit was not the quiet tour of Prague and meeting with a few of his Czech 'children' that they were expecting. The media had been informed of the story of the children's rescue and of their arrival, and wanted to celebrate a good news story, with photos of white-haired women throwing their arms around an even older white-haired man. Politicians had also heard the news and decided to make their own response, leading to a flurry of unexpected formal events: an invitation to Prague Castle to meet Václav Havel, the President of the Czechoslovak Republic, and, even more historical, a chat with Alexander Dubček, Czechosolvak leader at the time of the Prague Spring in 1968. There was also a formal ceremony at the

Town Hall with the Mayor of Prague who bestowed on Nicky the Freedom of the City.

It was quite overwhelming for both Nicky and Grete, unused to cameras following them, journalists asking for interviews, politicians making speeches and constant attention. Despite the intensity and pressure, they found it incredibly interesting too. One of their common interests was European politics and friendship. Grete was a founding member of the Maidenhead Women's Group for European Friendship, and both she and Nicky were involved in the Maidenhead Twinning Association, making new friends in four European countries.

The family atmosphere at home when Nicky was young was European, involving frequent visitors arriving from the continent, especially Germany. He became comfortable in the company of a wide spectrum of people, getting stimulation from their diverse views and outlook. The ease with which he entered different social and cultural groups gave him a taste for new places and experiences, which has never left him.

## 1926–38

At the age of seventeen, Nicky left school and prepared to start his banking training as a clerk at Japhet's Bank. His new status as an adult began with him getting an allowance from his father of six shillings per week (about £15 today), leading him to note he must take care what he did. Obviously this was not considered an adequate sum to fulfil his social life. He was soon also in receipt of a latch key for his family home – his first.

They were a tight-knit family. He regularly went on outings with his mother, his sister Lottie and sometimes his father and Bobby. Though Nicky remembers little of his father's interests and hobbies, one that stood out was Rudolf's life membership of London Zoo. This led to many family visits there, though Rudolf's enthusiasm did not transfer to Nicky. He enjoyed the visits but did not become absorbed by wildlife in particular; he was more interested in people.

Throughout his early life, when away from home, he would write reams of letters to his mother, many of which she kept and returned to him as reminders of his adventures. How lucky for me! Though his letters were to his mother mainly, his father obviously remained close, though less available. For his twenty-first birthday in May 1930, while he was in Berlin, his mother came to visit with Lottie. His father, unable to leave his work, sent him a long letter starting 'My darling old Nicky', describing his feelings of pride for his son at this important landmark (twenty-one at the time being the age when you became an adult legally). It must have been a wonderful letter to receive, for a son keen to have his father's approval.

One line in particular shows the deep affection held: 'I cannot tell you how deeply happy I feel at the thought that you have turned out a man as I or anybody else would always wish to have as a son, and if all men turned out similarly, this world would be a much better place to live in . . .'. He also gave him £100 worth of bonds as 'a foundation to your future fortune!' (which is about £5,000 today).

The family social life included dinners, both at home and out, and visits to the theatre, cinema and opera. Cinema trips were often several times a week. It was an exciting time for film as the first talkies were being made and the Hollywood film industry was really beginning to take off. Nicky's comment on the trend, in his diary in March 1929 when he was nineteen, was not at all percipient of the future: 'We all went to a talkie film with the Hetheringtons. It has wonderful possibilities but I am not at all sure if it will catch on. The Americans are, however, making a large market by only producing these films and ceasing to produce a great number of the ordinary kind.' Trips to the opera also make an early appearance, though it was only as he matured that this became one of his most cherished pleasures.

There were more intellectual outings also, such as in January 1927 when Nicky accompanied his parents to a debate on 'Leisured Women'. It was between G. K. Chesterton, the writer, and Lady Rhondda, a successful businesswoman, but Nicky attests to Shaw (George Bernard) who was chairman, as the most articulate: 'He has got a wonderful figure and face and though just seventy he is lively. He doesn't smoke or drink.' Two days later he goes to see his first Shaw play, *Pygmalion*, and gushes effusively about Shaw, getting tickets for *Man and Superman* (another Shaw play) for a fortnight's time and deciding to read all his works. Five days later he is already reading *Man and Superman* in preparation.

Shaw's plays, though veined with comedy, contained serious themes related to prevailing social problems, including education, class privilege and moral choices. Shaw was a member of the Fabian Society, a socialist political organisation whose aims were to transform Britain into a utopian socialist country through education and legislation rather than by Marxist revolution. It was instrumental in the founding of the Labour Party at the beginning of the twentieth century.

Nicky was attracted to his views regarding social equality and, as his parents were not interested in politics, reading Shaw's works may have been one of his first introductions to political ideas as well as to his developing left-leaning viewpoint.

At school his English studies had included Shakespeare, particularly *Hamlet*, and it was a play he read again regularly through his life. With its themes of death, revenge and uncertainty, he was gripped by the ethical dilemmas it explored. Some of the beautiful speeches within it moved him with their simple direct philosophy and he can still recite a few when the right moment occurs.

His strong feelings for maintaining close family ties and friendships have often led him to quote to his own children and grandchildren, 'The friends thou hast, and their adoption tried, grapple them to thy soul with hoops of steel', said by Polonius to his son Laertes, who is about to leave for France. Polonius follows this with more wise words to his son, which Nicky may also repeat on occasion: 'This above all: to thine own self be true, And it must follow, as the night the day, Thou canst not then be false to any man.'

Other regular quotations to us would come from the poetry he had read and learnt by heart. These would come out at apposite moments, along with his Shakespeare, even into his nineties and hundreds when his memory for other things had faded.

Many of Nicky's hobbies were solitary ones and some were downright quirky for a boy who seemed so outwardly conventional. At some early age, he took up graphology, the study of handwriting as a tool for assessing the psychology of the writer. Nicky took it very seriously, bought the main books on the subject and practised in his own notebooks. His father had friends who would never employ anybody without receiving a hand-written letter where they could look at the script to enable them to assess the writer's character, so it may well have been his father who believed in and introduced him to it. Despite it generally falling from favour as a valid science, Nicky to this day believes in it and occasionally will comment on the character of a person on receiving a hand-written note from them.

A life-long hobby was photography, which started while he was working in Germany aged twenty. He bought himself a Leica, a top-quality portable camera, and an enlarger to make full-size prints from the small negatives. Once home at Stonecroft, he made a darkroom where he spent many solitary but happy hours developing, enlarging and printing his pictures. However, his pride and joy was soon no more. It went missing, seemingly stolen from the flat he, by then, was sharing with Stanley. Its disappearance had coincided with visits by some of Stanley's more dubious women

friends of the time. Anyway, however it went, it seems Stanley felt
responsible for its loss and bought him a replacement – a newer
version of the same camera. In later years it was housed in a very
handsome leather case, which also came through Stanley in the
early 1950s.

The story that Nicky tells is that Stanley was working at
Harrods and discovered that they were making a special case for
Princess Elizabeth to carry her Leica to Kenya on safari. Seizing
his chance, Stanley asked them to make a duplicate case, which
he then proudly presented to Nicky. So Nicky's case is supposedly the only other identical Leica case that Harrods made
specially for the Queen.

His photo albums still fill one cupboard of his home, starting
from his youthful snaps in the 1930s of family, friends, outings and
longer adventures, including a trip to South Africa for his bank,
and continuing up to photos he took of his own growing family in
the 1950s. Sadly there are none of his adventures in Prague in early
1939. Though he did take photos on his arrival, his intense activity
then and later may have led to them being abandoned undeveloped
and forgotten.

Yet another solitary activity was building up his stamp collection. This was a very popular hobby for children at the time and,
most likely, his friends would have been making similar albums
themselves and swapping duplicates with each other. It seems this
was confined to his childhood and teens but he kept his albums
amongst his possessions all his life. However, despite the collection
starting in the early 1920s, his albums have not become valuable
over time, and recently were declared 'worthless' by a visiting
expert, much to Nicky's disappointment. He had been hoping for
a windfall from his youthful hobby.

As a youth, he was not totally focused on his own little world,
though; there is early evidence of a burgeoning social conscience

and involvement in the wider world. Beginning to read Shaw and perhaps other political and social writers, he got involved in his own community activity. In 1927, aged eighteen, having recently left school and started work, he was involved in the opening of a Boys' Club in Penfold Street in the Marylebone area of North London, funded by Stowe School to provide activities for disadvantaged boys. It was called the Stowe Club for Boys but nicknamed the Pineapple Club after the pub, then defunct, where it was housed. He helped find the premises and, once up and running, would attend with another ex-Stowe boy and assist where he could. A manager was employed, and there was a snooker room, ping-pong tables and other activities. Though Nicky was active helping out at the club, he was not a member of the committee running it, made up mainly of Old Stoics. As well as sports and games at the club, trips were organised for fishing, canoeing and even summer camps in the grounds of Stowe School.

Nicky noted in his diary his attendances there and occasionally mentioned innovations such as on 28 January 1929: 'went to the Pineapple Club which is getting on very well. They have just had a boxing ring erected which they hope will stimulate interest in this sport.'

However, he is obviously not in his comfort zone with the actual games and activities, as he writes shortly after, 'At the club all went as usual. In other words, both Leon and I went there with good intentions but found very little we could do, especially as we have no experience of how a club should be run.'

There is no evidence that Nicky continued to help out beyond the first early years and he cannot remember the duration of his support there, but the club itself continued to run, with regular fundraisers held at Stowe into the '80s and '90s. Stowe House still exists as a ground-breaking youth centre on the Harrow Road, Paddington. Nicky has no memory of his parents being in any way involved in volunteering in the community, or that they encouraged him to do so. This impulse most likely came primarily from Stowe's influence of encouraging moral and socially beneficial behaviour in the pupils.

Another tantalising glimpse into his developing outlook came when he was only seventeen in a short diary entry in March 1927, one month after starting work. He was spending the evening with Stanley, having dinner and 'a debate. He said his ideal is to get a caravan and some books and live alone. I explained this was running away from the world and not doing his share in the community. He apparently does not understand that, although he is running away from the world, he is still dependent on the community.'

At the age of nineteen, Nicky started his first relationship with a girl called Elizabeth, aged seventeen, whose guardian was a family friend, and who seemed to think that Nicky would be an acceptable suitor. They met quite often during the six weeks before Nicky left for his banking training in Germany, though always with a chaperone as was the norm in middle-class families in those days.

On an early occasion, he 'went to lunch and tea at Mr Sala's. I danced with Elizabeth to their gramophone, and Miss Anderson [her governess] did a few spiritualistic stunts in which she seems to believe' (and obviously in which Nicky didn't).

More outings followed, then two weeks later, a note in the diary: 'Out for tea with Eliz – I think she is pretty and certainly interesting.' His final jotting before leaving for Germany: 'I went to Eliz for supper after which we went to the Empire to see one of the new talkie films. I shall be sorry to leave E as we have got very friendly in a very short time and three years of correspondence well – perhaps I can?' At the time, Nicky was expecting to be spending three years abroad, though in the event it was only a year and a half. He did continue the romance by letter and rekindled it on his regular holidays home, but it did not last and gradually after his return they saw less of each other and it fizzled out.

Thereafter there were quite a few friends who were girls, particularly those who were his sister Lottie's friends. However, his relationships with girls never lasted or developed into marriage, despite his father's best attempts to introduce him to 'suitable' partners, often the daughters of his business contacts from Germany. Nicky has admitted that, at that age, he was not particularly interested in girls and generally preferred the company of his male friends with whom he could be frivolous or serious but always relaxed.

At the age of twenty-two, on returning from his time learning banking in Europe and obtaining his first properly paid job, Nicky was ready to start out on independent life. He and Stanley, still best friends, rented a flat together in Belsize Park, a few miles from his parents' home in West Hampstead. They enjoyed each other's company, having a similar sense of humour and urge for adventures and high jinks. The description of Nicky at school and in his rather solitary hobbies makes him seem a very serious and quiet young man, but there was another side to him. He had a wicked sense of humour and loved having a good time socialising with his close male friends when he could relax, forget about behaving maturely as his parents and their friends expected, and let his hair down.

A youthful outing I learned about from the son of another friend, Maurice Lovell, involved a trip to the fair on Hampstead Heath, where Nicky, Stanley and Maurice stood together near the bottom of a helter-skelter and took bets on the likely colour of underwear worn by each of the young women as they emerged, tumbling off the end of the chute. Laughter was a frequent sound emanating from his group, all through his life. Nicky's friendship with Maurice continued throughout their lives and, only a few years after their fairground escapade, they were sharing a common passion for left-wing politics. Maurice was to be one of Nicky's life-long friends, who went on to study languages at King's College

London, becoming a journalist for Reuters for most of his career, meeting up with Nicky whenever they were both in London at the same time.

It was in his early twenties that Nicky bought his first car; this was just before driving tests were introduced and a licence could simply be applied for. Therefore my father never did take a British driving test; he obtained his licence and held it until he gave up driving – to his regret but to our great relief, at the age of ninety-nine.

Cars were one of Nicky's and Stan's joint hobbies. The most they ever spent buying a car was £5, and their goal was to get it up to 60mph. Usually after a mile or two the engine would give up or they would get a puncture. Their biggest challenge was taking an Austin 7 to pieces to try and eliminate all the rattles and squeaks. This kept them busy for some time, but on reconstructing it the electrical system was all wrong. The horn worked the lights and the light switch worked the indicators; it was never fixed.

In the flat above theirs lived a policeman from the Flying Squad and his wife, with whom they became quite friendly. As they were often tinkering with cars, a system was developed with their Flying Squad friend that if they wanted to road-trial a car, they would let him know and he would pretend to chase them down the Edgware Road, so they could give the car 'a good test', and prevent other less obliging police stopping them for speeding. Nicky's social conscience did not extend to anti-speeding laws!

Around this time, in 1934, the highest ever numbers of road casualties – 7,343 deaths and 231,603 injuries – were recorded in the UK despite there being only about one million cars on the roads (this compares with 2,538 deaths and 228,367 injuries in 2008 with thirty-three million cars in use). Half the deaths were of pedestrians, and of these, three-quarters occurred in built-up areas. Hore-Belisha, the Minister of Transport, spoke of 'mass murder'. It led to the driving test in 1935 as well as Belisha beacons

Camping friends, Stanley at top.

First car circa 1932

being posted at road crossings. Luckily Nicky has no stories of ploughing down pedestrians during his youthful escapades.

One day they were having drinks with their friendly policeman neighbour when he suddenly launched into a diatribe against the Jews, saying how his mother had been swindled by a Jew. Neither Stanley nor Nicky responded, but sometime later they invited him to a party at their flat, the only other guests being friends they knew to be Jewish. When, the day after the party, he told them how much he and his wife had enjoyed themselves, they said to him, 'We hope you didn't mind that we had invited Jews.' He just didn't believe them and for some time after, when they brought up the subject, he would say, 'I don't know why you keep on pulling my leg about your friends.' Anti-Semitism showed itself in the strangest places.

As well as cars, another of Nicky's more extravagant interests was the new innovation of aeroplanes. Perhaps having seen Geoffrey de Havilland Jnr arrive in one while at Stowe stimulated his passion, but whatever it was, he took the opportunity his increasing income gave him to take up flying. At the age of twenty-four, he enrolled at the London Flying Club at Stag Lane aerodrome, in Kingsbury, North London, five years after Amy Johnson had taken the same step there. He met her there from time to time as he learnt to fly and obtained his pilot's licence. Despite his obvious enthusiasm for flying, he did not become as obsessed as some of the other early pilots, and his other hobbies and social and cultural activities continued alongside this new passion.

Nicky went frequently with Stanley to visit his parents who had moved to Cumberland Terrace in Regent's Park, central London, where they had lavish fun-filled Christmas parties. Though he visited his parents often too, he wasn't involved enough in their lives to have been seriously aware of the ongoing breakdown in their marriage. When looking back to that time, he remembered that his mother had several close male friends who went with the whole family on outings and came to visit, but he registered them as family friends, rather than his mother's. Her intellect was frustrated by the dullness of her life as a businessman's wife, especially with her children no longer needing her attention. Her siblings were all high-achieving professionals and yet, despite her being the eldest and equally as able intellectually, her main stimulation, apart from regular theatre and concerts, was playing bridge. She

Nicky learning to fly at Stag Lane aerodrome

loved a good discussion and debate and these visitors provided that stimulation where her husband did not.

Her first male friend was a man named Alfred Hicks who was brother to the Conservative MP, William Joynson-Hicks. Joynson-Hicks became Home Secretary in 1924 and had some involvement in the aftermath of the Lizzie Wertheim spying case. He may well have known Lizzie's relationship to his brother's friends. Alfred was often with the Wertheims, writing to Nicky at Stowe and accompanying him and his mother to the seaside or to theatres. A few years later she formed a close friendship with Frederic Handl who, on her instigation, married her sister Ida so she could stay in the UK after fleeing Germany in 1933. Ida's foot-dragging in agreeing to the planned annulment between her and Frederic led to a split between the two sisters which remained for life. However, eventually Ida let him go, and Barbara and Frederic's relationship developed. Nicky remembers that both Alfred Hicks and Frederic

Handl were intellectual, erudite men, enjoying stimulating argument and discussion, whereas his father Rudolf was more pedestrian and, obviously to his mother, boring.

In 1934, Rudolf and Barbara separated, and in June that year their lovely house in Cleve Road was sold. Rudolf moved to a flat in Hampstead and Barbara to a smart apartment in Ivor Court near Baker Street, where she lived for the next forty years. Despite all this family turmoil, Nicky's memories of it are hazy to say the least.

He can't remember any discussions about the sale of the house or his parents' separation. Whether he was so involved in his own burgeoning life or just shielded from it all by his parents' reticence is hard to tell. He was certainly busy with work and his social life, fencing, flying and other interests, but it seems surprising, with his very strong ties to his parents, that he would be untouched by such an event. However, as it was the custom in his family to suppress and control emotional reactions, it's likely that his parents kept their responses to the event low key, at least in front of their children.

In 1937, his father started divorce proceedings, based on his wife's adultery, citing Frederic Handl as co-respondent. In those days a divorce could only be obtained on the grounds of adultery or violent behaviour, both of which needed proof. His petition gives dates and locations of their adultery and was filed on 3 June 1937. However, it was abated (withdrawn) in September, as Rudolf died on 8 July, barely a month after petitioning. His health had suffered during the First World War and he had been gradually succumbing to a kidney disease originating from that time. Ida, his sister-in-law, was his doctor and looked after him through his increasingly rapid decline.

At that time Nicky was busy with his work on the stock exchange, and his nascent political activism, making new friends and attending meetings, as well as his continued fencing practice and matches and his busy social life. Ida suggested to him that his father could do with visiting but he did not understand the signals she was giving him regarding his father's fast-deteriorating health. He died before Nicky realised what was happening. It's hard to imagine how someone so seemingly close to his parents could ignore his father just at that critical time. His busy life was obviously one factor and his ignorance of the seriousness of his father's condition another. However, for someone who prided himself on his moral behaviour, it was a hugely negligent oversight and a sign that he could be self-centred at times and put his own interests before those of others. Remorse at his lack of attention to his father's deterioration filled him, but he kept these feelings to himself, tucked them away and carried on as before.

By then, Nicky did not have Stanley to himself anymore to console him for his loss. Stanley had met Maudie Roy a few years into their flat-share. He married her in June 1937, and left their bachelor pad, moving into a nearby apartment with his new wife just a month before Rudolf died. Nicky had also been busy finding new lodgings and by July had also taken his leave. Wanting to remain in the same location, he found a terraced house, 20 Willow Road, beautifully located in sight of Hampstead Heath, which he could just afford to rent with his slowly increasing salary.

Before long, his brother Bobby, having qualified as an engineer and started work at Mullard Electronics a few years earlier, came to join him there. However, Nicky's memory of their cohabitation was of them leading pretty separate lives, without the togetherness and joint enterprises he had shared with Stanley. This seems to be supported by Bobby who, when interviewed about Nicky's work on the Kindertransport in his later years, professed to have not known anything about it, despite living under the same roof for the nine months of the operation and having gone with Nicky to Liverpool Street station to meet one of the trains arriving with its young cargo at that time. Thus he obviously did have some idea of what his brother was up to in his evenings, but his own interests kept him busy and it was not on his radar enough for him to remember it later on.

In his mid-twenties, going on alongside his work in the bastion of British capitalism, and his rather middle-class hobbies, and while still sharing the flat with Stanley, Nicky began to develop his interest in politics. It was a topic he never discussed with his parents, but one which a couple of his friends were immersed in. He joined – not the Conservatives as you might have thought from his background and work life – but the Labour Party.

Nicky's whole worldview and convictions were much more towards the left than the right, and based particularly on British politics and the objective of social equality. In the 1920s and 1930s, hunger marches were occurring, including the Jarrow March in 1936. In the wake of the First World War and then the Depression, the marches were protesting the lack of employment and poor rights for the unemployed, particularly in the North East of England. Several of the marches ended in violence on the streets of central London as the police attempted to prevent the protestors reaching Westminster to hand in petitions. His reaction to what he saw as unjust and unethical treatment of workers further supported his feelings for the need for social justice and equal rights.

He was not influenced by Russia in the way that others were at the time, who were shown the idealistic portrayal of the peasant collectives while the real facts of suppression and purging of Stalin's enemies were hidden, and he had no interest in the fledgling British Communist Party. However, he was influenced by events in Europe and his views were as much anti-fascist as pro-equality. He was concerned about the Spanish Civil War and his beliefs were amplified by the tense situation developing in Germany, with acts of discrimination and injustice by the fascist National Socialists under Hitler.

During his earlier time spent in Germany in 1929–30 while doing his banking training, he showed no obvious interest in the politics there and Hitler's speeches were not even on his or most people's radar then. It was only at the end of 1930 that the National Socialists won seats in the German parliament and began to be noticed as a growing force. Five years later things were very different and so was Nicky in terms of his maturity and beliefs.

Getting to know stimulating left-wing people finally cemented his views. He had begun attending meetings on topics of the day. It is likely it was at one of these that he first met the people who would influence his political thinking for the rest of his life. These included Martin Blake, a master at Westminster School, who would later be the one who called him to Prague in 1938 instead of going together on their usual skiing trip escorting his Westminster School pupils. Maurice Lovell, already a friend of his, was actively left wing and would have been a spur to his growing convictions.

Probably through Martin, Nicky was introduced to active figures in the Labour Party, including George Russell Strauss, Stafford Cripps and Tom Driberg. George Russell Strauss was, I think it's fair to say, a 'champagne socialist', being from a wealthy family and having a large house at the northern end of Kensington Palace Gardens in the centre of London, as well as a cottage in a village called Slaugham, south of London. Nicky attended Strauss' frequent and, in his words, 'riotous' parties at the cottage, where he met other like-minded and compelling individuals, particularly Aneurin Bevan and Jenny Lee.

He was stimulated and inspired by Bevan, MP for Ebbw Vale in South Wales and an eloquent campaigner for workers' rights, considering him a 'political giant' and 'the most exciting person I have ever met'. Jenny Lee, married to Bevan and a Labour MP herself, was 'one of those people who was full of joie de vivre, more than life size'. His prevailing and future political views were obviously strongly influenced by the conversations he had with these vivacious and idealistic characters.

The late 1930s were for Nicky a very exciting and intellectually stimulating time, when his ideas about life began to coalesce. His involvement in politics extended to walking round Marble Arch wearing a sandwich board, advertising some Labour Party convention. Hard to imagine what his parents would have felt if they had seen him then. It is likely that many in his social group would also have been horrified by his left-wing activities as, like his work colleagues, they were mostly right-wing, middle-class types. Stanley, his long-time flatmate, was right wing as were Stan's parents who Nicky had become close to. His own family, though not overtly political, probably were more right than left leaning in their urge to blend in with their middle-class social group.

So, as at school when his Jewish-German roots were kept separate from his apparently English Christian surface, now his left-wing views and friends were mostly kept separate from his social and work life of right-wing middle-class privilege.

His intensive activity within this level of the Labour Party was for a relatively short time around 1936–39, but his connections continued to a degree during and then after the war when Nicky remembers being asked by Russell Strauss to keep an eye on his sons when Nicky was living and working in Paris and they were also there studying French. He also kept up contact intermittently with the others.

The Labour Party won the election held two months after Victory in Europe (May 1945) in July, and Nicky lost no time in writing to congratulate his friends. He kept in his files an informal, friendly letter from Bevan thanking him for his note, which is dated 8 August 1945 from the Ministry of Health, Nicky probably writing to congratulate him on his appointment as Minister of

Health five days earlier. Another letter from Bevan in June 1947 declared his wish to meet up before Nicky left for his post-war job in Geneva. Nicky was even with Bevan the evening before he was due to present his Health Service Bill before the House of Commons, and recalled Bevan saying to him that there were many faults with the bill but it had to go forward then or the time may not come again. Could he have been conscious, that evening, of the enormous significance of that bill and how it would shape the welfare of the nation up to the present day?

That moment was, in effect, the beginning of the National Health Service as we know it today, though it had been in development over a number of years without reaching fruition. Previously, medical services had to be paid for, either by the individual or through medical insurance, with premiums deducted from wages, but which mostly did not cover the family of the worker, only him or herself. The government during the war had agreed that the Health Service should be funded by national taxation rather than through insurance and would be free at the point of use for everyone. However, there were many who disagreed, not least the medical practitioners themselves. After the Health Service Bill was passed, Bevan's triumph was to manage to get the medical profession to agree to it, though he admitted he had made concessions to get their agreement as well as having to 'stuff their mouths with gold'.

Nicky's own foray into local politics (which I will describe in Chapter 13) occurred in the early 1950s when he settled down to married life in Maidenhead, but he never seemed to want to enter the frenetic politics of Westminster.

Nicky alleges that his political discussions amongst this group leading up to 1939 were what primed him for the task of rescuing children from Prague. He and his friends were very aware of Hitler's expansion plans, laid out in *Mein Kampf*, and could not understand that the National Coalition government of the mid-1930s, and the later Conservative government, seemed unable to see how great the Nazi threat to Europe was.

In the mid-1930s, Cripps, Russell Strauss and Bevan attempted to form an anti-fascist alliance across the left-leaning political parties in the UK, to try and prevent the spread of fascism in Europe and in reaction to what they saw as the appeasement by the British government towards Franco as well as Hitler. As this did not follow party policy, they were eventually expelled from the Labour Party in March 1939, though once war was declared and they agreed to follow the party line, they were reinstated.

Nicky would have been privy to their discussions about the threat from fascism and the naivety of the British government in relation to Hitler and his promises, and he certainly was of the same mind. So, in September 1938, when Chamberlain came back after signing the Munich Agreement with his 'peace in our time', which sold Czechoslovakia down the river, he was outraged, certain that his government was being wilfully blind.

Therefore Nicky's arrival in Prague three months later was not as an unknowing bystander. He was fully aware of Hitler's danger, having spent so much time in intense discussion with other anti-fascist colleagues over the previous years, and was in no doubt that war could not be far away. His sense of urgency was not felt by officials in the UK Home Office, however, or by his employers or work colleagues. His family's experiences and his recent political awakening had given him the insight that many did not have in Britain at that time.

Chamberlain's return from Munich was the catalyst for a major decision in the Wertheim family, which had been brewing for some time. Having a German name through the first forty years of the twentieth century had not been easy. Germans were, for obvious reasons, viewed with suspicion, despite the fact that many with German surnames had been in the UK for a generation or two, or had come as refugees from anti-Jewish action in Germany in the 1930s.

During the First World War, the anti-German sentiment led to Nicky's parents deciding to change their name to a more anglicised one. They chose Wortham for reasons Nicky did not know, but which was also the name his uncle Bruno chose. However, once the war ended, Nicky's parents changed their surname back to Wertheim again, unlike his uncle who retained his new name.

The sense that another war was brewing made them look again at the idea of a new name. Nicky remembers: 'We became Winton when Chamberlain came back and made his speech and said "peace in our time". This triggered us at last to change our name. We had had a family conference when problems with Germany were brewing – that is my mother, brother Robert, sister Lottie and myself. We discussed our family going through a second world war with a German-Jewish name, whereas we were in fact British and brought up as Christians. Up to then it had always been decided that it seemed an almost cowardly thing to do to change one's name. However, when Chamberlain set off for Munich to meet Hitler, we had a meeting and decided that if he returned to this country and there was going to be a war, or it looked like there may be a war, then we were really stuck again fighting the Germans with a German-Jewish name. But it was decided that if he came back and it looked as if war had been averted, then we would all change our name.

'So when Chamberlain returned saying it would be peace, we met to discuss the change. I phoned my best friend Stanley Murdoch to ask for suggestions. He said, "Wait a minute while I fetch the telephone book. You will obviously want to change your name to something beginning with W so as to keep your initials the same", and he read through W in the book till he came to Winton and said, "Winton sounds good". I agreed that it was fine and, as I was in charge of this, I went to the solicitor and we changed our name by deed poll. I can't remember that there was any disagreement and I remember it as being fairly quick and straightforward once the name was suggested.'

So our family are called Winton thanks to Stanley and his phone book.

## 6

## *Working in the City*

### *1998*

In January 1998, Nicky received a phone call that was to change his life yet again. It was from a Slovak film director called Matej Mináč who had come across the Kindertransport story while researching historical material for his next film, *All My Loved Ones*. It was to be based on his mother's Jewish family just before the Second World War and the harrowing story of what happened to them. He wanted a ray of light at the end and decided that, in the film, a child from the family should escape the Nazis. Researching ways this could have happened led him to a memoir by Vera Gissing, called *Pearls of Childhood*, which mentioned her escape from Czechoslovakia in 1939 on a train organised by Nicholas Winton.

He took his completed script, including the child's escape on the train, to a well-known translator in Prague, to transform it into English to help him obtain funding. The translator, Alice Klimova, read it with interest, then told him he had made some mistakes regarding the train episode. When he demanded why she should think so, she told him that she had been one of those who escaped that way. Stunned, he pressed her for information, but as she had been only four years old at the time, she suggested he speak to Mr Winton himself. Alice had met Nicky and Grete several times by then and handed over his phone number.

Matej was dumbfounded that this historical figure in his story was still alive and immediately set about making contact. The phone call led to a meeting and Matej arrived at Nicky's home in mid-February full of questions. To his dismay, Nicky was dismissive of what he had done and seemed unwilling to talk about it all. It was so long ago, how could he remember? Not one to give up easily, Matej invited Nicky and Grete to Prague the following month so as to revisit places that might jog his memory and stimulate his interest.

Mid-March saw them sitting in the Hotel Europa once more, being interviewed by Matej in front of his cameras. The atmosphere in the hotel, unchanged in its *décor* since his pre-war visit, helped unlock Nicky's memory much to Matej's delight. His work as a stockbroker in 1939 had allowed him time to work on the Kindertransport after the stockmarket closed at 3.30 p.m. That profession, as well as his banking training, had equipped him to work quickly and accurately to deadlines, both necessary skills for the task he undertook with the refugees. Something interesting is how, since the story entered the media, Nicky has always been referred to as a stockbroker; in fact, he was only in that profession for three years. His route there was dictated partly by his mathematical aptitude and partly by the economics of the time.

## 1927–39

While still at Stowe, Nicky had suggested to his father that he might like to be a solicitor. His father's reply, that you had to be very clever to be a solicitor, crushed Nicky's fragile confidence. He took that to mean he wasn't up to it and it was never mentioned by either of them again. The family finances were going through a rocky phase as he finished his time at school, and his father decided he needed to start his working life rather than continuing in education. Though Nicky much later expressed regret at never having attended university, at the time he seemed resigned, or happy even, to be diving into the adult world of work.

With no other particular idea of what he would like to do, Rudolf suggested banking, his own and his father Nicholas' occupation. Thus in February 1927, at the age of seventeen, Nicky started as a clerk at Japhet's, a new private bank in London, where Rudolf had contacts. The work involved starting some of the bank account books. At the time a bank account was opened as an individual 'book' for each account holder. It was the beginning of a three-year apprentice-like training, which was common for young men at the time, with each placement organised through his father's contacts. He received a small salary of about £5 a month (today's equivalent of £60 a week), which made his allowance from his father stretch a good bit further.

The month before commencement he had done a Pitman shorthand and typing course to prepare for life as a bank clerk. He was obviously excited about starting work, writing in his diary on his first day, 1 February, 'BUSINESS!!!' and the next day, 'I worked very hard and feel that I am getting on well. I am beginning to understand the work. It is tedious sitting in a chair for eight hours but work is work. Father explains all I do not understand in the evening.'

He often met his father for lunch during the working day and got answers from him to all his questions about the mechanics of a bank. After only one week the reality of starting work had begun to sink in, as well as the implication of living on a small income. Lunching with his father was always pleasant, but on his own he had to be frugal. He wrote, 'I had a 1/ 3 ½ lunch at Lyons (one shilling and thruppence halfpenny). It is a cheap but dirty place and although you get served fast, one is uncomfortable.' A better choice was soon found, a sausage shop: 'cheap, clean and better than Lyons though the only hot dish is sausages, mash and beans.'

It was while at Japhet's that Nicky met a young German, Hans Wollshläger, over in London learning the (banking) ropes, who became a close friend. They met often through their lives, the only lapse in their contact occurring during the Second World War, Hans being enlisted into the German army. However, this did not keep them apart for long, and after the war ended, Nicky was soon in contact again. There seems to have been no great agonising between them about it, though discussions obviously took place. Hans' son-in-law Dirk Ippen remembers them in later days, wreathed in pipe smoke, discussing Nicky's Prague pre-war evacuation of children, among other topics of European affairs.

After two years in London, Nicky was sent to Germany to expand his knowledge of international banking. It seems likely this was also arranged by his father through personal contacts, as they went together to his initial interview at L. Behrens & Söhne in Hamburg. Rudolf then saw to finding him accommodation. They both agreed the first place they saw was 'A1'. The following day Rudolf took him to tea with Dr Eberstadt, Nicky's employer at Behrens. Nicky ended the three days with his father by noting in his diary, 'I don't think I have said a word for a few days.' It sounded like Rudolf did all the talking and Nicky was feeling out of his depth.

His mother, also there to see him settled, left for home with his father the day after he started work. His diary notes 'a very sad parting' and the same day, 'Wrote a most sentimental letter home', show clearly the close family bond and his anxiety at being in a strange place aged twenty. However, homesickness seemed soon reduced and he quickly settled into a life of work and play. It was play that seemed most on his mind – he was twenty, after all, and meeting lots of young men his age, as well as girls. It was obviously a beautiful hot summer and they swam, canoed, played ping-pong and went out in the evenings to the theatre, cinema and opera in a huge social whirl of activity. Within a month he wrote in his diary

'I myself am happy but the only thing that makes me a little sad is the thought that they might by [sic] sad at home'. Why would he think that? Were there intimations of problems there or was it just the 'sad parting' which had unsettled him?

His mother's brother, Paul, only nine years older than Nicky, was living in Hamburg and quickly became his main support and confidant. They met often, went to the theatre, ate out and talked for hours together, with Uncle Paul acting *in loco parentis*. Paul taking Nicky to task at one point, for socialising too much and working too little, served to focus Nicky a bit more. The work he was doing was not stretching or interesting him, and he asked to be moved to another department where he could learn more. He also decided to enrol at the university for a few classes in economics and statistics. His German was improving rapidly and he was pretty fluent by the time he left Hamburg.

However, the socialising continued apace, mostly with boys of his age and older and a few girls, though none seemed to replace Elizabeth in his affections. They continued to write to each other regularly and he noted by September that they had written for longer than they had seen each other in London. He did attempt a few small romances but nothing lasting or serious. One girl he took out was the maid of his hosts, aged eighteen. 'I took Gretchen for a walk. She works very hard and has very few friends here in Hamburg. She is very nice and very good company. Anyway she corrects all my mistakes. If I have not mentioned G before she is our maid.' However, Gretchen seemed able to handle Nicky and kept his attempts to become more friendly at bay, saying '*Das beruhren des figuren mit den foten ist verboten.*' Nicky's translation of this slang is 'Keep your hands off my body!'

He was also chased by various girls, but wrote after dancing with one named Dodo: 'It was quite nice but I am in no way *begeistert*' (enthusiastic). According to Nicky, Paul was horrified at his lack of sexual experience, and tried to set him up with various girls,

without success. It was a few more years before Nicky's relationships with girls were anything more than chaste or unsuccessful.

At one point, caught up with enthusiasm for sailing, he bought a
share of a racing sail boat, which could hold him and five friends.
He used it for regular escapades through the late summer and
before long had bought it outright.

His peers appeared to be from similar backgrounds to him,
mostly German, but some, like him, living in Hamburg to learn
banking or trade. At one point he was introduced to Louis Dreyfus,
the son of the owner of the giant French trading company, with
whom he went for drinks, tea or dancing from time to time.

Soon after his arrival, he joined the local fencing club and wrote
'Fenced with Herr Halmann and seemed to cause quite a sensa-
tion', his skill being much better than most there. He considered
the master who taught there much less capable than his London
teacher, Captain Gravé. The club was obviously delighted to have
him and soon asked him to compete on their team against the
Danish Copenhagen club, which he readily agreed to. However, he
was soon deciding to move to a different club, the Hamburger
Fecht Klub where 'No foreigners are really allowed but they take
me as a guest without entrance fee and I pay 30DM (deutschmarks) every three months.' He continued fencing frequently and
did well later in the year in a major tournament in Hamburg,
coming second in the final of the foil.

Theatre, cinema and opera featured large in his life as well, and
he attended such cultural events three or four times a week. One
week he saw three Wagner operas, which he considered 'rather
much but I would do it again any day'. It all sounds very extravagant for someone on a minimal income, but opera viewed from the
'gods' was cheap and available. He and a friend used to go to the
opera as a cheap evening's entertainment involving a game between
them. Buying the cheapest tickets in the 'gods', they would look

down into the next gallery for an empty chair. In the interval they would move down to occupy that seat, and again try and move further down at the next break, the winner being the one who got nearest the stage by the finale. Having soon attended many operas in this way, he became hooked and developed a passion for the art form, which has continued his whole life.

Hamburg Fencing Championship, October 1929.
Junior Foil L–R: Itnner 1st, Behnken 3rd Wertheim 2nd

An interesting aside in his diary relates to an invitation to Friday dinner at the home of family friends, the Meyers. 'Before dinner there was a small Jewish ceremony and later on one of the men, a Zionist, discoursed on the Jews all over the world. Apparently they all thought I was Jewish so I tactfully put them right.' It is not surprising they thought him Jewish, what with his German-Jewish name and family history. They must have been most surprised at his rebuttal, though he obviously had no sense at all of Jewishness, not even seeming aware of the regular Friday evening Shabbat ritual. They obviously did not hold it against him, as he was invited again a few months later. 'After dinner at which Herr Meyer said prayers as per usual, we talked or rather they talked until eleven when I was able to escape,' so for Nicky, and probably the Meyers, these visits were an obligation rather than a pleasure. Here again is another example of Nicky not quite belonging. These were family friends, but they were very different to who he felt he was, a British Christian, and he showed little interest in their religion and its rituals. It was obviously politeness that kept him accepting their invitations.

He remained closely in touch with his family, showing concern for Bobby's decision to get confirmed, which Nicky thought should not be rushed, though Bobby did not follow his advice and went ahead. Nicky was impressed by Bobby's school progress, declaring him 'the brains of the family'. Another missive from home, from Stanley Murdoch, caused him great distress: 'I received very bad news from Stan. His parents have divorced and he is very miserable. His Pa apparently drank and had a woman. I am so terribly sorry for him!' As the only legal cause for divorce then was adultery or violence, such an event was uncommon and carried a real social stigma. For Nicky, so close to his own parents, this must have seemed unbearable. At this time he was blissfully unaware of the fissures in his parents' own marriage and their separation came as a complete shock only four years later.

Stanley's story was soon discovered to be a false alarm, as his parents remained together. However, real tragedy was to come for the Murdochs. During the Blitz, early in the Second World War, they were living in a suite at the Hyde Park Hotel where they were instructed to decamp to the downstairs ballroom during air raids for safety. When a bomb made a direct hit on the ballroom they, along with other guests, were killed outright. Nicky and Stanley were both in London at the time and went straight to the hotel together. They discovered the terrible fact that though the hotel, especially the ballroom, was badly damaged, Stanley's parents' suite was untouched.

It is safe to say, looking at his diaries of 1929 and 1930 (the latter only filled in until May, and no further diaries written), that he threw himself into life in Hamburg, mixing with a wide group of friends rather than a particular one or two. However, his partying had limits. Having spent the evening drinking and playing bridge with two other boys, he remarks that he won't see much of one of them in future: 'I am too tame for him and he is too much of a vulgar lout for me.' His Uncle Paul remained a steadying influence and was obviously stimulating company; they talked about many things, including politics and economics.

There was much of concern to talk about. The German economy had been under great strain since the First World War, though by the late 1920s it seemed to be improving at least on the surface, and life for most Germans had got better. However, the Wall Street Crash in the USA in late October 1929 precipitated Germany into financial crisis due to US demand for loan repayments. Hitler's National Socialist Party had almost gone bankrupt the previous year and was hardly visible during the time Nicky was in Hamburg, but Germany still had many problems, particularly financial, which got seriously worse that year.

Paul seemed intent on educating Nicky further, and as well as their long discussions, he took Nicky to various lectures, one on war reparations, another on politics and economics in Russia. A few comments in early 1930 showed that things were getting tough. His employer was cutting staff and reducing the size of the bank. He wrote on 28 February, 'There is nothing to do in the

office. Things look black over here.' And a few days later:
'Business is very bad and the policy of the banks is to do as little
as possible.'

However, these storm clouds brewing did not at all alter his life
– a steady round of work, fun and games. His time in Hamburg
was up after nine months, his next stop being Berlin. Before he left,
Paul had one last long conversation with him, this time about
himself. This he took most seriously and he wrote, 'I must . . .
look interested when talked to' as well as 'Have developed enormously in the nine months I have been here.' Having made his
leave-taking visits, he departed by train, making a detour to spend
a happy few days with his friend from Japhet's, Hans Wollshläger,
and his family who lived in a little village, Westerkappeln, near
Osnabrück, before arriving in Berlin in late April.

Hans and Nicky cycled to Osnabrück one day, where Nicky was
introduced to various high-power friends of the family. One, Herr
Meyer, who was director of a large factory, was considered by
Nicky 'a typical die-hard, with curious opinions and theories on
politics as well as business'. No further explanation is given but
could it have been the first person alluding to the National
Socialists in any other than a dismissive light?

In Berlin, Nicky was again near family: his '*Grossmama*' and
his aunt Ida and various other relatives of his mother's family.
They lost no time in introducing him to their social group.
Lottie's best friend Desiree was also in town, teaching English to
a young girl and improving her German. Des, as Nicky called her,
helped him find rooms in Mommenstrasse, after rejecting a place
further out near the Wannsee, a large lake used for swimming,
sailing and recreation just on the south-west edge of Berlin. His
boat, making a reappearance from Hamburg, was found a berth
on a northern inlet of the Wannsee at Pichelsdorf, and Nicky
wasted no time in taking his friends, new and old, sailing on day-
long excursions around the magnificent lake. It's hard to believe

that a mere twelve years later Wannsee would become an infamous place, as the location of the meeting to determine the 'Final Solution to the Jewish question' under the aegis of SS General Reinhard Heydrich.

His work in Berlin was at Wassermanns, a merchant bank, perhaps through some connection with his family friends Wassermann in London. There are no further diaries or notes to colour his time in Berlin. As in Hamburg, the clues of what was to come just a few years later with the rise of the National Socialists were practically invisible and it was mainly the economic turmoil that was apparent, though even this did not seem to affect Nicky's work. He was, after all, only a trainee. He had no sightings of National Socialists in 1930 but his photo albums show some pictures of marching Brownshirts and Hitler Youth from a visit to Germany in 1933. Even then Nicky did not find the march to be particularly menacing, more of a curiosity.

After about five months in Berlin, Nicky moved to Paris for a similar short posting at the Banque Nationale de Crédit, which lasted until February 1931. He had a room on Rue Villebois-Mareuil, in the seventeenth arrondissement, just north of the Arc de Triomphe and the Champs Élysées, in the centre of the city.

There are no diaries or letters home from Paris but it's hard to imagine he did not behave here as he had before in Hamburg and Berlin, making use of familial contacts to build an active social life. Paris was the absolute centre of the cultural and artistic world in 1930, with people like James Joyce, Salvador Dalí, Man Ray, Sartre and de Beauvoir living, working and socialising in the cafés of the Left Bank. Nicky's inability to remember anything of his time in Paris suggests that he stuck to his previous social formula, rather than seeing any of that artistic world. His interests of the time being economics, theatre, opera and cinema as well as fencing and sailing, his universe ran parallel to those engaged in art and philosophy.

Hitler Youth march

He had hoped to follow his nearly two years in Europe with some time in America, but the effects of the world economic crash took their toll. His father could no longer afford to support his training. It was early 1931, he was twenty-one and it was time for him to earn his living back in London.

His European banking training and fluency in French and German made him eminently employable and he obtained a position at the Anglo-Czech Bank, this time seemingly without parental help and for the princely salary of £100 per year. This state of affairs was not to last. He had been promised a salary increase to £125 after three months if he undertook the bank's French and German correspondence, which he duly did. Applying for the agreed rise led to an unexpected response: instead of receiving it, he was promptly dismissed. The ongoing depression had led the bank to trim costs on a 'last in first out' basis.

Before long he found another post as a foreign exchange operator with Ullmans, a new bank opening in London. Starting a bank in the middle of the downturn must have been quite a challenge but it succeeded. Nicky continued working there for around five years gaining experience in different areas of banking and eventually moving into their stock exchange department.

In 1937 he left banking and joined the stock exchange, initially with Vandervelts. There he worked as a dealer, specialising in arbitrage with South Africa. Arbitrage is the practice of taking advantage of a price difference in a share between two or more markets. The area Nicky worked in was gold shares and his job was to make a profit based on the price difference between the same shares dealt in London, Paris and Johannesburg. As at the time communication between these centres was difficult, even the phone lines being tricky to obtain, there could be a considerable time-lag in getting information.

Whichever stockbroker had the speediest communication, therefore, was able to get the best bargain and make the greatest profit. It's hard to imagine in these days of instant communication that days could elapse before news arrived from another part of the world. One enterprising stockbroker at the time noticed that the result of a major horse race in Johannesburg was in the London papers the next day, which intrigued him, as stock exchange communication to South Africa normally took two to three days. He sent an envoy down to find out how this was done and discovered a fast communication line within the states of South Africa. He took advantage of this and for some time, until others found out his trick, did extremely well in his dealings.

Nicky obviously had flair for this work, relishing the fast and furious atmosphere in the broking room, and using his maths skills and quick thinking with gusto. His expertise drew attention and he was soon headhunted by another city broker, Crews and Company, who wanted to get into the arbitrage business with South Africa. This entailed finding a partner in Johannesburg and Nicky's first assignment was to be sent there to fix up an arrangement.

The journey involved taking one of the first ever flights to South Africa with Imperial Airways, the pioneering British airline. In June 1937 they commenced commercial flights to South Africa by flying boat. Aviation had been kick-started by the pilots of the First World War and was entering its golden age with innovations and new routes opening up for commercial flying. These amazing flying boats were used on this route as there were very few runways in Africa, but long stretches of water were easier to find (one mile was needed for take-off). The plane held forty passengers on two decks with promenade areas from which passengers could see out over the landscape. Nicky, who loved flying since obtaining his private pilot's licence four years earlier, jumped at the chance to make such an exciting but madly expensive journey, paid for by the company. The voyage took five days, flying only in daylight. Each evening the passengers disembarked from the plane into a motor-boat for transportation to a luxury hotel for a night of comfort and a good meal. The pilot was considerate of the passengers' sightseeing requests. He made an extra loop around the Pyramids so they could get a better look and take photos, as well as flying over other monuments and natural wonders, including the dormant volcanoes, Vesuvius in Italy and Mount Kilimanjaro in Kenya. Nicky returned with a mass of photos to develop in his amateur darkroom, producing pictures of African wildlife from the air – elephants and flamingos, as well as the Pyramids and breathtaking landscapes.

(For those interested in such things, Imperial Airways' first through flying-boat service to South Africa left Southampton, G-ADHL Canopus on 2 June 1937. The route was Marseilles–Rome–Brindisi–Athens–Alexandria–Cairo–Wadi Halfa–Khartoum–Malakal–Butiaba–Port Bell–Kisumu–Mombasa–Dar es Salaam–Lindi–Mozambique–Beira–Lourenco Marques–Durban.)

On top of his photography spree during the day, the evening stops gave plenty of opportunity for adventures of all kinds. His first night was in Brindisi, in the 'heel' of Italy, where they spent what Nicky described as 'a pretty rough night' with Mussolini's fascists shouting anti-British slogans outside their window, their landing on the sea and passage to the hotel no doubt drawing unwanted attention to the British influx. Leaving in the morning was another ordeal, as their exit was through the customs hall, which had a large portrait of Mussolini on the wall. Their party were instructed to salute it before they would be allowed through. With no way out of this dilemma they all conformed, including Nicky, despite his great discomfort. His politics by then were firmly socialist and he was dismayed about the fascism extending across the arena of European politics. He was therefore distinctly unhappy to comply but refusal would have jeopardised the whole trip and so pragmatism won the day.

Flying boat

On they went, arriving the next evening in Alexandria. He and another young man on the flight had by then decided that the opportunity to see the sights was more important than sleep, so they decided to go out and explore. The hotel commissioner advised them to leave all valuables at the hotel and take only minimal currency for safety. They wandered off, eventually finding a nightclub where, in the early hours, they were presented with a bill for drinks, for more than the limited cash they had on them. Nicky, leaving his new friend as 'hostage', had to run back to the hotel, retrieve his money and return to pay the ransom. A couple of hours' sleep and they were off again.

En route to another stop at Naivasha in Kenya, they flew low over Lake Nakuru, home to an enormous swathe of flamingos gloriously visible from the plane. Landing on Lake Naivasha, their hotel was an enormous wooden bungalow, said to be where Rider Haggard had written *She*, the famous nineteenth-century adventure story of a lost African kingdom.

A few days later after more stops in exotic locations, with many canisters of film taken, they arrived in Johannesburg. Several weeks later, having found the ideal firm to partner their London company, he returned to Britain. The new contact was immediately fruitful, leading to great success in Crews' arbitrage business from then on. For Nicky, it had been a wonderful adventure. By then he had become a much more confident young man and could make the most of the unique opportunity.

A later trip to Brussels was not so successful in outcome. Nicky was again sent by Crews to fix up somebody to run a joint account with them, but this time was given the name of a specific firm that wanted to start an arbitrage business with London. They met at the Belgium office in a room with curtains covering all the walls. It was explained to Nicky that the firm operated using graphs for all possible interactions and behind the curtains were the graphs. He recalled, 'Deutschmarks plotted against dollars, dollars against pounds, pounds against the share price index, share indexes from one country against another country, and graphs for each share traded. Everything was graph, graph, graph. The Belgian told me that what he really wanted was to work with Crews by using the graphs to tell us when to buy and sell.'

Nicky was taken out to dinner and, whatever the topic of conversation, the Belgian would pull a graph out of his pocket that somehow related to the situation. All his staff worked to keep the graphs up-to-date, and the wall graphs were replicated in miniature on cards, which he carried about with him. On his return to Crews, Nicky reported back. He had not been impressed and suggested the Belgian was not a suitable partner for them. Luckily they accepted his advice as, a year later, on reading the financial papers, they discovered this particular stockbroker had gone bust.

In Kisumu, Kenya

Nicky thrived in the competitive and fast-paced atmosphere where he could act independently and make his own business, not just 'writing numbers in a book', as he described his work in the bank. He was obviously good at it, as when he went abroad to set up an office he received a letter from his boss, encouraging him to get back to London quickly to carry on trading there. In fact Nicky had several letters on the same theme, even when he was in Prague helping to set up the children's transports. His boss obviously wanted Nicky in the office making money for him.

An added dimension to the competitiveness of the work at Crews was the difficult relationship he had with one of the 'jobbers' who made the price in gold shares. Nicky found him a bully and the jobber took it on himself to sneer at and insult Nicky whenever possible. There seemed to be an element of anti-Semitism to the bullying, as Nicky's surname Wertheim came in for frequent contempt.

Nicky did not shrink from this challenge and his great aim at work was to do deals with the jobber whereby he would make money and the jobber would lose. This he mostly achieved, causing him quiet satisfaction. He considered the jobber 'a nasty piece of work' and the only overt anti-Semitic bully he could remember ever encountering. His upbringing and schooling, as well as his developing self-confidence, seem to have given him the ability to stand up quietly to such intimidation.

Nicky had spent twelve years working in banking and the stock exchange, during which time his views on life and politics had developed and matured, alongside his confidence. As war came closer he began to feel at odds with some of those who employed and worked alongside him. His boss had reacted callously to his work in Prague, suggesting that he should be resting at home during his holiday so he would be better able to come back and earn money for him. This, as well as the constant view that human disasters were a money-making opportunity, turned him cold. For nine months in 1939, as war loomed and his long evenings after his day at the stock exchange were spent on what he considered his real work – the Kindertransport – he began to feel more and more like a fish out of water.

To make the children's rescue successful, Nicky needed some of the skills he had built up from his years in banking and the stock exchange: clear thinking and quick action, attention to detail and independence of mind. However, these skills were underwritten by the drive to give aid to those in need without any financial reward involved, an ideal not shared by his colleagues at work.

His close friends and political acquaintances, like him, believed in living a moral life. The other volunteers helping him with the Kindertransport were also putting morality and compassion before personal advancement. Indeed those remaining in Prague were also putting these ideals above their personal safety.

Nicky had absorbed the influences from his school of giving help to those in need, and from his reading and political discussions had developed his views of social responsibility and equality. He had come to realise that living a moral life and giving support to others in need were more important ideas to him than the exciting, lucrative but seemingly amoral world of financial dealing. None of these ideas seemed to be held or supported by his City bosses or those he worked with. The clash became too great for him to tolerate.

The final straw for him was after the war started and he was in the Red Cross, just returned from the evacuation at Dunkirk. He had been four days on the water trying to get back to England and he turned up in his old office to look up his ex-colleagues, looking much the worse for wear in his grubby Red Cross uniform. On greeting an old colleague and asking how things were, he was told, 'Oh Nicky, things aren't too good; gilt edge are flat today' (gilt edge being government bonds). A director of the company saw Nicky and came over for a chat. Without preamble he said, 'Look this is bloody ridiculous, we can't win this war. The sooner the government realises it and we make peace with Hitler the better.' The contrast between Nicky's recent Red Cross work and Dunkirk evacuation and the self-absorbed focus on money of his ex-colleagues could not have been greater. Nicky had enjoyed the work, the challenges and excitement but that attitude, of callousness and money above people, was the end for him. He knew he could never go back to work with such people. He had thought this world would be his career for life, so his disillusionment with the ethos – the lack of morality and greed he had discovered there – led to his abandoning the City forever.

## 7

# Refusing to Fight

## 1998

The spring and early summer of 1998 were a busy time for my parents, involving that whirlwind trip to Prague and the filming involved. Other activities also kept them occupied and my mother's odd health issues, itchy skin and tiredness, seemed unimportant in the hurly burly of their active life. A June trip to France had been planned with their close friends, Ric and Sheila Fontaine, pootling around Normandy, past the Second World War battlegrounds and paying a visit to Giverny, the home of Monet, and a magnet for fans of his paintings of the gardens and lake. The visit was memorable for the wrong reasons – Grete, by then so exhausted that they were using a wheelchair to ferry her around the site, suddenly collapsed, vomiting a large amount of blood. The director of the gardens called an ambulance and accompanied them to the hospital at Evreux. Nicky, though outwardly calm, was beside himself. Her collapse had seemed at first to be fatal and though she was still alive, he did not know what was happening to her. He spent an anxious week lodged in a local hotel, while the doctors tested and treated her. Eventually she stabilised and was allowed to be taken home by their stalwart friends who had remained with Nicky.

Back in Britain, she was taken straight to their local hospital, where the doctors looked at the Evreux hospital notes and delivered the devastating verdict. The scans showed a mass on the pancreas, diagnosed as pancreatic cancer. The prognosis was poor, not only due to her age – seventy-eight – but also due to the cancer, a very difficult one to treat. Nicky and Grete had had their final visit to France together. It was the place they had first met, lived together after their wedding, and before that, where Nicky had done war service in the Red Cross in 1940 and begun his irrevocable change from pacifist to recruit.

## 1939–41

In September 1939, war came – a war that had seemed to Nicky and his political friends to be inevitable. He felt that Hitler, time and again, had done exactly what he had said he would do and yet, time and again, the British politicians appeared to be taken by surprise. Over the previous year Nicky had been a member of the St John Ambulance Brigade, feeling that when war came he 'would be willing to help clear up the mess but not take part in the slaughter'. He explained, 'I was not a conscientious objector in the true sense but I was utterly disgusted and confused to see politicians time and again trying so hard not to see the signs and portents that to me and my friends seemed so self-evident.'

So, when in August, Hampstead Borough Council sent forms out to all members of St John Ambulance asking what service they were willing to undertake in the event of war (i.e. a few hours part-time or full-time), Nicky volunteered for full-time service. Thus it was that while still working in the City, Nicky was asked by the Medical Officer for Health of the Borough Council to set up an Air Raid Precautions (ARP) depot. When he asked why he, as a junior in the St John Ambulance, should be given this post, he was told it was because he was the only one to put himself down for full-time work.

As he was still working on the Kindertransport every evening at home and feeling a sense of urgency that war could not be far away, this request was opportune. He could not continue his daytime job as if nothing was happening, so he accepted the post and resigned from the City. His employers at the stock exchange treated this resignation in the same way they had previously responded to his work on the Kindertransport. He was told that, as he was leaving voluntarily and not waiting to be called up, he should consider that he had left the firm for good and would receive no retention payment from them during the war if it came. He was not surprised, recognising the money-first attitudes and having already come to the conclusion that the world of stockbroking was not for him. He had pretty much decided by then that he would never go back, though some pay would have been a help! The final insult of his visit after Dunkirk was yet to come.

The ARP depot was set up in a school on Rosslyn Hill, Hampstead, just a few hundred yards from his home on Willow Road. Once installed in the depot, and with war now declared, Nicky's first task was to requisition vehicles and select other volunteers to man the post. Having accomplished that task, the initial adrenalin rush of preparation for an onslaught that didn't arrive soon turned to boredom. The other warden volunteers were an unusual group, including musicians from the Royal Opera House and other London orchestras and barmen from central London clubs. They trained and trained for the eventualities of bombings but none came. Before long, the musicians were bringing in their instruments and people passing by sidled in to listen to the lovely music being played.

One day, at last something happened: an urgent request to give aid for a man just outside on the pavement who appeared to be having an epileptic fit. Nicky instructed his group to go and administer first aid as they had been trained to do. This they did, restraining the man to prevent him hurting himself, and eventually putting him in a car and taking him down to the nearby hospital.

A few minutes later Nicky received a call from the matron at the hospital, asking for the man in charge of the depot. She informed Nicky that, rather than saving the man, their intervention had nearly killed him, as he had fallen over and got his false teeth stuck in his throat and was trying to get them out, thrashing around, when the wardens came out and stopped his movements. Her sharp rebuke dampened their spirits; his first attempt to help had been an almost fatal failure.

The Phoney War, the name given to that early period before bombings and military engagement really began, which lasted from September 1939 to May 1940, left Nicky feeling that he was not doing any work of value. Six months of low-level activity was not how he had foreseen his new role. He decided to get more involved and by March 1940 he had joined the Red Cross as an ambulance driver, where his decision to 'help clear up the mess, not take part in the slaughter' would be even more usefully employed, especially as his language skills would be helpful in France.

He quickly became good friends with his co-driver, a man called Mummery. Their ambulance crew was one of the first sent across to France that March, and before they left London they were inspected by Queen Elizabeth, wife of King George VI, at Buckingham Palace, their ambulances all polished, with shiny bright chrome.

On arrival in France, the first thing they were told to do was find paint and cover over the lovely shiny chrome as it was visible from afar, making them an easy target.

The first weeks spent stationed at Wimereux, just outside Boulogne, were quiet. Occasional practice runs and drills but no action, led Nicky to suggest to his commanding officer that his team would benefit from first-aid classes. Despite them having almost no basic medical training at all, this was refused. The lack of preparation and the incompetence Nicky witnessed drove him crazy. Morale in general amongst the ambulance crews was dismal. However, before long, the Phoney War ended and the real one started. They listened with anxiety to the radio, which was reporting news of the German advance through Belgium during early May. The British forces were deployed along the Belgian/French border and, as the German army advanced, the British were driven back down into France.

Ambulance crew 1940

After some days, the order to retreat came for Nicky's crew and they travelled in convoy towards Calais. While in Wiemereux, Mummery had developed acute lumbago, which for the previous few days had left him completely unable to move. Nicky had to carry him into and out of the ambulance when they drove. En route for Calais they were attacked by German aircraft, having received advance instructions that, should this happen, they must abandon their vehicles and take cover in the ditches either side of the road. Nicky, without time for thought, leapt out of the

ambulance and threw himself into the nearest ditch. On remembering Mummery, he looked round and found his co-driver also
sheltering close by. Neither man could explain how he had got
there by himself, as when the alert was over, Nicky had to, as usual,
carry him back to the ambulance.

They later discovered bullets from the German guns lodged in
the blankets that were stored in a compartment above the driver,
which had probably saved their lives. They camped that night in a
field near Dunkirk, being continually awoken by gunfire. In the
morning, their accompanying officers went to reconnoitre in
Dunkirk. As they didn't return that day, the next morning, another
group set out to discover what had happened. They were told their
officers had embarked for England without informing their men.

With ongoing air fire and bombs dropping, they continued to
attend to the wounded, as well as to the feet of soldiers who had
marched for days to reach Calais. At last they clambered on board
a destroyer, which took them to a cargo ship waiting a few miles
offshore. Nicky and the others in their team felt they were nearly
home but it took a very uncomfortable four days to reach England,
herded on deck with no food, just quantities of cigarettes. The
ship's crew had food but there was none for them. 'To start with,
the sailors came up from the galley carrying trays of food for various crew members. On the second day hardly any of these trays
reached their destination, as the carriers of the food were tripped
up and a dive made for the food scattered all over the deck. After
that, the crew went to eat in the galley.' Eventually they landed at
Plymouth and bread was distributed under armed guard, which
was 'more welcome than any food I had ever tasted at the best
restaurant'.

He was sent back to France again within a few days, but not for
long. As the remains of the British and Allied troops further south
in Brittany, who had not left during the Dunkirk episode, continued to be pressed by the German advance, their evacuation was

ordered. This time it was from St Nazaire in southern Brittany, where Nicky joined his second evacuation within two weeks of his first. Once again, 'packed tight like sardines', he made the four-day journey home 'with not a crust to eat on board'.

In 1944, when he next set foot on the continent after the liberation of France, he wrote down some of his thoughts of his previous experience there. They had remained crystal clear in his mind: 'Two days and two nights in an enormous field near St Nazaire where 25,000 troops had collected and were waiting to sail home. They had nearly all marched there from long distances and some could hardly even stand on their sore and aching feet . . . Two days and two nights of tending and bandaging sore and bleeding feet. A more stinking job can hardly be imagined. I can smell it still. The second day, a Hun aircraft came over. We knew the game. Spot at day and bomb at dusk. We knew we had been spotted and the shells being fired by the guns must have been directed by the thought waves of 25,000 tired and anxious men: "The news must not get back." We all watched in silence and the atmosphere was charged as I have never felt it before or since. Silence – just the guns speaking and the aircraft now seemingly making its getaway. And then what a yell – it was hit and was falling. Joy such as this born of relief from fear and expressed by shouting and clapping from such a vast crowd was an ever-memorable scene.

'Party by party we moved from the camp to the port . . . "OK, let's nip into this establishment and have a quick one. What is the old barmaid jabbering about?" you ask. I translated, "She says the English are abandoning France to her fate and she will not serve us." "Oh, she's mad, let's go next door." Same story: "There is no armistice, we are not defeated, why are you deserting us, I'm damned if you can drink here." What terrible, horrible and tragic confusion it all was. We belonged to the machine, we got orders, we obeyed. What did we know of the political or even the military position for that matter. No drinks.

'Perhaps because if we had got it, that drink would have meant so much and also because of the tragic reasons that lay behind the refusal to give it to us, this episode stands out more vividly than any other at that time. The French were in despair . . . It must not be forgotten that it was into this mentality that the Germans marched.'

The remembrance of that episode in such detail demonstrated the impact it had on Nicky. Not just for the fear and discomfort of it, but also for the shame he and his compatriots felt at leaving the French to their fate. Having no say in what they could do and being forced to follow orders did not suit him, though he acknowledged that for others the problem was reversed. 'It is this complete irresponsibility, this helplessness of the individual to decide his own fate which has made the return to civilian life so hard for many. To be ruled for years by a vast machine and then suddenly to become one's own master.'

Back again in England, and recovered from his second getaway, Nicky's Red Cross work continued from his new base in Crawley in the Sussex countryside south of London. He and his crew drove their ambulance throughout the south of England as the Battle of Britain raged in the summer of 1940. During their frequent night-time missions they were allowed to use only their side lights to prevent them being targeted by enemy aircraft. Even these lights had to be blacked out, leaving only a one-eighth-inch hole for a pinprick of light. They navigated by the co-driver looking up to see the lighter sky between the trees or houses beside the roads while the driver looked ahead to spot oncoming vehicles. Luckily there was little traffic on the roads and they got through these episodes unscathed.

He heard first-hand the German triumphalist propaganda to their own troops. They saw many German aircraft shot down during several aerial battles, one day picking up a wounded German pilot. As he was put into their ambulance, he said to Nicky, 'At least I have the honour of being the first pilot to be shot down over England.' In reality, by the end of that July the Luftwaffe had already lost 268 planes.

On another occasion, he collected a severely wounded German crew member who asked where he was. On being refused this information by Nicky, he stated, 'Well, I know I am somewhere in the south of England, which is a pity because if I had been shot down north of Birmingham, I would be in the part of England already occupied by our troops.' The German officers were obviously encouraging their troops with these fables, as well as misleading their citizens.

His Red Cross work continued for over a year and a half altogether, but, by late 1941, Nicky was ready for a change. His level of activity in the Red Cross was no longer what he felt he should be doing. There was not enough real action and he was not doing enough good, and on top of that he was bored. His steadily increasing urge to get more involved in the battle to protect his country made him ready to take a yet more active part.

Nicky's trusty motorbike

# 8

## *Joining Up*
### *1998*

In the late summer of 1998, our family's thoughts were not totally focused on my mother's slowly declining health. There were more uplifting issues to discuss. Nicky had, before Grete's illness, been formulating plans to have a big party in 1999 to celebrate his ninetieth and Grete's eightieth birthdays that year. Now this seemed too far off. Instead he set his sights on another landmark date: their golden wedding anniversary, due at the end of the coming October. He and Grete decided that if a party was to happen, it should be soon, and early October was decided on. Suddenly lots of party plans had to be put into action, a real distraction for us all.

In the event, it was a wonderful occasion with a big marquee in the garden filled with golden balloons, a harpist playing and lots of food and drink. All Nicky's and Grete's friends and family were invited and a wonderful time was had by all. Grete looked frail but happy, and many photos were taken by Sheila, her close friend, to remind them of the occasion.

Three weeks later another occasion arose: Nicky had been awarded the T. G. Masaryk Medal, the second-highest honour in the Czech Republic, by President Václav Havel, and was invited to Prague to receive it. He at first hesitated, not wanting to leave Grete who was too ill to travel. A bit of persuasion from her was needed for him to go, accompanied by my brother Nick, while I looked after my mother at home. It was a magnificent affair, which took place in Prague castle, with massed soldiers, the President and lines of recipients, Nicky in their midst.

The castle stands in an imposing location, atop a hill overlooking the old city. From the castle terrace, Nicky could look down into the British Embassy gardens, lying just below its walls. The Embassy, housed in the grand Thun Palace, was a place he'd never visited in 1939 during the three weeks of feverish activity he'd undertaken so nearby.

He had, however, visited it once before when he had played bridge with the Ambassador in 1945 when he was staying in Prague as a representative of the Royal Air Force (RAF).

The war was ending and he was travelling through Europe in the wake of the victorious Allied troops, with an exhibition on the work of the RAF during the war. It was his second visit to Prague, six years after his first, and occurred as a result of his move from the Red Cross into another war role.

## 1941–46

In late 1941, Nicky applied to join the RAF. He had got over his anger at the politicians – their betrayal of Czechoslovakia and blindness to Hitler's intentions – and, having seen first-hand what was occurring on the continent, had decided that he must engage fully with the war effort.

His flying training in the '30s made him feel equipped to make his contribution in the RAF, so he was dismayed when he was turned down for both pilot and air crew service due to his wearing glasses.

The refusal was a blow and, discussing it with his old friend, Martin Blake, led to the suggestion that Nicky should join him at the British Council, as they needed help in their Cairo office. His old Prague colleague Doreen Warriner, now at Balliol College,

Oxford, produced a reference for him and he began his new position. However, this soon turned out to be another non-starter. After a few months learning the ropes in London and with no transfer to Cairo in sight, Nicky reapplied to the RAF. This time he was accepted as a flight trainer, his flying experience now seen to be valuable to their pilot training programme. It was not quite the active role he had hoped for, but he was happy to be at least now using his flying skills to aid the war effort.

Around July 1942 he was sent to Hatfield to learn to become a Link training instructor. The Link was a recently developed innovation: an early flight simulator, developed in America. It was used to teach night flying in particular, by training the pilots to fly using only their instruments. While there, he met his old schoolmate, Geoffrey de Havilland Jnr, already a Spitfire pilot. Geoffrey offered Nicky a flight in his Spitfire, and they set off, Nicky sitting squashed on the floor next to him in the tiny cockpit. Geoffrey decided to have some fun and undertook a series of aerobatics, which sent Nicky falling all around the cockpit, luckily without serious damage to him or the plane. Having qualified, he was posted to South Cerney aerodrome in Gloucestershire to instruct pilots in instrument flying using the Link Trainer machine.

In the early war years, very few pilots were experienced in the methods needed to fly at night and accidents occurred when pilots did not set or read their altimeter correctly, hitting the ground while believing they were still at some height. British pilots gained their wings in Canada during the war, but many returned home with no instruction or experience in night flying. According to Nicky, instrument flying was a very different skill: 'In fact some of them who were then taught night flying with the aid of the Link in this country never became proficient in this and so one had some pilots with wings who were, in fact, never used in actual combat and spent their life doing clerical jobs.'

He was mainly assigned to teaching French pilots due to his language skills. By then the Germans were in control of the whole of France and many French airmen had escaped to Britain. He developed great respect for their low-level flying prowess, being flown by some who were keen to demonstrate their dexterity. He described it as an astonishing and nerve-wracking experience, at one point dipping sideways to fly between two trees in a field and flying under a bridge over the Bristol Channel with their wheels in the water. However, he found that they were lost when it came to night flying or flying in clouds and it was his task to make them competent to do this using the Link.

After several years at South Cerney and as the war was slowly being won, he was selected as a representative of the RAF to accompany an exhibition about its work through Europe. His fluency in both French and German had again come into its own. Why this exhibition took place while the war was still being fought is hard to understand, but it was obviously considered a valuable propaganda device, as it progressed across Europe in the wake of the Allied advance through Belgium, France and Germany. Nicky's role with the exhibition was mainly to demonstrate and lecture about the Link Trainer, with one such being brought along to use. However, he was also one of those in charge of getting the exhibition to each location, which in Germany could involve finding American personnel who could give them petrol for their vehicles. He was in fact the second in command, the first being Flight Lieutenant Kenneth Wolstenholme, a bomber pilot who flew over one hundred missions and was awarded the Distinguished Flying Cross with Bar. Wolstenholme went on to be a football commentator for the BBC. He will be forever identified with his comment at the end of the 1966 World Cup final: 'They think it's all over . . . it is now', which has entered mainstream culture.

Siblings in uniform.
L–R: Nicky (RAF), Lottie (WRAF), Bobby (Royal Engineers)

Their first location was Brussels, and they arrived there to set up the exhibition on 4 or 5 November 1944. This was five months since D-Day on 6 June, and only a few months after the Allies had made sweeping victories, pushing the Germans back from France and Belgium to within their own borders, leaving only a few pockets of resistance in France. Paris was liberated on 25 August and Brussels on 3 September. Fighting was still continuing ferociously in Germany, as Nicky and his team arrived in post-liberation Brussels with all the equipment for the exhibition. He wrote frequently to his mother during this period describing his string of engagements and lectures, as well as making requests for luxuries such as coffee to be sent from home.

His first letter, written a day or so after arriving, gave his first impressions of Brussels. 'Dear Ma, This is all very exciting. Instead of coming to a city which is stricken down and suffering, at any rate on the surface, this is very far from the fact. Brussels is crowded, not only with natives but of course as well with crowds of service personnel. The streets are packed but travelling is precarious as the only transport available is trams. These we are allowed on free and so far each trip I have made I have been precariously perched on one of the running boards. All that I write here is of first impressions and therefore may possibly be inaccurate. The shops all seem to have plenty to sell and jolly good stuff too. Beautiful watches, binoculars, bags, dresses etc. etc. I am told that a great deal of it was hidden and only appeared when the Germans left and, further, the beautiful dresses in the shops are only models and you have to bring your own material. On barrows in the streets you can buy the most wonderful fruit very cheaply. I have just eaten a pound of grapes, which cost me about 1/6d. There are all the cosmetics that anyone could possibly require, but I am afraid that the money I am allowed will not permit me to do much spending.

'We (that is all the Exhibition people) live in a hotel together. Quite small but OK. We go out to the Hotel Metropole for all meals. This hotel is really the Officers' Mess and is magnificent. They get army rations delivered to them but the chef must certainly know a thing or two as the meals are A1. Everyone is very kind and helpful and seemed to be most pleased to see us around. It really is most amazing to be in a big city up till recently in German hands and find not a piece of glass cracked in the windows and the place buzzing with life . . .'

He also admitted to her that at one party he'd attended he had got so drunk – two gins, half a bottle of champagne and a liqueur – that he had bought a fox terrier puppy in the street. After eighteen hours, during which it had obviously made itself a nuisance in various houses, he resold it, though 'it was with me long enough to be christened Pickles'. It's good to see that five years of war had not dampened his capacity for high jinks, though as a representative of the RAF his superiors would not have agreed.

Five days later, the next letter is sent: 'The exhibition has been opened. It is impossible to describe the rush of the last morning. Even one hour before the opening ceremony was due to take place it all seemed quite impossible. We all really worked very hard and enjoyed it and all of a sudden it all was finished. In fact we had plenty of time, as when the last exhibit had been put in its place we had still five minutes to go! My Link section is quite fantastic. A hole has been made in the floor under the machine so that the turbine which makes all the noise could be put in the cellar below. There is a floodlight trained on me at the desk and one trained on the Link itself. In addition there are two projectors which give an effect of moving clouds on the semi-circular wall that's painted blue. It looks as though I am going to be very hard worked; after the official ceremony with all the big nobs – Belgian and British (headed by Air Marshal Conningham) – my room was packed. I had a loud speaker fitted up through which I could give explanations and there was naturally a continuous stream of people who wanted "to have a go".

'My first client was the Air Marshal's pilot and whilst giving my lecture and demonstration I was able to give him a lesson; he especially asked for this as this is the only Link in Belgium and is coming again. Never has my voice (not I expect will it ever again) been heard by so many important people as it was during that first demonstration ... On Monday the exhibition is open to the public. For the rest, all goes well. I have met in diverse ways a

number of people whom I shall be seeing over the weekend and
their cordiality is such that it will no doubt snowball as it goes
along. It is good to be amongst people who are so evidently pleased
to see one and who in so many ways go out of their way to show
their pleasure.

'The extraordinary thing about Belgium is the Black Market.
This is not hidden but on the contrary quite open. You go into a
shop where sweets are marked at seven francs and say that you
want to buy some but that you have no coupons. The price is, say,
fifteen francs. All quite open. There is in fact a regular price for
everything with and without coupons. In the street cigarettes are
sold quite openly without coupons at a price far exceeding the
correct price. With food, this is just the same. All very strange,
especially as presumably those who ought to be enforcing the regulations should have learned enough in England about how these
things ought to be managed.

'I can now see that the food situation is bad as is also the coal.
There is no hot water in the hotel and I have not as yet been able to
organise myself a bath . . .'

An extraordinary fact is that while the exhibition was going on in
Brussels, the Battle of the Bulge was beginning. This was Hitler's
massive re-offensive pushback into Belgium to try and split the
Allies' advance, which took the Allies by surprise and inflicted
huge losses, particularly on the American troops. It was a long and
costly battle, which continued through December and most of
January before the German troops were finally overcome.

While Nicky was merrily showing officials and the Belgian
public the work of the RAF, their planes were busy attacking the
last massive offensive of the war. He can remember nothing of this
being known to his team at the time and cannot imagine now how
it was possible that they were able to continue with their display as
the Germans approached and the fighting increased, at its nearest

only about forty miles from Brussels. It's probable that the exhibition finished in Brussels before the attack got really close, as by January it had transferred to Paris.

The exhibition itinerary was Brussels (November 1944 to January 1945), then Paris (January 1945 to March 1945), Lyons in the South of France (March–May 1945), The Hague (August–September 1945), Oslo (September–October 1945) and Prague (December 1945 to January 1946), with returns to England in between locations. The whole operation went on for over a year. At each venue, important local dignitaries including royalty, representatives from the armed services, government and businessmen, as well as members of the public, came to visit. Nicky gave lessons in the use of the Link Trainer to all and sundry, including many of these VIPs. His reputation among his team was of a cool, calm and unflappable person, though when times were tough he did occasionally lose his composure.

RAF exhibition main hall, Brussels, November 1944

Explaining an exhibit

The Paris exhibition was right at the start of January 1945, some four months before the final German surrender. Amazingly, a record (literally) of the exhibition remains. While searching my father's cupboards, I found some old 78 rpm shellac discs in a sleeve labelled '*République Française, Ministère de l'Information: 8/1/45, L'Exposition la RAF au combat*, Lieutenant Winton'. They were hard to play but we did get some sound out of them by putting them on a modern turntable and spinning them as fast as we could. First, we heard a French reporter introducing the exhibition and then Nicky's voice still recognisable through the crackles, talking about teaching French pilots in South Cerney and how the Link worked, all in completely fluent French.

A highlight of their time in Oslo was witnessing a football match between the UK and USSR army teams, both countries having troops there to oversee the German surrender, as well as the first post-war international match between Norway and Denmark.

There was a happy atmosphere as Russian soldiers sat amongst the crowds just four months after Norway's liberation.

The Oslo episode involved demonstrating the Link to members of the Norwegian Royal Family, recently returned from exile. Nicky has pictures of Crown Prince Olav listening intently with the young Princess Ragnhild and Prince Harald alongside. Like many eight-year-old boys, Prince Harald was most fascinated by wooden models of the RAF planes that were a central part of the exhibition. His eyes lit up as he looked at them and he spoke excitedly to his father, the Crown Prince. He was asking if he could be given one: the Spitfire. His father, indulging him, passed on the request. Nicky had no choice; this was the future King of Norway after all. So it was that for the rest of the life of the exhibition, there was no Spitfire model on their display. I wonder if Prince Harald, now King of Norway, still has that plane?

The journey to Prague and his time there was particularly memorable, taking place in the winter of 1945. To get there, they drove in a convoy of five vehicles through a defeated Germany, filled with Allied troops. Germany had surrendered in May and had been divided into four zones of occupation by the Allies. Their journey took them first through the British Zone and then the American as snow and then rain fell, making the roads treacherous.

Reaching Nürnberg near the Czech border, they found complete destruction: mountains of rubble ten feet high on each side of the road. They had been refuelling at US bases across Germany under the Lend-Lease agreement, through which America had been funding Allied countries during the war, even though the agreement had officially ended on 2 September 1945, more than two months earlier.

At Nürnberg, however, the Americans informed them that their authorised papers, which had got them full tanks this far, were not sufficient here. Therefore, there was little petrol on offer and what

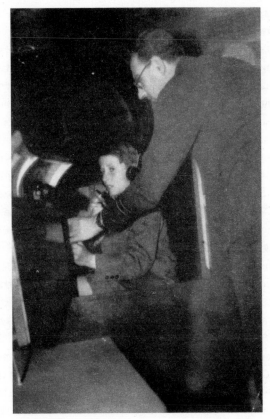

Prince Harald trying out the Link

they eventually received after prolonged negotiation, would not be enough to get them all the way to Prague.

Nicky remembers, 'It was late in the evening, it was pouring with rain. We were all extremely tired after our long journey and I am afraid my resultant bad temper did not help in these discussions.' At the point when his team felt this time they had really had it, a US soldier came up to him and asked, 'Anything to exchange, pal?'

Nicky immediately offered some cases of food rations they had on board, which were accepted at the rate of one case of rations against two five-gallon drums of petrol; anyway they got enough to see them to Prague. There is no mention by Nicky, in his letters of that time, of the fact that he had been to Prague before, or any reaction to revisiting the site of such heart-rending scenes as he had witnessed in 1939. He gets on with things, though he obviously does re-engage with some of his previous contacts. A telegram sent by the Air Attaché to the British Air Ministry on 22 December reads, 'Much regret Winton's posting [elsewhere]. Is it possible to defer this at least until the end of the run in Prague? Winton has valuable pre-war contacts which are proving of immense help ... Will therefore hold Winton until advised by you.' These contacts were obviously helping with arrangements for housing and publicising the exhibition.

He met up again with Martin Blake and his wife, out there on British Council business, and later with his friend Maurice Lovell, working there for Reuters news agency. The main currency he used to thank people for favours was cigarettes and, in his letters home, he regularly exhorted his mother to send more.

Then a tragedy occurred in their little team: the sergeant was struck down with diphtheria and rushed to hospital but the drug needed for his treatment was lacking. Within thirty-six hours it had been sent from Britain but to no avail, and the man died. Arrangements were made for Nicky to take the body home and an enormous coffin was produced, with the explanation that it was a coffin inside another box due to the death being from a highly contagious disease. Nicky was instructed to keep both boxes closed for burial to prevent spread of the infection. The special plane due to fly them back was cancelled and so, suitably camouflaged, the coffin was put onto a scheduled service flight to England where Nicky met and attempted to comfort his colleague's distraught widow. Having agreed the coffin could spend the time before the funeral at her house, he returned four days later with an

RAF contingent to take it to the church. The widow invited Nicky inside and he was horrified to see that both coffins had been opened and the body laid out. There were luckily no adverse consequences to this and the funeral went ahead, with Nicky flying back to Prague straight afterwards.

Before leaving Prague he had fallen in love with a beautiful set of etched Czech wine glasses, and he used the tragic occasion to bring them with him back to England. Of course, as the head of the group escorting a coffin, he was waved through without question by Customs, avoiding the inevitable problems of that period regarding bringing valuable items into the country without the correct authorisations, which could even have led to confiscation. Self-interest was not totally foreign to him, even in such tragic circumstances. He has the whole set still; they were too good to use!

After one year, three months and six cities visited, the tour finally ended. A week or so later, in February 1946, he was posted to La Rochelle, on the west coast of France, as a French-speaking Link trainer, once again using the simulator to train French pilots in night and low-visibility flying. With the war over, this was a more relaxed time than his previous training in Gloucestershire, and it showed.

The Links were complicated machines that needed constant attention from mechanics to keep them working. However, mechanics were in short supply, being needed for other tasks as the monumental work of rebuilding Europe began, and so the units on which Nicky was supposed to be teaching pilots were predominantly out of action. Therefore Nicky spent most of his time free to follow his own impulses, which mainly involved befriending the local fishermen, going out fishing or collecting mussels with them or even on occasion decamping with a duck-shooting party. After the bustle of the previous years, relaxation and enjoyment were high up his agenda, and with the RAF officers 200 kilometres down the coast at their regional headquarters in Bordeaux, there was no one to take him in hand.

A British pilot, Airlie Holden-Hindley, who had volunteered to teach RAF methods to the French, became a great friend. He had flown across from Northolt, bringing Tiger Moths for the flight training, and spent some months at La Rochelle in the small but friendly British contingent.

He flew Nicky in his Tiger Moth at intervals down to Bordeaux to report to his commanding officer stationed at the British Consulate there and to collect provisions from them. It was here that Nicky met, in passing, a young WAAF officer called Heather Charlton, who was the secretary of his superior. A few years later she was working at Mullards in the Tottenham Court Road in central London, where Nicky's brother Robert also worked. She said to a colleague, 'That man over there looks like someone I worked with in the WAAF' and when she heard his name was Winton, she asked to be introduced to him. This chance encounter led to marriage and Heather becoming Nicky's sister-in-law.

In the Tiger Moth with Airlie

Nicky and Airlie visited the oyster beds, sharing the local fishermen's early morning breakfasts of coffee washed down with strong red wine. Other fraternisation involved collecting mussels with the locals and going back to their homes to cook them outdoors on wood fires. The shells were planted directly onto the ashes; when they sprang open, they were ready to eat.

There was, though, even more drinking than there was eating. One episode with Nicky's hard-drinking fishermen friends involved a bottle of absinthe. This is an aniseed-flavoured spirit derived from plants including wormwood, which could be devastatingly strong – up to seventy-five per cent proof. It had been popular amongst bohemian society for its supposed psychoactive effects and, due to these, had been banned in the USA and much of Europe, including France, in 1915. However, that didn't stop its consumption, especially amongst the artists, writers and painters in Paris in the early twentieth century. One evening when Nicky was with his local friends, they introduced him to absinthe. He had never tried it before and it led to him becoming 'the most drunk I have ever been in my life'. He lost twenty-four hours entirely, having no recollection of what happened. He didn't try it a second time!

For Nicky, his months in La Rochelle after the war had ended were more often than not like being on holiday. He had always enjoyed having a good time and partying and this period with so little actual work to do led to him carousing rather too much. Heather's story about a visit she made to La Rochelle shed light on his relaxed mode. She once accompanied his commanding officer there to a meeting with the trainers. On arrival at the meeting, Nicky was nowhere to be seen and she was dispatched to go and track him down. On walking into the port, she came across Nicky just leaving a fishing boat, rather the worse for wear and carrying a brace of ducks, having had a merry time duck shooting and drinking with his fishermen friends. He was lucky to get away without severe consequences but somehow he did.

Nicky found his knowledge of French and German incredibly enriching and valuable throughout his life, allowing him to teach in the RAF in La Rochelle, to mix with the locals there, to get work in Germany before the war and after in Geneva and Paris, and most importantly to have been able to communicate in Czechoslovakia while he was there in 1939. Most Czechs spoke some German and despite their antipathy toward Germans, it was vital for Nicky to communicate with, as he spoke no Czech.

Another of Nicky's La Rochelle stories shows he wasn't alone in treating it more like a holiday than work. 'One incident at the time, which caused considerable upset, was when an engineering section of the RAF, with about six large trucks filled with engineering instruments, was brought to our airfield, and the group captain in charge of this particular transport walked into the mess room and he walked up to the first officer he could see and said, "I've just parked six valuable trucks in your yard and you are in charge of them" and then disappeared.

'It so happened that the man he put in charge was the most happy-go-lucky member of our particular group and, as far as he was concerned, as long as he could look out of the window and see the trucks there every morning, there was nothing more he had to do. However, we then suffered the most severe winter on record and when spring came and an officer arrived to retrieve these important vehicles, he found that all of them were out of action: the severe winter had cracked all the cylinder blocks. As a result, the lieutenant who was responsible for them was hauled down to Bordeaux to receive a dressing down from the commanding officer. He said in his defence, "I didn't know that I had to drain the tanks of these vehicles" and when he was quizzed that it was impossible that he should not know this he said, "well, I haven't got a car and I have never been asked to drain the water out of my aeroplane". So somehow or other he got away with it.'

Duck shooting with the fishermen

He also talked about his life-long friendship with Airlie, his accomplice in his La Rochelle escapades. 'The one friend I made, Airlie, I really knew nothing about what his background was before the war but when we parted, he said, "If you are ever up in Cumbria, look me up." Months later I did just that and found that, instead of him living in just an ordinary little village in a little house, he lived on a vast estate in an enormous country house.

'Since then we have remained great friends, he being the godfather of my daughter. I got on well with his parents, who were in the fabric business. Whenever I was there they gave me material to have my own shirts made and his whole family made me welcome. I suppose he was happy to fly me round; we just seemed to get on together and I felt relaxed in his company. We went on holiday together to Cannes after the war and waterskiied together there. Airlie was as disinterested in girls, at the time, as I was. We were both mainly interested in sport – waterskiing, fishing – and we had an easy, relaxed relationship. I was a late developer as far as interest in girls went.'

Thus his RAF career came to a relaxing end; he returned to England in mid-1946 and was demobbed at the beginning of July with the rank of Flight Lieutenant. He was not looking for a career in the RAF, as demonstrated by a letter he sent to his old headmaster J. F. Roxburgh that month stating that he had got out just in time before he was promoted. His thoughts now were on other areas that he wished to pursue.

## 9

## *The Grim Aftermath*
### *1998–99*

The winter of 1998 was a quiet time for my parents. They were coming to terms with Grete's declining health, while continuing their life, albeit at a less hectic level than previously. Christmas, which had often taken place at our house in Herefordshire, was celebrated at Maidenhead with Nick and me, my husband Steve and the grandchildren, Laurence and Holly, now ten and eight. It was an unspoken thought for us all that it would probably be our last with Grete.

As spring arrived, there was another flurry in the slowly building recognition that Nicky was getting for his pre-war work. The local council had somehow heard of his Czech acknowledgement and decided that they should follow suit by awarding him the Freedom of the Borough. Being the Borough of Windsor and Maidenhead, it meant that honours were awarded in the Guildhall in Windsor, just outside the castle. The ceremony occurred in April 1999 and the council had made it a family affair, allowing Nicky to invite all his family, as well as the usual officials. Grete was well enough to attend, though frail, and it was a lovely day. Nicky was presented with his scroll by the Mayor in the ornate Chamber, under the watching portraits of Queen Elizabeth and previous monarchs, where almost exactly six years later Prince Charles was to marry Camilla Parker Bowles. He joined a distinguished list of local freemen, the most well-known being Queen Elizabeth, Prince Charles, the Queen Mother and Prince Philip.

As well as family and local dignitaries, a local resident, Ruth Drahota, attended – another 'Winton child' not known to Nicky until that day who had come to the attention of the council organisers. She had discovered her Kindertransport history eleven years before when watching *That's Life!* but had not come forward, being an unassuming lady and someone who did not focus on the past. At the Freedom ceremony she was introduced to Nicky who quickly made her feel welcome.

'Goodness, you kept quiet!' were his first words. He followed up with an invitation to visit, saying, 'We must get together and talk. Ring me, and if I haven't heard from you by next week, I'll be ringing you.'

She and her husband Jaroslav have since become close friends of Nicky and two of his most frequent visitors. She told me, 'The fact is in the back of my mind all the time that he saved my life and none of my family would be here if not for him. But over time I have got to love him for his own sake; he is a lovely person.'

We have no idea exactly how the selection of Nicky for this award came about and who in the council brought his pre-war rescue to the attention of fellow councillors. His connections to the council were slight and occurred mainly through his local charity work when permissions were needed for some event or building, but he himself had never been involved in working for them. His work life never led him into the civil service on a local or national scale. You might think from his experiences with the Czech Kindertransport that he would never have wanted to work within a government organisation thereafter. He had discovered that the wheels turned very slowly in big organisations and government departments, and that being subject to committees and their rules and regulations did not suit him much.

However, despite this, soon after the war, he did in fact spend just over a year working for a branch of the United Nations. Despite being inside a huge institution, he undertook, with remarkable freedom, a task that no one would readily volunteer for and which is little known about to this day.

## 1947–48

Having been demobbed from the RAF, Nicky began to think about what his next step would be. His thoughts were on post-war recovery in Europe and how this would be achieved. Remembering those endangered children he had helped bring out before the war, the plight of refugees was at the forefront of his mind. He wasn't thinking of 'his children' though, as he assumed the Czech Refugee Trust Fund and guarantors had dealt with their return home or future life elsewhere. He was in no position now as an individual to go round Britain chasing them up. However, he knew that repatriation was a necessary part of the future of all refugees and so he applied for a job with the International Committee for Refugees in London, thinking he could perhaps help with the resettlement of those leaving Britain. He was accepted and became part of quite a small team, about half a dozen, who were to assist refugee repatriation.

Before many weeks had passed, however, they were told that their agency was being integrated into the International Refugee Organisation (IRO), part of the new United Nations (UN), which was formed at the end of the war. The IRO was still being developed and so was initially known as the Preparatory Commission for the International Refugee Organisation and was based in Geneva, Switzerland. The city had a history of humanitarian concern; the Red Cross was initiated and headquartered there, and the Geneva Convention was the first international legislation on treatment of prisoners of war. Humanitarian organisations had congregated there during the war and so it was a natural home for the (PC)IRO.

The London-based Refugee Committee was informed that those who wanted to continue in their work would need to move to Geneva. Only three of the six-man team accepted the offer, and those three, including Nicky, travelled to Geneva to report to an officer of the new organisation. On arrival they were told that as they were becoming part of the UN, they would receive American rates of pay with no income tax – a huge rise from their British salary for the same work. Nicky suddenly found himself unexpectedly well off, though he soon found that he had little time to make the most of it as he plunged yet again into a hectic work environment.

Switzerland had remained neutral during the war and so Geneva had been protected from the devastation wrought on many European cities. The IRO offices were modern, with new technology like copying machines and teleprinters (often known as telex, which worked a bit like early email but using the telephone system) – a far cry from the old-fashioned and basic lodgings and equipment of their London base.

The work was initially as Nicky had expected. His first job was to aid the resettlement of refugee families from a displacement camp near Frankfurt, inside the US zone of occupation, working alongside the Vatican representative at the IRO, Father Killion. As in many of his previous exploits, Nicky wrote and kept notes of his experiences at the time, which have helped piece together this frenetic episode.

Arriving in Frankfurt in August 1947, Nicky discovered the city looking much the same as on his previous visit two years earlier, when he'd been on his way through to Prague with the RAF exhibition. Rubble still filled the streets from the bombings of the war, with seemingly no attempts being made to rebuild. The US troops were firmly in control of the roads, and he and Father Killion were stopped regularly to have their credentials checked as they approached the city, a machine gun trained on them until they were given the go-ahead. Once, they were stopped briefly just to be told their speed by a group proudly brandishing a newfangled radar gun.

After settling into his miraculously undamaged hotel, Nicky had to obtain some money. The only legal tender in the US sector was called 'scrip', more formally known as Military Payment Certificates, which was used as currency to buy goods and then on return to the USA exchanged for dollars. It was illegal for soldiers and civilians to deal in dollars but a thriving black market in them and other 'currencies' was soon to become obvious to Nicky. No officials seemed able to help him, and he was advised by the American Express office, which would only accept travellers cheques which he did not have, to 'Stop a GI, he will help you out'. To Nicky, 'this seemed strange as GIs are not allowed to possess dollar bills and here was I officially being asked to step in to the unofficial market, a very close relative indeed to the black market if not the same man'.

Leaving American Express, he bumped straight into a US sergeant and told him the situation. 'He said that he was a bit tight, but hastened to explain that this did not by any means mean that he had no money on him. In fact he confided he had $1,600 in scrip in his pocket, but he was just going to buy a Chevrolet. I showed interest and so he gave me the details. He had negotiated the purchase of a brand-new Chevrolet, which had just been shipped from the USA to Antwerp, and the clock would only show the mileage from Antwerp to Frankfurt. He did not intend to use the car in Germany but the Army would ship it to the States for him free. The biography of the car, including how it figured to start with in some priority order and then by passing through its own black market was bought by a top sargeant [sic] in Frankfurt with the proceeds of another black market and finally its return unused to the US, would make interesting reading. Well, after all this we were real buddies, and he helped me out with twenty dollars of scrip.'

The next task was to get travel papers to their next location: Berlin. This proved even more taxing – lots of waiting around in offices and, on being asked to return, finding said office closed.

Father Killion had fared no better amid the chaos. An extra day was needed before they both received all the correct papers. In the meantime the real reason for the trip occurred: attending a conference regarding the displaced persons, and this time, success! Up to one hundred families were authorised to leave their transit camps and start new lives elsewhere.

Nicky was free after the meeting and soon his natural curiosity led him into the ruined city for a look round. Before long he was chatting to an old man who told him he was sixty-three and had been called up to fight at the age of sixty. He offered to show Nicky the old town, where they found an area even more devastated than that near the railway station where Nicky was staying: '. . . near the railway station seemed a wilderness but what he showed me was beyond description. It seemed impossible for so much nothingness to exist.'

All the major buildings in the old town were flattened, with just the Paulskirche in the process of being rebuilt. This church was the seat of the first freely elected German parliament, which met there in the mid-nineteenth century. Nicky walked through the rubble of the Römer, Frankfurt's town hall, one of the city's most important historic buildings, dating from the fifteenth century.

'In the centre of the square in front of the Römer and otherwise surrounded by complete devastation, stands undamaged a fountain called the Gerechtigkeitsbrunnen (the fountain of justice) in the centre of which stands a maiden holding a pair of scales. Here within a radius of kilometres no building is undamaged and here stands Justice with a fragile pair of scales in her hands. Is there some guiding power which has left this as a sign?'

That comment gives a clue to the dramatic impact this devastation had on Nicky. He was no believer by then in a 'guiding power', but the symbolism could not fail to move him and stir up his emotions, usually so well concealed.

With George Wicks, in their Geneva apartment

Fountain of Justice in front of bombed cathedral, Frankfurt

Many of the population he saw seemed to be living in cellars underneath the ruined buildings, but at night, after he again ventured out into the town, he saw lights shining in houses which seemed to be empty shells. This time he came across a crowd of people, and as he looked and spoke like a German civilian, he soon found out that this was the real black market in action. There was buying and selling of bread and meat coupons, also chocolate bars, but mainly cigarettes. Whenever any police appeared, the crowd would melt away, only to reform immediately as soon as the patrol had rounded the corner. The group was mainly young men aged between seventeen and twenty-one, many of them disabled, with only one leg. While Nicky was speaking to one of them, a well-dressed girl came up and asked them for cigarettes. She told them that she and her family had had to escape from East Prussia (a province of Germany separated from the rest of the country by a part of Poland) in front of the advancing Russian Army in 1945. The soldiers were known to be committing atrocities on the local German population, and they had fled, leaving everything they owned behind. They were now living in the countryside outside Frankfurt and could only obtain food from the farmers by exchanging goods with them, cigarettes being the most sought after.

She eventually obtained two packets of cigarettes for the equivalent of her earnings for one month.

On his return to the hotel, and writing notes of his experiences, a sense of anger rather than sorrow seemed to come out. 'What a contrast between luxury and destitution. The . . . American-run hotels are like oasis [sic] in a desert. One can see from the service stripes that most of those who work in the oasis were not in Europe when the desert was created. I wonder if it is a good policy to send over young lads for whom the easy profits to be made are far too tempting. These are the real profiteers of the war, and big profits are being made. If someone has to take advantage of this state of affairs, I should prefer it to be the men who know what war is and who fought, and not these lads who were 10–12 years old when the war started. It may not be possible to stop all this but the Americans indirectly actually encourage it. In the PX store (The American NAAFI – Navy, Army, Air Force), one can for example buy soap and chocolate unrationed. Both of these are commodities just right for the black market. I have seen GIs go in and buy over 100 tablets of soap at a time. No one buys a bar of chocolate but a box of six bars and most purchasers buy many boxes. And apart from this, one can buy jam, honey and an untold number of different kinds of tinned foods. All these things the Germans are prepared to pay (barter) anything for.

'In the hotel I met an American civilian. He had just come from Berlin where he had visited an art dealer whom he had known before the war. The art dealer had just sold to a GI a Van Dyck (painting) for two million marks and the GI admitted to having made all this money by the sale of cigarettes.

'I went to bed with a thought in my mind that the basic problem here was food. I cannot see how any successful reconstruction program can be put into operation before the people can go about their work without having to fight the daily battle against hunger.'

His feelings towards the German population were mixed. He saw that many were traumatised, starving and injured, and yet he also knew that many had supported the Nazis in their aims of establishing an enlarged and racially superior German population throughout Europe, while ridding the country of those considered inferior in the most terrible way.

However, his notes not only point to the injustice of what he was witnessing, but also to solutions that could be found and should be acted on fast. He was not one for the wringing of hands, but was always looking for solutions, a way of channelling his emotions into action. This, however, was not his current focus and he did nothing to put these thoughts into any kind of action. He was focused on his task of the moment of resettling refugees.

After this first assignment, however, the nature of his work changed dramatically to a more mind-boggling task. This was to assist the American director Abba Schwartz in organising and supervising the liquidation of Nazi loot, stolen from those the German army imprisoned and over-ran during the war. Schwartz was a lawyer who, after two years as Reparations Director at the IRO, became an adviser to Eleanor Roosevelt, and later to both John and Robert Kennedy. He spent much of his life working for refugees and encouraging the US government to allow greater immigration of Eastern European and other refugees. Schwartz asked Nicky to be his Deputy in Reparations, possibly having discovered his banking background.

Despite being based in Geneva, Nicky spent most of his time travelling to Germany, Britain, France, Switzerland and America to carry out his role, making forty-three journeys over an eight-month period, by car, train, lorry, boat and plane. The job involved collecting loot found by the Allied troops, storing it securely, then breaking it down into basic materials – gold, jewels etc. – so they could be easily sold. He then had to organise the sale, tally the income and forward on the money obtained according to what was initially called the Paris Agreement but became the Five Power Agreement of June 1946.

This agreement between the governments of the USA, Great Britain, France, Czechoslovakia and Yugoslavia was to make $25 million available from the liquidation of Nazi assets for assistance to victims of their regime, 'not for the compensation of individual victims but for the rehabilitation and resettlement of persons in eligible classes . . . The available data indicated beyond any reasonable doubt that the overwhelming majority of eligible persons were Jewish' but 'in recognition that a small minority of non-Jews fell into the eligible category' the sum of $2.5 million was set aside for those non-Jews who 'could prove that they were persecuted for religious, political, or racial reasons'.

On top of that sum, ninety-five per cent of the value of the non-monetary gold (NMG), as it was called, that had been found and which the Reparations team was dealing with, was to be given to the Jewish Agency and five per cent to agencies helping other persecuted groups. The Jewish Agency, originally set up by the League of Nations to represent the Jewish community in Palestine and to enable the setting up of a Jewish state, was the body that administered funds for Jewish resettlement.

The background to the loot was grisly and Nicky could only cope with it emotionally by detaching himself from the knowledge of its history, though on occasion the reality broke through the shield he'd erected to protect himself.

A large portion of what he had to deal with had been found by American troops close to a liberated concentration camp, stored in salvaged military boxes. In particular there were crates and crates full of valuables and jewellery, all of which had been taken from the Jewish and other victims on their arrival at the camp. Along with the valuables were more horrifying hoards: crates of false teeth and glasses, cigarette cases and, unbelievably, gold teeth and fillings removed from the corpses in the gas chambers. Other boxes of similar loot were found as Allied troops had moved through Germany – all taken to the Reichsbank in Frankfurt and deposited in the vaults.

Nicky's first task was to go to see what was there and arrange for its sorting. His photography hobby, now an integral part of his life, led him to take pictures of the opened crates in the vault. It was these photos, many years later, that he thought would be of most interest to historians rather than the Kindertransport scrapbook. He was astonished to find little curiosity for this pictorial record amongst those he discussed it with in Britain, and so these prints were given to Yad Vashem at the same time he donated his scrapbook to them.

Case of false teeth

Cases of jewellery

Having assessed the crates' contents, Nicky had to supervise the sorting into items that were easily saleable and those that were financially worthless. Jewels had to be separated from their mountings and saleable metals melted down. Then the best price for them needed to be found on the international markets to enable the money to be distributed as per the Paris Agreement. Nicky worked on this feverishly, finding it all-consuming and at times complicated. Experts had to be brought in from the USA to separate real from false diamonds, and to separate metals into gold, silver and lower grade. This examination resulted in piles of smashed up jewellery, watches and clocks, with the valuable parts removed and the remnants which were deemed worthless – but which had to be disposed of without any of it entering into the German economy as stated in the Paris Agreement – packed up again for transportation. The diamonds examined and then valued at $500,000 (equivalent to $5.5 million in 2013) were the first part of the loot to be sent, by air, to the USA for sale there.

His next job, after the sorting, was to transport all the items that could not be broken down, such as paintings, furs, china, silverware and other luxury goods, over to America to be auctioned

there. Again, these had been found throughout Germany, seized by
the Nazis from their Jewish victims and with no way now of tracing ownership. Nicky left Geneva for Frankfurt where these items,
packed into 844 crates, were stored at the Reichsbank.

Dismantling clocks

To get a sense of the magnitude of the valuables discovered and
now being transported, here is the list of the crates' contents:

- 334 chests containing silver bowls, candlesticks, silver plates
- 198 chests containing table silver
- 132 chests containing rugs
- 130 chests containing china
- 34 chests containing watches, clocks, jewels, cigarette cases
- 16 chests containing valuable postage stamps

Dealing with all these items, the testament to the brutal genocide which had occurred so recently and so nearby, was a disquiet-
ing proposition. Nicky was ideal for the job, not because he was

unfeeling, but because he was able to separate and suppress his emotional response, at times overwhelming, in order to get on with the job. The complex problems and logistics kept his mind occupied and helped keep his thoughts on the practical issues involved in his task.

Accompanied by two US army officers, he inspected and sealed each crate and had them loaded onto a train, seventeen coaches being given over to their transportation. The coaches were sealed for the journey and had to be inspected on arrival at the port of Bremerhaven, near Hamburg, by Nicky and Captain Wikle, the Freight and Movements officer there. Then further seals were affixed and an armed guard posted with orders to shoot any unauthorised persons coming close to the train, which was floodlit through the night, with an electrician on standby close at hand in case of power faults. The guarded train coaches were then left for about two weeks until the US ship, the *SS General Sturgis*, arrived.

Loading crates of valuables onto train

Nicky returned to Geneva to continue other work for those few weeks, but was back in time to join the ship when it sailed on 1 December 1947, with the cargo safely stowed, destination New York via Nova Scotia. The ship was also carrying a group of refugees under the IRO resettlement agreement, which was organising new lives for displaced persons. This group of 856 was the sixth the ship had transported and they were headed to Canada, where most had relatives. The ship was one of three operated by the US War Department on behalf of the IRO for this purpose.

The crossing was a rough one, but nevertheless it enabled Nicky to solve the problem of disposing of the crates of unsaleable items, which were also on the ship alongside the crates of property for auction. These items, including the innards of watches, alarm clocks, glasses, false teeth and such like, though seemingly worthless, had been forbidden from entering the German economy in any form, though there was no ruling of how this was to be achieved. He was required to dispose of them somehow and he found a solution to this problem based on expediency that fitted the bill. In mid-Atlantic, the crates were brought on deck and, along with his American escorts and the ship's officers, he watched two sailors with axes smash them open and throw them overboard. No mention of the effect of witnessing this destruction has remained, but with a ship full of refugees, it must have been a poignant episode for all who witnessed it. However, it fulfilled Nicky's remit of preventing all such materials from remaining in Germany and therefore for him, whatever the emotional reaction, it was another job done.

Nicky wrote a few pages about the trip which described the stormy weather in some detail, as well as commenting on his fellow passengers: the 'displaced persons . . . They are a good-looking well-behaved bunch of people. The crew are delighted to carry them as, instead of creating work, they are all eager and willing to help and the escort officer has no trouble in getting volunteers for the 101 odd jobs that have to be done. Having worked at a distance from these people for so long it is good to be amongst them on their trip to final freedom. Canada should certainly benefit greatly from the work all these people will be giving in the years to come.'

Breaking open crates of 'worthless' items for disposal at sea. Nicky on right wearing glasses

He played cards in the evenings, and managed to eat well despite the rolling of the ship; at one meal he careered back and forth the length of the room on his chair, having failed to grip onto the table at the right moment, knocking a waiter for six as china crashed around them, and finally ending up back at the table: 'A real Laurel and Hardy scene.'

Daytimes were spent watching the dramatic seascape, and he reflected, 'I have not lost the art of doing nothing.' It must have been a welcome respite after the hectic previous six months: 'My chief occupation remains eating and sleeping and all the same I remain continually hungry and tired.'

Due to the rough seas, the trip to Nova Scotia eventually took eleven days instead of the expected seven and after the disembarkation of the refugees, the ship sailed down the coast to New York. Once there the unloading took two days with the crates being stored on Staten Island to await customs clearance. Nicky's responsibility ended when he handed the crates over to the UN-designated organisation dealing not only with their sale, but also the passing of the proceeds to the various agencies.

The most surprising thing about Nicky's notes of the crossing was that he didn't mention in them the episode involving the destruction and disposal overboard of all those crates of pitiful items, reminders of lives destroyed due to hate and insane ideology. Perhaps it was too difficult to write about and ignoring it was easier. Nicky, never prone to introspection, can still not explain this omission. However, he had already demonstrated his ability to suppress emotional responses that hindered his ability to get on with things.

In an interview given many years later about this voyage, he stated, 'I was able to detach myself from my responsibility for the gruesome cargo in the hold of the ship and, although the crossing was very rough at times, with passengers disappearing to their cabins for hours, even days, at a time, it was all very social. There were parties and I was invited to join games of bridge and poker; I actually won 25 cents! Two army officers, both Lieutenant Colonels, who had been assigned to me to assist with security, were good company. We sailed through the Gulf Stream where the cloudless sky allowed a brief, but welcome, warmth from a winter sun. Seagulls and a porpoise leaping out of the water were the only signs of life. Such serenity produced an amazing feeling of apartness – I felt a long way from the misery of Europe.'

*       *       *

Degussa gold smelting

Back in Germany, Nicky was thrust straight back into his next task: dealing with the precious metals – taken from jewellery, watch cases, spectacle frames, cigarette cases – which had been removed from victims before they entered the gas chambers, as well as gold fillings extracted from the corpses before cremation. The company given the task of smelting the metals was Degussa, the biggest European smelter and dealer in precious metals at the time. They were a German company based in Frankfurt, and only a few years earlier had been melting down precious metals for the Nazis, presumably from the same source.

Nicky organised the movement of the crates of precious metals from the vault at the Reichsbank where they were stored, across Frankfurt to Degussa, to be made into gold bars before arranging their sale. His banking background enabled him to use contacts at London banks to discover the best sale price of gold, which he remembers being about $35/ounce, and then spend hours haggling on the phone to get an extra few cents out of the buyers. (As I write in 2012, the price is $1600/ounce.)

650 kilos of gold and 150 kilos of silver needed to be taken to London to be sold there and that transportation became one of his most dramatic adventures. Arrangements were made by Samuel Montagu merchant bank for the material to be transported on a regular British European Airways flight from Frankfurt at 1900 hours on 9 February 1948. A write-up Nicky made of the whole episode gives snippets of farcical aspects, mixed with the drama.

Firstly there was one bar of gold needing collection from the smelters before the cargo could be packed. As the smelter was delayed, the gold bar was delivered to the bank after the vault had been closed for lunch, 'so I had to take it with me to lunch – Midas had nothing else but gold and starved as a result, but I made a hearty meal with the gold bar as a footrest.'

Afterwards at the bank, as Nicky and two military policemen set to work removing the twenty boxes out of the vault, containing $750,000 of gold, a Mr Keller of the Reichsbank and a US Army officer sat on chairs in the doorway and watched. 'So many people check what I do, although they have little or no responsibility in our affairs, that I am used to it although at times it is a bit embarrassing. However it suits me to be watched and checked . . . So they watch me and I watch the bullion and take all the responsibility and everyone is happy.' Documents releasing the boxes from the bank's responsibility were signed and exchanged. The cargo was now Nicky's responsibility, as it was taken under escort by five military police to the airport.

He recounts, 'The van with the bullion, followed by a jeep with its red light flashing and its siren blaring, sped along the near deserted roads, scattering pedestrians in its midst; any vehicle in sight was ordered to slow down and pull in to the side of the road.

'We arrived at the airport, happy to find the plane scheduled to leave on time, but there followed a period of uneasiness and uncanny silence. It was then announced that all flights were cancelled! Bearing in mind the bank having washed their hands of the whole procedure once we had signed the documents, I decided to load the boxes into the wire enclosure at the airport, ask for the airport police to stand guard and stay locked in with my "freight" for the night. That was not to be. The escort of Military Police (MP) were anxious to be on their way and the airport refused to provide extra guards.

'After numerous telephone calls, it was decided to reload the boxes back into the van, drive back into the city and deposit them in the main hall of the bank where I would stay with them for the night. The bank had day and night guards. We reload, speed back to town and begin unloading only to be told that Lieutenant Colonel Emigh, of the Provost Marshall's Department, US Military Headquarters, had now been alerted and instructed us to bring the cargo round to his flat, offering me a bed for the night where I could sleep with the boxes surrounding me and two MPs on duty outside my door all night.

'We reload once again and speed through the town to his flat where I slept, my cargo beside me and did not even wake for the "changing of the guard". My escort returned at half past eight the next morning, and ten minutes later we set off for the airport. We loaded the plane and took off arriving at Northolt at lunchtime. Formalities on our side of the Channel were minimal!'

On arriving in London, he was met by a representative of Samuel Montagu who had made the gold transaction, plus one solitary policeman. The money from this cargo was destined for the Jewish Agency in Palestine and sent to Eliezer Kaplan, its treasurer, who shortly after became the first Finance Minister of the new State of Israel.

Nicky has since reassessed this episode and come to believe that the flight delay was not an accident. 'The authorities were highly suspicious of me, an English civilian, in charge of a large load of gold bars attempting to leave the American occupied zone. My credentials must have been checked pretty thoroughly.'

The telegram Nicky sent, sometime in February 1948, to inform his boss Schwartz in Geneva and Kaplan in Jerusalem of the culmination of the transaction, has survived. It states, 'Many months work NMG culminated today my arrival London with kilograms 650 gold formerly gold teeth etcetera sold for approx seven hundred thousand dollars stop This ends one chapter concentration camps and opens new one for resettlement survivors nazi terror stop Three hundred thousand dollars expected from sale silver near future Winton' (NMG being non-monetary gold).

The telegram encapsulates the job done, but does not shrink from making a clear statement of the origins of the gold and the moral use to which it was now to be put. After all, this was why Nicky had volunteered for the IRO in the first place: to help resettle refugees. In amongst all the bartering and logistics, he still had his mind focused on the end results and reasons for doing this work: to assist real human beings who had suffered terrible crimes against them.

A telegram to Dave Rolbein was more succinct: 'The gold has been delivered and $700,000 is being paid to us today on account.' When interviewed by Muriel Emanuel in the '90s about this episode and the business-like nature of this note, he said, 'I look at those words now and do not feel as I did then. But then what else was it but a business transaction? I had the goods, I transformed them into manageable cargo, I arranged for their transport and they were paid for. Today, I think not only of all those innocent lives, senselessly and horrifically cut off, most of them in their prime, but of the depraved minds obsessed with the material gains to be obtained from pitiable items so small and so personal as gold fillings. A million wedding rings alone. When I think that if I had a handful of gold fillings and weighed them on my kitchen scales, it would take three or four fillings before the scales would register and there I was handling thousands of kilograms. There you have some idea of the scale of this mighty operation. At the time it was a job I had to do and I suppose I had a sense of pride and achievement in having succeeded in my mission against such extraordinary odds.'

Nicky seemed to be suggesting that the difficulties and complexities of the job were more than enough to focus on. He had huge personal responsibility and had to put all his skills to work to get the job done. To really take on board the source and significance of the gold would make it impossible for him to function effectively and so he consciously shielded himself from thinking about its history.

There was yet more to do. Following this major consignment was that of the silver: 119 crates which were going to Sheffield for smelting, as well as another transaction involving 6,000 kilos of silver being sent to Tangiers, Morocco. Nicky sent numerous letters to Abba Schwartz who was, by February 1948, back working from the IRO New York office. These detailed the complex and often frustrating arrangements and negotiations regarding the silver, but eventually by mid-March the shipments were made satisfactorily.

Dealings with the Reichsbank throughout his time at the IRO were often fraught, as they seemed, to Nicky, to be intent on being unhelpful and at times petty. However, he was not intimidated by their officials and he was prepared to stand up to them. There were frequent arguments between them in which Nicky forcefully overcame their resistance, thanks to his fluent German and ability to convey authority, this latter coming from his long experience in the world of banking as well as the ethical conviction he carried about the job he was doing and the moral ambiguity he saw in these officials, so recently doing similar tasks for the Nazis.

It was an exceptionally difficult, tiring and stressful job. Nicky's aptitude for it came exactly from his ability to separate out his emotions and mostly suppress them, and to stick to the mechanics of the job rather than getting sabotaged by the horror those goods revealed. His banking knowledge and contacts in that field as well as his fluent German were clearly vital to the task. No wonder Abba Schwartz saw in him the qualities and skills he needed to get the task done. He was glad to leave this chapter behind though and move on, to new pastures and fresh adventures.

# 10

## *Romance in Paris*

### *1999*

As 1999 drew on, Grete slowly became weaker. She and Nicky continued with their quiet life, often interrupted by visitors, mainly friends seeking to help and offer any support they could. Right into the summer, Grete continued to cook and behave much as normal, though without making many trips out and none far afield. She was uncomplaining about her many physical indignities and pains and kept a brave face to the world, including to Nicky. Any thought she gave to her deterioration and her wishes for how her death should be handled were kept to one-liners at intervals. We had to keep our ears open for these; they would not be repeated. Mid-August came, with no obvious change. In the third week, however, just after Nick had gone away for two weeks' holiday, she took a sudden turn for the worse and was taken into hospital at Wexham Park, near Slough.

I rushed up from my Herefordshire home to find her very weak, having been vomiting blood, just as she had when the illness was first diagnosed. After a few days, Nicky and I were given the awful news that there was nothing to be done and she had very little time. Nick was sent word and set off for home, made complicated by being on a remote Greek island. Grete's close friend, Frances Slade, was summoned to say goodbye, and left in tears.

Those last days in the hospital were very mixed; Grete was at times very weak and tired, but at others quite alert and talkative. It was heartbreaking to witness her and Nicky talking together, saying their goodbyes without actually saying it. There was a lot of reminiscing – all the good times they had had. When Nicky went home to bed in the evenings, I stayed on, sleeping or trying to, on a blanket in the corner of the single room she was given. It was during those quiet precious hours that she told me things about her early life I had never heard before.

She held on, sleeping more and more, until two days later Nick arrived straight from the airport, still in his shorts and sandals. He took over that night watch and twenty-four hours later she gave up. Late on the night of Friday 28 August, she died in her sleep, with Nick and I both holding her hands. We faced the awful task of breaking the news to Nicky when he woke the next morning.

Their fifty-year love affair was ended and he was bereft. Despite their different characters, experiences and nationalities, they had been an impregnable unit. Nicky saw his own life as clearly divided into two parts: before and after he married Grete. They had met and started their life together when he was already nearly thirty-nine and Grete was twenty-eight, and in a city foreign to them both, but where their individual drives to do constructive post-war work had brought them, and a place made for falling in love.

## 1948–50

As Nicky's work with the IRO slowly came to an end in the spring of 1948 and he was beginning to think about what came next, he was approached to take a job in Paris at the International Bank for Reconstruction and Development (IBRD).

Nicky saw this work as a 'continuation of the efforts of the world to try and put itself together after the traumas of the war. I was lucky in this offer insofar as they required the two bits of knowledge which I had: a) a banking background; and b) a

knowledge of French. And so I found myself in Paris being interviewed for a job and was immediately accepted.'

Looking back, he says, 'I suppose that this posting, of all the
things which I have done in life, had the greatest consequence,
insofar as it was there that I met my wife.'

In 1947, another Lend-Lease type agreement was made between
the US, France and Britain, which became known as the Marshall
Plan after the then US Secretary of State, General Marshall. This
loan was to help Europe rebuild itself using around $20 billion,
lent between 1947 and 1953. There were conditions on how the
money could be used and Nicky's job at the bank, as a supervisor
in the Treasurer's department, was to help oversee that the $250
million loaned by the IBRD to the French bank Crédit National
adhered to these conditions.

'It's all a long time ago but I think I remember rightly in saying
that the conditions of the money given were not set out as to what
they could do with the money but specifically what they could *not*
do with the money.

'What they could not do with the money was to use it for any
military or warlike purposes whatsoever and so from time to time,
I was closeted in one of the French (government) departments,
looking through all their paperwork and if I found ... that
particular consignment of money had found its way to look like
that it could be used for anything resembling a warlike action, I
had to query it. I can remember perhaps only two occasions when
this occurred and I think my memory is correct in saying that I was
then told that the particular document to which I was referring
had got into the wrong basket. And they would see to it that it was
removed from that basket and put into one to which I could have
no objection.'

So for Nicky, compared to his previous IRO job and his work at
the stock exchange, it was a fairly straightforward and mundane,
even boring, job, even though it was still a post that aided the

international efforts to assist with the reconstruction of Europe. Perhaps after the emotional and mental strain of the work at the IRO, he was satisfied to have a quieter post for a while. It was certainly not his usual stimulating work environment. Nevertheless he had accepted it and on arriving at the bank on 1 April 1948, the first two people he met were the director and his secretary, a twenty-eight-year-old Danish girl who spoke good English, French and German, called Grete Gjelstrup.

Grete's first real memory of Nicky was not that favourable. He did not have a secretary himself, so he came in one day and asked her if she would type a letter for him. As he began to dictate it to her, she discovered that it was not business but a note to his mother thanking her for a coffee pot she had just sent him. What a cheek! She was incensed that he should assume it was OK to ask her to write this personal correspondence for him. Anyway, she obviously did not hold it against him as before long they were seeing each other socially. Though at times superficially restrained and circumspect, Nicky was in general a confident, fun-loving character. While Grete was altogether quieter and more reserved, she had strong views about life and values that matched his. She also possessed an enormous curiosity about the world, which had brought her out of Denmark to Germany, where she worked for a Danish Red Cross unit, and then to France.

They quickly found they had lots of interests in common: music including concerts and the opera, exploring Paris – its churches, galleries and cobbled back streets – and discussing life and current affairs while rowing on the lakes in their plentiful spare time. Nicky joined the local fencing club, having been unable to pursue this interest throughout the war years, and before long Grete was accompanying him to all his countrywide competitions. As fencing is really not particularly a spectator sport, her attendances showed an early commitment towards him. Their romance developed quickly, unlike any previous liaisons Nicky had, which had mostly tended to remain fairly casual. A fun-filled holiday they took with friends in August to the Pyrenees made clear to him that they were well-suited.

He was already thirty-nine years old, but though he obviously felt that this relationship was in a different league to any he had previously known, he hesitated about taking the next momentous step. Five months into their courtship in early September, Nicky was having dinner in a restaurant near the Gare du Nord with a British friend, Stephen Burnett, who was visiting Paris. He obviously poured his heart out, as towards the end of the meal, Stephen said, 'Well, after all you've told me, why the hell don't you ask her?'

Thus galvanised, Nicky jumped in a taxi and sped over to her flat. It was late and she had gone to bed, so his proposal was conducted with Grete in her dressing gown and a disapproving landlady not far away.

'Our memorable joke, which neither of us really remembered if it were true or apocryphal, was that when I eventually summoned up the courage and asked her to marry me, she said "yes, please". And neither of us can really remember if I invented this or if it really happened.'

Then, as Nicky put it, 'that's when it all began'.

'Then started all the business of when, where and how we should get married. This was by no means as easy as it sounds in retrospect. Eventually after much discussion and much letter writing it was decided that we should get married in Denmark. Little did we realise that an Englishman marrying a Danish girl but both living in Paris would cause any complications, but indeed it did. The date, whom to be invited, who would send out the invitations, how the invitations were to be worded, what kind of ceremony it was to be, in what church it should take place, in what language it should take place, all this meant a huge amount of correspondence.' (In fact the wedding date was only seven weeks after they got engaged, so little time was allowed for all the complications Nicky recalled.)

'First of all who should be invited? Then how long should they be in Denmark, then where were they to be put up and who was going to pay, where was the actual ceremony to take place? Who of Grete's parents and relatives were to be the ones providing the major entertainment? In the end the various authorities had to agree the paperwork so it would be a valid wedding and at last four days before the wedding was due to take place in Vejle (where Grete was born and her parents still resided) and we thought everything had been organised, a letter came from Grete's father asking us to let them know what music we would like to be played as we left the church.

'This was one question too much for me and I said we had been corresponding about this wedding and answering questions for a very long time. Any further questions such as this one, they must work out for themselves. The result of this quite innocuous remark however proved a disaster. My best man was Stanley Murdoch and according to him, "everything had to be done as it should be done". The wedding took place in the British church with everybody in full evening dress according to the Danish custom. When all was over and we both stood erect in front of the altar ready for the music to start for us to march out of the church, to my surprise, but to Stanley's absolute horror, they played the British national anthem. He of course stood rigidly to attention, nobody moved and everything came to a full stop. So we thought they had learnt their lesson and when they came to the end, what happened? As nobody had moved, they played the national anthem again. When they started playing it for the third time, I think it was Mother who could bear it no longer and said something to Stanley and we did in fact march out of the church to the strains of the national anthem.

'Thereafter followed three days of banquets, each member of Grete's family doing their utmost to make their lunch or evening the highlight of the wedding. Our return to Paris in my Citroën was made easy by two things: firstly I had bought some CD plates to put on the car to which nobody whom I asked at the bank seemed to know if I was legally entitled to or not. The second was by putting Grete's wedding gown over all the parcels on the back seat, which did in fact seem to make a great impression on the functionaries at the frontiers.'

There was no immediate honeymoon, no reason why remembered now. On their return to Paris, they set up home together in an apartment on Rue de Passy, in the west of Paris, with primitive cooking and bathing facilities. Once a week they would walk through Passy in their dressing gowns to the local bathhouse for a proper bath, doing some shopping on the way home. They had a blissful time, cooking duck on a grill in their fireplace and entertaining an international group of friends, including Jean Weidner, head of the Dutch resistance in France during the war, and Rafael Kubelík, the Czech conductor, who Nicky remembers turning the spit to cook a chicken over their open fire, while they prepared the rest of the meal. Grete took her duties as a wife seriously and Nicky was old-fashioned in that respect too. The kitchen was her territory, so she signed up for a Cordon Bleu cookery course at the famous cookery school in Paris, which soon led to her life-long reputation as a tremendous cook. They started as they meant to go on, and throughout their lives regularly invited friends and acquaintances to come for meals which Grete meticulously planned, writing down the menu and what she would need to buy.

Their beautiful old Citroën was kept in a local garage used by all the nearby residents. One day while driving it, Nicky leaned over to get something from the glove compartment, only to discover someone else's belongings there. His car key had opened and started another identical Citroën kept in the same garage.

Wedding day, October 1948

Vejle, Denmark 1948. L–R: Grete,
Nicky, Kirsten (Grete's sister)

In their spare time, they drove all over France, visiting cities, ancient cathedrals and archaeological sites, as well as to Nicky's regular fencing tournaments. On the way to one competition, they happened on a vineyard in mid-harvest. Another new experience beckoned. They responded by spending several happy sweat-filled days picking grapes and chatting to the *vigneron*, Stephan Foin, his family and workers. They got on so well that, as the day of the tournament dawned, their new friends accompanied them, taking a day off from the harvest to watch the action.

However, all good things come to an end, and Nicky's work at the bank came to an end in October 1949. The job he had been taken on to do was completed and the bank had nothing else to offer him. His reference from them stated, 'In the course of his work Mr Winton has had to follow up the delivery and utilisation of aviation, railway and other equipment. He has shown ability and a capacity for hard work, as well as tact and a gift for getting on well with the French officials he has had to deal with.'

Having no immediate next step in mind, they decided that now was the time to have their long-delayed honeymoon. They agreed to explore America using the glut of US dollars in which they had been paid, rather than lose out on the unfavourable rate of conversion into British pounds. They had already more or less decided to live in England, and before leaving for America, spent a few months at Lottie's flat in Belsize Park, Nicky's and Stanley's old stomping ground. Stanley was living with his wife Maudie nearby, enabling them to spend more time together again. As their discussions involved where and how they were going to live in the future, Stanley put forward a scheme to Nicky which entailed buying a large run-down property overlooking Hampstead Heath, called The Logs, and converting it into six flats, so they could have one each and pay for them by selling off the other four.

The Logs is still a landmark off East Heath Road in Hampstead, and was Grade II listed in 1974 for its 'eccentric mixture of Gothic,

Italianate and other styles'. Nicky was enthusiastic and Grete obviously offered no objections, as for about one year this plan was put into action. Stanley was in charge of all the admin and Nicky, supposedly, the finance. However, just at this point, Nicky and Grete went off to the USA for three months on that belated honeymoon, leaving Stanley in charge.

Helping with the grape harvest at Foin family
vineyard, 1949. Nicky second from right

Nicky and Grete with their beloved Citroën

Nicky's savings were not enough to buy and convert the property, and Stanley could not make up the difference, so much of his time and effort went into trying to raise funds for their joint venture. Letters flew to and fro across the Atlantic updating Nicky on progress or, more often, the lack of it. Mortgages were promised then refused, and a last-minute scramble for funds involved Stanley asking Frederic Handl, Nicky's mother's lover, for help. This he reluctantly supplied, though asking for it to be short term. Therefore when the work was finally completed on the building, to their dismay they found that neither of them could afford to keep a flat after all. The whole development had to be sold to pay back their creditors.

The honeymoon trip began with a liner across the Atlantic, Nicky and Grete travelling in Third Class 'in the bottom of the ship'. They both had misgivings about spending so much on so frivolous a thing as a holiday, but somehow neither went so far as cancelling it. Changing dollars into pounds at that time led to a large loss of currency and so seemed uneconomic. By chance, Nicky's wealthy second cousin Ernest Friedman, who lived in America, was also travelling back on the same ship but in First Class. He was 'surprised but delighted' to see them and, knowing they were in Third Class, often invited them up for meals and drinks. It was while dining with him on several occasions that they witnessed Errol Flynn, the famous Hollywood actor, propping up the First Class bar. The crossing was rough and Grete spent a fair amount of time in bed feeling ill, though most evenings they managed to see a film, one such being *How the Americans Won the War*. One meal in First Class that Grete recorded was 'extravagant luxury . . . And quite amazing food, starting with caviar and ending with crêpes suzette. Dancing afterwards made almost impossible by extraordinarily bad weather.' Nicky expressed delight in a letter to his mother that even in Third Class they get a five-course dinner with wine included. He adds, 'Every morning at 11.30 Ernest comes "slumming" and meets us in the (Third Class) lounge.'

They had enough money to make their holiday last for the three months they wanted, only if they were frugal in their outgoings, and so First Class was a real treat. Ernest Friedman was going on holiday, deep-sea fishing in Florida, on his return and so he lent them his car which they were to drive down from New York to Key West in the southern tip of Florida to collect him and drive him home. As their intention had been to see as much of the country as their money would allow, this was a huge boost to their plans. Exploring new vistas was something they both loved and doing it on the cheap was no great hardship. Their inclinations were similar; comfort was less of a priority than adventure.

While in New York, they looked up several of Nicky's work colleagues from his post-war work at the IRO. They also tried to see Nicky's uncle Friedl, by now an eminent and somewhat controversial psychiatrist who had changed his name to Fredric Wertham on arriving in America in 1922. He was too busy to meet them but his artist wife Florence Hesketh was free. He was apparently in the middle of his involvement in work on violence in comics and Nicky told his mother, 'The Canadian government have just passed a law banning a great number of children's comics based on Fredric's work and in fact the government sent someone to him so that he could help draft the bill.'

In the same letter he comments on the 'magnificent' shops, but reckons prices are two or three times what they are in England. Grete adds her input on the impressive scale of New York, but follows with, 'you need not fear, we are not staying here; we don't fit in. I understand why Nick is so keen on settling in England; that is the kind of life we both like.' Magnificent shops and the consumerism they discovered in America were not great draws for either Nicky or Grete. Their joint plan was for a simpler life, based around community and family relationships rather than possessions. To drive in America Nicky had to take a driving test, which he passed without problems – the only driving test he ever took! They walked many miles exploring New York, to the great amusement of their US friends who never walked anywhere, and made simple meals in their hotel room to economise. Then, having spent nearly two weeks in New York and seen all they could, Nicky and Grete took to the road for their 1,500-mile drive down to Florida in Ernest's car.

Their first stop was Washington, where they spent a day with Nicky's old boss at the IRO, Abba Schwartz, and his wife, and were shown the sights. One aspect of American life that irritated yet intrigued them both was the enthusiasm for advertising and the focus on money and the cost of everything. 'We have a wireless in the car and between the advertisements it is occasionally possible to listen to some music . . . So many people *talk* like advertisements. You say you have a cold and they set about selling you the qualities of the cold cure they have . . . They open the fridge and extol the virtues of all they have inside.' On taking a guided tour of the capital, Nicky comments, 'It was all extraordinarily interesting but we could not help but smile to each other when our guide set a price on every picture he showed us. No doubt this impresses the Americans but we wondered how a price could be set on anything which could never be sold.' Even later on he comments, 'The road itself is greatly spoiled by all the advertisements . . . you are continually being told that you are driving the wrong car, using the wrong petrol and, of course, smoking an inferior cigarette.'

It showed how well-suited Nicky and Grete were, that they were in agreement that this way of life was not for them. Money was not the prime goal and materialism not of great interest, though they were intrigued by some of the novelties America was producing.

Nicky was on the lookout for possible future business ideas, which seemed to have been sparked by talks with his uncle Emil about his plastics business: 'I hope to return to England with a large quantity of gadgets and if I can't make my fortune out of them I shall at any rate be able to use them . . . I have my eyes open (Emil) for plastic gadgets and am now looking for a gadget which enables one to dispense with gadgets! This in America should be possible.'

Having taken their leave of the Schwartzes, they drove into Virginia to the Blue Ridge Mountains, continuing with big detours to visit particular sites via Tennessee, Alabama and New Orleans, then finally into Florida. They could not afford to eat in restaurants, so all their meals were picnics, making coffee on a little primus stove. As they moved southward, the weather improved, the sun shone and the picnics became more pleasant affairs.

Nicky's letters to his mother were full of glowing descriptions of the beauty of the landscape and the friendliness of the people, but the cultural differences between the USA and Europe demonstrated to both him and Grete why they did not want to make America their future home. Though the landscapes delighted them, there were not the historical depth and aesthetics that they loved in Europe. Moreover, the focus on material gain and the drive to 'get ahead' that they observed did not sit well with their chosen lifestyle. It felt foreign to them and their beliefs. Perhaps what they saw was a superficial view of the American way, but their experiences while there left them in no doubt of where their future home should be.

Nicky felt English through and through and had a deep attachment to the country, his friends and family. He had escaped the City where, in his work at the stock exchange, he'd felt that the relentless greed for advantage and money without any ethical integrity was dominant. America seemed to show a similar push for material gain and so did not appear to offer him the more socialist and equitable life that he felt was now being built into society in Britain. The Labour Party, having won the 1945 General Election with a landslide, was busy putting into place the foundations of the Welfare State that Nicky had spent so much time discussing with his hero Aneurin Bevan and his other left-wing political friends. He wanted to live in a country that built institutions such as these, open to all. Though he was not to know that within a year and a half the Labour Party would lose an election and the Conservatives would be reinstated, at least the main welfare provisions would remain in place as the framework for a more equal society.

Once in Florida they met an American couple, also on holiday, and became quite chummy with them and some of their friends. They found all the Americans they met extremely friendly, but also firmly of the belief that America was the best place on earth. None of them could believe that Nicky and Grete were there on holiday and intended to return to Europe. All other foreigners they knew of had come over as immigrants and they could not understand why anyone would not want to remain in their land of opportunity if they could. Nicky, having been offered several jobs while in Washington that he had refused, was considered incomprehensible for wishing to turn down such a chance in order to return to a ruined continent.

At last they reached Key West and Nicky enjoyed a few days deep-sea fishing with Ernest while Grete turned first pink, then red and sore, then brown, strolling along the sun-baked streets. Their leisurely return up through Florida with Ernest was frequently interrupted by more deep-sea fishing trips, which Nicky loved despite never catching anything, though he witnessed others landing impressive trophies. They got redder and redder, with descriptions to his mother of continuous peeling and sore skin, long before the days when this was considered unhealthy.

Having left New York in mid-February and arrived in Key West three weeks later, they returned to New York at the end of March, en route to three more weeks in Canada before sailing home from Quebec at the end of April.

Already by the time they were back in New York, their thoughts were turning to home. Another letter to his mother declared, 'We continue to have a good and full time but I am eager to get back and find some work.' Grete added, 'We are wondering whether any of the jobs materialised?' It looked like he had already put feelers out for work before leaving England or at least had got his mother on the case.

Their final stop was in Ottawa, still in the midst of a freezing winter, staying with another friend from the IRO, George Wicks. Having seen the 'majestic and thrilling' Niagara Falls, and enjoyed tapping syrup from the maple trees in the snow, they were at last at the end of their trip. Nicky had received a letter from his brother Bobby giving fencing news, and he wrote back asking Bobby to try and lobby for him to get a place in the national team again. He described how he had been fencing in New York at the Fencers Club the previous week and had beaten their champion fencer, Lubell, 5–4, so he hoped he would be good enough to be accepted once more. Sadly this wish, for whatever reason, never came to fruition. He never fenced again at national level.

Their return journey was less luxurious than their outward one, as they travelled on an unconverted troop ship, the SS *Samaria*. Nicky wrote to Airlie, who had sent them a welcome-home telegram on boarding the ship, that 'men and women are separated, and I am in a dormitory with eleven other men and Grete has eleven women companions!' He found the behaviour of some of his cabin mates to be inconsiderate and discovered that it was typical in the rest of the ship: 'there are about three out of the twelve occupants who make the lives of the rest uncomfortable. They come to bed late, put the lights on and chatter until the early hours.' It leads on: 'It makes one almost despair of one's fellow creatures. This "I'm OK, damn you" attitude merely costs me and many others a few hours' sleep each night but when I realise how such people must act in their daily life, it is not difficult to imagine why there is so much misery in the world which need never be and which is brought on by the selfish egotistical minority.'

Key West, Florida. L–R Ernest Friedman, Grete, Nicky

Once back in England, with their great adventure over, reality hit home. They were once again lodging at Lottie's flat while she, in turn, was touring round France in Nicky's Citroën, which had been garaged in Le Havre since their departure. Nicky loved his car and was soon off to collect it to bring over to England.

On arrival back in Dover, the unexpected occurred. Nicky had believed that, as he had used the car for some years in France, the import duty would be negligible. He was aghast when the Customs demanded a huge sum from him due to his recent three months in the USA not using the car. He had to pay up or go back. So with a heavy heart Nicky took the car back to France where it was sold. It was some years before he once again laid hands on another beloved old Citroën. Now Nicky needed to find work, and soon, as ever, help was at hand in the shape of his devoted mother and her wide social contacts.

# 11

## *A New Family*
### *1999*

Grete's funeral was held in early September 1999 with all her family and friends in attendance. Nicky was bearing up, being his stoic self in front of everyone. I can't imagine how he was when he was alone, but he soldiered on.

Around 1996, while Grete was still well but getting older, she had decided she needed help with the house. A neighbour recommended her cleaner, Babs Armstrong, who came to see Grete and was taken on instantly. They got on like a house on fire, making the bed together and chatting about this and that. Once Grete became ill and knew that Nicky would have to fend for himself before long, she asked Babs to continue to help him if she could. This Babs has done, and fourteen years later helps more than ever to ensure Nicky can remain independent in his own home.

Only six weeks after the funeral, Nicky was invited to Prague again. This time it was to the premiere of Matej Mináč's feature film, *All My Loved Ones*, which included the escape of the young son of a Jewish family on the Czech Kindertransport. Though it was a distraction from his grief, Nicky was uncertain about bearing up to the task. There would be interviews and people to meet and he was not feeling strong. In the event, he asked me to accompany him and support him through it. We went and it was indeed a real distraction; lots of his 'children' attended, journalists asked questions, meals were given and the film viewed.

Matej had got so excited about the Kindertransport story that he had decided to make another film on the subject, this time a documentary. Nicky had agreed to participate, so time was taken up with filming questions and answers and creating shots of Nicky in Prague amongst his 'children', some of whom had come over from the UK for the occasion and others who were living in the Czech Republic.

*All My Loved Ones* was based on Matej's mother's family of Slovak Jews who had lived a happy middle-class life before the Germans invaded, then been torn apart during the war and sent to concentration camps. The film showed the juxtaposition of a loving family way of life with the torment of their slow recognition of its destruction. Some of Nicky's extended family living in Germany and Holland had gone through their own terrors before and during the war. However, his knowledge of their experiences was second hand. Despite enduring the ravages of First World War bombings in North London during early childhood, his strongest memories of his own upbringing had been of a happy and secure family life. It was this benign family environment that he wished to recreate for himself and his new wife after their marriage.

Therefore after their belated honeymoon and move back to England in 1950, he and my mother had been determined that their incipient family life should be settled and sustaining, and they set out to put down roots and begin this new phase. Having both gone through the war years in varying degrees of stressful, tumultuous and hectic settings, they were looking forward to a calmer life, while still keeping their minds open to new interests and challenges. The self-imposed task of rescuing children from Nazi-occupied Czechoslovakia, having been followed by ten intense years of war and then post-war reconstruction work, was, by now, a distant memory for Nicky. Meeting and marrying Grete encouraged him to continue to look to the future and not the past.

He was looking forward to the next stage of his life as a new beginning, and to family life as another great adventure.

### *1950–88*

Nicky's mother, having put out feelers for job prospects for her
now-unemployed son, soon discovered that one of her regular
bridge partners had a son, Guy Lawrence, who was a businessman
looking to take over an ice cream factory in Maidenhead, and in
need of a financial director. Before long a meeting between Guy
and Nicky was organised and he was offered the post. Having
looked around the town, he and Grete agreed that Maidenhead,
just twenty-five miles west of London, would be a fine place to
start a family. As 'The Logs' conversions had finished, they were
no longer tied to Hampstead.

Maidenhead suited them perfectly; they wanted to be near
London within easy reach of the other members of Nicky's close
family. Bobby was in North London, as was Lottie. His mother
Barbara remained in her elegant apartment near Baker Street.
Maidenhead was a thriving town on the River Thames with a
population of around 40,000, surrounded by woodland and open
countryside, and yet within an hour of their family and all the
cultural delights the capital offered.

Having accepted the job of financial director for Glacier Foods,
house hunting was the next step. By early 1951 they had found a
small detached house in a quiet leafy lane a few miles from the
town centre, which suited their plans for their new domestic life.
As by then they had used their modest savings to live on over the
previous six months, the house was purchased for £1460 with a
full mortgage at the low interest rate of two per cent with no
deposit. Having moved in, their initial living expenses and furni-
ture costs were paid for by a generous gift from Nicky's old
German friend, Hans Wollshläger.

Having bought and moved into the house, called Dodbrook, and Nicky having started his new job, they were ready for their next stage of life. They did not want to wait long to start their family. Nicky by then was already forty-one and Grete, thirty-one. So it was only one and a half years later that their first child was born, on 27 July 1952, and named Nicholas Paul – Nicholas, as is the way in certain middle-class families of naming after the father, and Paul after Grete's brother.

Only fifteen months later their second child, Barbara Ann, was born on 23 October 1953 – Barbara after Nicky's mother, and Ann . . . ? No one knows. It must have been a combination in the air at the time as my best friend at school was also Barbara Ann.

As was the norm back then, there was never any thought that Grete would be anything but a housewife and mother. We children and Nicky were her full-time occupation and looking after us all kept her fully employed. Unlike Nicky's own mother, there was never a sense that Grete wanted anything else from her life at that point. Then in 1956, on 14 August, their third child, a boy named Robin Christian was born. It was some months after he was born before the concerns they felt became a certainty. He, though healthy, had a condition that was then called mongoloid and now Down's syndrome.

It is hard to imagine now, when there is so much knowledge of the disorder, that at that time so little was known and understood about it. What was explained to Nicky and Grete was that such a child would have some physical problems but more especially serious mental disabilities, which would preclude him from developing into an independent youth and then adult.

Down's syndrome is a genetic condition caused by one extra chromosome. It leads to a range of medical problems and mental disabilities, but symptoms vary widely among individuals ranging from mild to severe. These days it is considered much the best to keep children with Down's syndrome within their families whenever possible and to respond to their needs on an individual basis.

However, in the mid-1950s the advice was the opposite. The common consensus at the time was that children born with this condition should be put into care, in homes which catered for their special needs and which allowed the 'unfortunate' family to get on with their lives without all the extra work and problems associated with looking after such a child. Indeed, Nicky and Grete were counselled to do that by some of their concerned friends and by the doctors involved at an early stage after Robin's diagnosis. However, it did not feel right to them. Though they were disturbed by the uncertainties of this condition, they loved Robin as much as the rest of us and did not want to break up their family. They accepted that there would be problems along the way, but were in agreement that Robin must remain within the family unit.

When asked in later years about it, neither gave any hint that they regretted their decision to keep Robin at home with us, though they had obviously thought long and hard, not only about the extra work involved but also about the effect on Nicholas junior (Nick) and me. They worried about whether Robin would perturb friends we brought home as we got older and therefore affect our own social development. The social stigmatisation that such disability could evoke illustrated the prejudices that existed at the time around what were considered to be defects rather than the genetic accidents they were. The discovery of a genetic cause was only made in 1959. When Robin was born in 1956, the cause was still unknown and it was common for the parents to be considered responsible for inducing the condition by some personal moral flaw.

However, as Nick and I grew up, we had no inkling of these problems. For us, Robin was a lovely younger brother, albeit one who could not join in our games in quite the way our friends could. He remained like a toddler – happy, naughty and sometimes infuriating, but an integral part of the unit. To me, it demonstrates how much Nicky and Grete focused on family life and the wellbeing of their children, in that we never felt any ripples – emotional or practical – about external pressures or prejudice. Another perspective might be that Nicky, having learned from his own parents how to keep emotions under wraps, was able to suppress his sorrow and anxieties so they were not visible. My mother behaved similarly, always keeping a brave face on whatever the situation.

However, Nicky later wrote about their experiences of that time as a way of offering information to other couples who found themselves in the same position. Having had suspicions there might be a problem with Robin, the meeting with the consultant who made the clear diagnosis and prognosis about Robin's future was the point where they had to make their decision about how to go forward.

'How suddenly the whole course of one's life can be changed – not only one's own wellbeing and comforts, but also one's whole outlook on the world. Up to then we could still dream that it would all be well, it wasn't true, it could be cured, we could live with Alice in Wonderland and make ourselves believe anything – anything except the truth. All that was past, the present was fact and a fact which had to be faced and could not be shirked and a decision had to be taken. Yes, a decision and one so important to us and vital to this child. And what about the other two? Nicholas was three and Barbara two. Would what was right for Robin also be right for the other two? We could get advice from everyone; in fact, this was too freely offered by kind friends and relatives.

'We listed, we discussed, we learned and still we were not sure. But soon we were sure of one thing: that this was a problem we had to decide for ourselves. Should Robin live with us or be sent away? Either way there were uncertainties and problems. How would the elder children react to having Robin in the home? Would they resent the extra attention he would get by virtue alone of his own impotence? And later, when they grew up, would they find it impossible to bring their friends home? Would they suffer by getting less of us and from us than they would have were Robin sent away? And what of us? Keeping the child at home would, we knew, involve not only a great deal of work as he would require constant supervision, but would also mean that we would be pretty well tied to the house as many potential sitters would prefer not to take on the extra responsibility of looking after such a child. Our doctor was clear and concise in his advice. "The extra work is great and this alone will completely disrupt your family life with possible serious results in your family relationships and it is by no means impossible; in fact, it is likely to react badly on the other two children, especially as he gets older. Send him away."

'We asked friends who had specific interests in mentally handicapped children. They were also clear and concise. "You must remember that these children are most loving and will give you great happiness despite the extra attention they require . . ."

'We kept Robin at home and have never for one moment regretted this decision.'

Nicky's mother seemed to find acceptance of Robin the hardest. Her family were high achieving and socially aware, and she felt her children to be of fine lineage and stock. She was initially very disturbed that her beloved son could have produced an imperfect child and seemed to blame my mother's bad genes for it. 'Nothing like this has ever happened in our family!' was her charge, which must have been an added blow to my mother at such a sensitive time. Her attitude was fairly widespread at the time; eugenics was on the scene, and breeding and intelligence were considered the result of a 'proper' family inheritance. The serious social stigma which could befall a family that produced an 'imbecile' – a diagnosis given at that time for those with a learning difficulty of any form – was something she was very worried about. Her own stigmatisation during the First World War had cemented her need for the approbation of her peers. This new challenge raised anxieties that were hard for her to bear.

Knowledge of genetics and the statistics around the likelihood of Down's occurring more frequently among older parents was only just becoming known at the time. Now, of course, we can see that both parents were relatively old, my father being forty-seven when Robin was born and my mother thirty-six and this makes the possibility of Down's occurring significantly more likely – with no other genetic history needed. (Though, of course, it can occur in younger parents too without known cause.) Nicky was firm with his mother and refused to listen to her opinions, trying to protect Grete from her disapproval. His priority was to maintain a happy family home with his wife and children all together, regardless of what others thought. His mother never became really comfortable with Robin. She seemed uncertain of how to relate to him and her interactions with him were never as relaxed and 'grandmotherly' as they were with Nick and me.

Having Robin in the family created for my parents a new avenue of life to explore. Not only did they learn how to cater for his individual needs, but before long they also found others with similarly disabled children. Many of these other parents became friends. From them, they learnt about the difficulties of families struggling to care for even more severely disabled children, as well as hearing from some who found coping with the emotional strain even more impossible than the physical one.

Nicky, who never liked to come up against a problem without seeking to find a solution, threw himself into the search for an organisation that helped families with mentally handicapped children (now termed learning disabled). He discovered the National Society for Mentally Handicapped Children, a small new national organisation, but with few resources to give the support needed to the families he had met. (It is now called Mencap.) He decided that a local branch was needed and became instrumental in forming one in Maidenhead. As the national organisation grew, so did the local branch, becoming a focal point for families like his in the town. It became his first foray into community action and volunteering; the first of many.

From 1951 until 1958, our growing family lived happily in our cosy home, Dodbrook, in Altwood Bailey, a tree-lined cul-de-sac. In our garden were apple trees, a vegetable plot and a good expanse of grass for games. A fairly relaxed atmosphere must have pervaded. As my mother had to concentrate on keeping Robin out of the trouble any toddler might get into, both Nick and I were allowed to play freely outdoors or when a bit older to visit neighbours' children for games. Early on, a playpen for us was put outside on top of a small sandpit so we could play unsupervised when my mother was otherwise engaged indoors. One day it was noticed that the sand seemed to be disappearing and on investigation my horrified parents discovered that the sandpit was located over a well and was collapsing; luckily we survived this incident. Nick remembers climbing an apple tree which he promptly fell out of, knocking himself unconscious; he must have been under five years old. Perhaps the relaxed atmosphere had been too relaxed.

On all sides were friendly neighbours. Next door an older couple, the Tanners, had a wonderful summer house in the garden, which was on a sort of rail that meant you could push it and turn it to face the other direction. Of course we children just wanted to push it round in circles and got shouted at, as the adults, drinking tea inside, didn't want a fairground ride. Beyond them were a younger couple with young children also, the Skelts, who have remained friends to this day, despite moving away from Maidenhead many years ago. Other neighbours were the Abreys, who remained in touch after we moved in 1958. Some years later, it was Mr Abrey who gave my father his last job before retirement.

Despite Nicky not having had pets as a child, except for his pigeons at school, it was not long before we began to collect a few. Perhaps this was my mother's influence, but they both obviously felt it was good for us to learn to look after a small creature and to enjoy its company. Our first was a lovely brown spaniel called Chip, introduced into the family around the time Nicholas was born.

Nicky and Robin circa 1960

Later we had a golden retriever, Whiskey, and a marmalade cat, Ginger, for company. These were lovingly cared for by Grete rather than us. Our responsibility was for other smaller pets, which Nick and I requested and promised to look after and who came and went over the years. First a budgie, then a guinea pig, rabbit, tortoise and hamster arrived on the scene in turn. Unfortunately before long each would either escape or die under mysterious circumstances. Perhaps, despite the theory that it would teach us children to care for other vulnerable creatures, in practice no one paid them quite enough attention.

Other activities were started from need, but became a way of life. Food rationing, started during the war, was still in existence in the early 1950s, only completely ending in 1954. Therefore chickens were brought in to facilitate a good supply of eggs for the growing family, as well as a vegetable plot established at the end of the garden. Not only did Nicky keep the family provided with fresh fruit and veg, but gardening also became a rewarding pastime for him and his main form of exercise. He kept it up for the next fifty years, only very recently giving up altogether.

None of his forebears had lived this kind of semi-rural life, but he and Grete took to it with relish. It must have been bemusing for their London and Paris friends to witness my previously cosmopolitan parents settling down to this *Good Life*-style existence, but it became an intrinsic part of their chosen way of life, while still keeping up their previous, more cultural interests when family and work duties allowed.

After we moved to our new house in 1958, we continued with chickens and at one time some geese, in the much larger garden. The geese didn't last long as they chased and pecked us whenever we dared roam into their territory and so didn't fit the idyllic relaxed life Nicky and Grete had created there.

Despite being fairly hard up, with all the bills to pay and mouths to feed, Nicky at the time was concerned over his mother who had little in the way of finances to keep her in her elegant flat off Baker Street. They had remained close, despite him marrying and her not being delighted in his choice of wife, though it's hard to imagine who would have satisfied her. Her dismay over Robin's disability was also calmly dealt with and their close relationship continued.

So in January 1957, Nicky resolved to help support his mother and drew up a deed that covenanted her £100 a year for the next seven years (a sum equivalent to about £2,000 today). How he managed this payment when he was supporting a wife and three young children, as well as being about to build a brand-new house, is unclear. However, his filial bond was stronger than any concern he had about his own impecuniousness.

Family ties were strong and remained so throughout all their lives. 'Granny' would visit frequently, as would Lottie as well as Bobby and his wife Heather and their own growing family. Bobby had graduated from Imperial College London in 1935 with a degree in engineering, then had served in the Royal Engineers in Egypt during the war. In mid-1952, he had married Heather Charlton, the WAAF Nicky had met back in La Rochelle in 1946. They went on to have three children – Peter, Andrew and Carol – of similar ages to us three, so our family get-togethers became lively affairs during our early years.

Bobby, younger than Nicky by five years, had followed him into fencing at Stowe and reached the level of junior *épée* champion just before the war, as well as coming third in the British championships the same year. Nicky had also continued fencing seriously through the 1930s, being in the English team, as well as attending matches all over the country for his club Salle Bertrand.

It was a shared interest between them that they kept up long beyond their competing years; Nicky for a time became Secretary of the southern section of the Amateur Fencing Association and Bobby, with more dedication, went on to serve on the Amateur Fencing Association Executive Committee for over fifty years, for which he was awarded an MBE. In 1950 they had agreed that an annual team competition between the regional groups would boost the sport and together founded an event called the Winton Cup. This competition still occurs every year and in the 1980s was extended to include cadets. In 2008 a Veterans cup was added, which Bobby presented at the inaugural match only five months before his death in February 2009.

Nicky, with his years of banking experience, helped Lottie with her accounts and she sought his advice on any financial matters. She had lived alone and then with a female friend for many years. In the 1930s she'd had a fiancé who she had met while visiting relatives in Germany. He was a well-known German-Jewish pianist called Heinz Fischer who had remained in Germany when war broke out to care for his sick mother, rather than make his escape while he could. This had led to his detention and murder by the Nazis. The trauma to Lottie must have been intense and she never mentioned him thereafter and never married. During the war she had served in the WRAF (Women's Royal Air Force) and listened in to conversations between German Air Force personnel, making use of her fluent German. Afterwards she earned her living as a dressmaker and developed a passion for hand painting china, making beautiful christening and birthday gifts for siblings, sisters-in-law, nephews and nieces.

Apart from fencing, Bobby and Nicky had different interests and led quite different working lives. Bobby remained at the same company, Mullards, as an engineer for most of his working life, whereas Nicky worked for quite a few different companies and organisations, though mostly in some kind of financial role. However, their mutual affection and respect remained strong and they always pulled together over family matters. After their mother died in 1978, her will left two-fifths of her estate to Nicky, the same to Bobby and one-fifth to Lottie – perhaps because the two men had families, who knows? Anyway, Nicky and Bobby were the executors and they decided that the inheritance should be divided equally between the three of them and that is what they did. It was not a huge sum – £15,000 – but the current equivalent would be £73,000, so not tiny either.

Back to the mid-1950s and our house move. This came in a roundabout fashion. As my brother and I were getting towards school age, my parents looked at the local schools and decided on two – Alwyn Infant School, which took children from four to seven years old, and Courthouse Junior School, from seven to eleven – which they liked very much. They were disconcerted to discover that we could not attend these as we lived on the wrong side of the main road to be in the catchment area. My parents must have kept trying though, as the headmistress of Alwyn eventually gave in and said that if Nicky promised that they would move house into the catchment area, then Nick could start there straight away. This they agreed to and immediately started looking for a place to match their dreams of a beautiful spacious family house. They could not find anywhere they liked, however, and somehow the idea of buying a piece of land and building a house came to them and they set out to find a likely plot.

Winton Family in 1956. L–R adults: Nicky, Lottie, Grete, Bobby, Heather, 'Granny', children: Barbara, Peter, Nicholas

In 1957 they heard about some ground, three miles out of the town, surrounded by a National Trust-owned common, some woods and farmland. However, the whole area for sale included not only the vegetable gardens and paddocks of a large mansion, which Nicky thought perfect to build a house on, but the mansion itself and a gardener's cottage. The whole site was being sold for £10,000, which was a massive sum, and my parents only wanted a part of the garden for their scheme. They found a friend who wanted the main house, but who cried off when someone else put in an offer for a part of the grounds. Nicky's networking skills paid off though as, through a work colleague, he was introduced to a Mr Loweth who was interested in the mansion but not the grounds, making them ideal partners.

Guy Lawrence, Nicky's Managing Director at Glacier Foods, offered their company buildings manager to organise the project. The house was built with a Scandinavian feel to Grete's specification and with the aid of a local architect, with lots of large windows, a gently sloping roof and wooden slatted upper section. It was open plan in the main rooms and felt spacious, light and airy. Despite having been built in 1958, it still has a modern feel, though the fittings have never been updated and remain of the era. It must have been a challenging undertaking for my parents, though Nicky maintains that the plan all went well overall. His memory is that it cost £9,000 in total to build and fit the house, a sum equivalent to around £180,000 today. A sizeable mortgage was taken out to pay for it, paid back over fifteen years. As usual with Nicky, lack of money or a low income was not going to stop him following the path he was set on.

Somehow he managed to pay back the mortgage, even despite retiring the year before its final settlement. One of the attractions of the land was that, as part of the grounds of the mansion, it had walled flower and vegetable gardens and an old swimming pool, a field with a ha-ha wall and some specimen trees, including a towering monkey puzzle tree and a huge unruly laurel hedge along one boundary, which Nick and I used to climb around inside hidden from the world. Right at the far end of the land was a privet maze, neglected and grown lanky, so you could see through the elongated trunks but only in some places squeeze through. When the house was built at the top end of this parcel of land, there was plenty of space for us children to play and disappear into, on top of the more formal garden and vegetable patch by the house. Nicky and Grete used the land fully, building up a large productive vegetable garden, filling the borders with shrubs, roses, dahlias and perennials, and lining the garden walls with espalier fruit trees. Pride of place was taken by an old fig tree, already sprawling across a south-facing wall in 1958. It still produces a hefty crop each year, as does the ancient mulberry tree by the terrace.

One of Nicky's favourite pastimes is having bonfires; initially he had a bonfire site and would spend happy hours getting it lit and feeding it with twigs and cuttings. In later years he became more sloppy and a bonfire would be started wherever the debris had accumulated with various smouldering heaps on paths or in corners, leading to largely ignored protests from my mother. Gardening became a great pleasure to him for over fifty years. The garden was definitely his territory, whereas the house was more my mother's. Though, after his retirement, they were at home together for long periods, they both did their own thing – Nicky outdoors, Grete inside – getting together for meals to discuss progress in their various activities.

The back field initially contained the chickens and geese. Later on, our neighbours who had bought the original garden-er's cottage from my parents were allowed to keep their horses there, followed by the ponies of two school friends of mine. From time to time the ponies would escape and we would be woken in the dark early hours by a phone call saying they had been spotted wandering on the common opposite and we'd all have to turn out to try and round them up, with torches and buckets of food.

Nicky's final animal flourish was to get some fan-tailed pigeons, white with fluffed-out chests and peacock-shaped fan tails, which lived in the potting shed and mooched about on top of the garden walls, cooing loudly. Now it occurs to me that these were harking back to his pigeon-keeping days at Stowe. They were fun for a while, but the mess built up and they eventually had to go.

The main draw for a visit from local friends and acquaintances during the summer was the swimming pool, in another part of our garden formed from the old mansion grounds. At that time these were rare, ours being the only one we knew of in the area. My parents extended an open invitation to everyone they knew, many of whom would turn up on sunny days to have a dip in the unheated water. At the start of the season the water would be icy cold straight from the hose pipe and would only really begin to get nicely warm just as it started turning soupy-green with algae and summer ended.

Swimming was often followed by games of croquet or badminton, glasses of squash and endless ice lollies from our big chest freezer, kept filled from the warehouse of Nicky's ice cream company. We never had to beg for ice cream, we just opened the freezer and there was masses! By the house still stands a gnarled but productive mulberry tree, which every summer drips with oodles of delicious dark astringent fruit. Picking and eating mulberries warm and juicy straight from the tree was, and still is, undertaken by any August visitors, but was best done in a swimsuit followed by a swim, as getting the juice on your clothes or skin meant an indelible stain and lots of cursing.

If it sounds wonderful, it was. Nicky and Grete were hospitable and sociable and enjoyed people dropping in and sharing our lovely garden. Over the years they developed a strong social network locally, as well as maintaining their previous friendships from their Paris time and the war and pre-war years too. Many friends attest to having learnt to swim as children in the pool alongside Down's children, brought along by their parents who had met Nicky at the Maidenhead Mencap centre. Nick Abrey, son of ex-neighbours in Altwood Bailey, remembers as a young boy being taught to dive by a patient and attentive Nicky. The family visitors book, which people signed when they stayed with us, attests to guests from Australia, New Zealand and America, as well as Germany, France and Denmark. Both Nicky's and Grete's friends from before they were married, along with their partners, soon joined the wide company of those who dropped in, or stayed a while.

Family at home circa 1960

Nicky loved having lots of visitors. He was never happier than with a house full of people. For my mother, it was more of a chore as she was the one responsible for the cooking and planning. Though she was happy with a certain level of visitors, she was more self-contained than my father, enjoying, most of all, time spent just with the family. This difference was replicated in their holiday choices. Nicky would love to go to places where they had friends they could stay with. Grete was more relaxed visiting new places, staying in a hotel and having their own space.

Grete had taken becoming a full-time housewife seriously after they married, learning to provide delicious dinner parties on top of the everyday family meals. However, she was never satisfied with her creations, always suggesting it could have been better in some way, while Nicky always professed that it had been perfect.

For Nick and I, the frequent invasion of visitors was a double-edged sword. We enjoyed playing with our friends and relatives, but there were expectations placed on us in terms of behaviour, which we sometimes dreaded, especially on more refined occasions and with less familiar guests. Nicky had had a formal Victorian upbringing, which stressed good manners, modest behaviour and deference to one's elders and betters. He expected his own children to behave politely and amiably, especially when there were visitors. As I grew up, and began to learn the piano, I used to dread their frequent dinner parties when I might be asked to play a tune and chat to guests before I was allowed to disappear to my room while they ate. Nick remembers the same anxiety, though his instrument was the clarinet. However we might try and escape, Nicky would insist. This did not always end well, especially as we got older and became less compliant. As he never played an instrument as a child, Nicky didn't know how mortifying it could feel to be asked to play. His expectation was that his children would enjoy conversing and performing. We should be polite and properly dressed and definitely not bite our nails, which I did, and continuously got told off about. He expected us to respect him and my mother as the authority figures in our lives and therefore to be happy to respond to his requests.

As a result of his upbringing, I think, Nicky has always had a default deference to authority figures. He would expect those in authority to be acting in the best interests of their electorate or clients and they should therefore be respected in return. This belief, however, would be dealt a severe blow if he discovered those leaders were not acting morally or in what he saw as the best interests of those they were there to protect.

It was this shock at discovering that the politicians had failed to grasp the reality of the National Socialist threat from Germany in 1938 and had behaved immorally in their betrayal of Czechoslovakia that made him furious with them, and led him to be a conscientious objector at the start of the war. In later years he would also become furious if he saw that the authorities were not supporting what he considered the moral course of action or the most effective for getting things done, when he put forward one plan or another for supporting one of his charities.

When we children were still very young, a series of au pairs came to live with the family and help Grete to care for us. These were invariably girls known through extended European contacts in Poland, Germany and Denmark. Some became long-term family friends, while others were not such a success. The trigger for this help came from a particular event. Both Nicky and Grete had smoked since they were young adults, which was the norm in those days before the health issues of smoking became well known. However, around late 1952, soon after the birth of their first child, Nicky came home one day to find that Grete had dropped ash from a cigarette, held between her lips, onto baby Nicholas's nappy while changing it. He was horrified and on the spot he bribed her by offering to get help with the baby in return for her giving up smoking. She agreed and the au pairs started to arrive soon after. It took him about ten years more before he eventually also stopped. By then he had recognised, along with the rest of the world, that smoking was bad for health so that when Nick and I were both teenagers, he bribed us not to smoke by offering money at a later age, which I don't think either of us ever received!

In the 1950s and early 1960s, our summer holidays consisted of an annual trip to the seaside; Swanage and Selsey Bill were two regular south coast locations. Sometimes Nick and I went with our aunt Lottie and grandmother instead, to give our parents a break. They would keep Robin at home with them, while we played sandcastles on the beach with Lottie. We had several memorable trips to Denmark to visit our Danish relatives, once in the mid-50s, the next some ten years later. Both Grete's parents were dead by then, but we visited her brother Paul and his family, travelling to Esbjerg by boat from England. Later on we went to Malta *en famille* and in 1969 a long car trip to Venice staying at hotels en route.

During one seaside holiday with Lottie, when I was eight and Nick was ten, our parents arrived to see us without warning. They had come to break the news that Robin had died suddenly from meningitis. It is hard to imagine how they must have been feeling and all I remember was the shock of the announcement.

As was considered right in those days, in order to protect children from difficult emotions, the funeral had taken place without Nick and I being present, but it meant that we came home to a different family and Robin was hardly mentioned. Life went on as before with our emotional responses to the tragedy remaining buried. This extreme event was an example of how Nicky and Grete dealt with difficult family issues. They were to be managed practically, rather than explored emotionally. Their Victorian-type upbringings were passed on to their children.

Nicky, to this day, keeps his emotions mostly to himself and finds intense demonstrative displays of emotion by others towards him very uncomfortable. He would not, by nature, kiss people on meeting except close family and friends, which does not mean he is not delighted to see them. It was not his upbringing to behave like that. He would, however, be too polite to protest if a stranger hugged or kissed him, saving his complaint until later when alone with Grete, Nick or me.

He and Grete would talk a lot, but if problems arose they would discuss the practicalities of the problem rather than the emotional impact of it. There were plenty of events in their lives that caused them great upset and yet, to outside eyes, this would not be apparent. News of serious illnesses and deaths in the family were received with sadness but rarely tears. In fact I have only one memory of ever witnessing my father cry and that was the day after my mother's death.

Despite neither of them being prone to outward displays of emotion, what is undoubted was that my parents' relationship was rock solid. They obviously loved each other, and in most photos of them together, Nicky would have his arm around Grete, both with huge smiles on their faces. They would occasionally disagree and sometimes bicker, but I don't remember any angry arguments between them. Nicky is, these days, fond of talking about the need in politics as well as relationships for compromise. However, he has also admitted that, in their relationship, Grete compromised more than he did, that is to say, he would want to do something and she would go along with it, especially in the frequent entertaining they did.

He would often invite people on the spur of the moment and she would be the one to do all the work involved. However, though she might grumble a bit, she never put her foot down and, all in all, I am sure that they both loved their life together. He was, and still is, fond of having parties. The house would often be full of friends, especially during the summer when people would spread out into the garden, either into a marquee, occasionally provided by the local Scout group, which would be a khaki army-type affair, or, for a more important event, a 'proper' marquee. The local Scout group who met in a hut very near our house were given the run of our large back garden for camps from time to time and were very happy to reciprocate when asked. In recent years when the garden began to be too much for Nicky to manage, he often obtained the assistance of an obliging Scout to do the heavy tasks – for a small wage.

Some of their friends not only enjoyed their sociable company, but used them as confidants to talk through problems and worries. They would listen, sympathise and make suggestions, sometimes based on their own experience. One close friend, Beth, who was also Danish like Grete, had a severely handicapped daughter. She confided in them once when her daughter, Annelise, was very ill, about what may happen and how she should proceed. Nicky advised her that if Annelise should die, they should get a doctor to certify it to prevent a post-mortem. Happily Annelise recovered, but Beth thought this advice was based on their experience with Robin. He must have been given one after his death and it must have been a harrowing experience for them, but neither ever mentioned it as fact.

It is notable that this guidance given by Nicky at such an emotional time for Beth was practical and about how to handle the situation should the worst transpire. It was not words of comfort and support, but about the best actions to take for her future well-being. His work for the Samaritans, discussed in Chapter 13, shows a similar disposition: to take action to make things better, rather than purely to sympathise or comfort.

Nicky, perhaps like his own parents, has never been particularly sensitive to others' emotional states and may say that someone was uncommunicative or unfriendly when in fact that person was in emotional distress of some sort or unwell. Another of his traits is a complete lack of interest in health and illness; he will know that a friend is ill, but when asked have no idea what is wrong with them, having not asked for any details. He left all that to Grete who was much better at understanding the emotions of others and responding sympathetically. Nicky's health until very recently has always been excellent; he would occasionally have bad colds and the occasional injury, such as a bad shoulder sprain from waterskiing which took six months to heal, but that was it. My mother, who had more than her share of bad health, would be looked after by Nicky, but it was her female friends who she would talk to about it.

When Ric Fontaine, one of his closest friends, was ill, Nicky did not visit but would phone from time to time to ask after him. Once, he asked Sheila if she and Ric would come out to lunch. Sheila replied that Ric was very poorly, to which Nicky asked, 'Does that mean you can't come?' He did not want to know the details. This trait sometimes causes friends to think he doesn't care about them, but it is not in his nature to enquire, believing health to be a private matter. He does, though, have a tendency to shut off thoughts about things he does not like. Illness is just such an area he would rather not know about or dwell on. He doesn't understand it and there's nothing he can do so he would rather ignore it.

Nick's and my early schooling was based on finding the best local schools on offer. However, Nicky, as the product of his own upbringing, felt that boys should be sent to public school to obtain the best education and life chances. So Nick, aged eleven, was duly sent as a day boy to the local prep school, a couple of miles down the road, and then at thirteen dispatched to Abingdon, a minor public school thirty miles away in Oxfordshire. Nicky, having gone to Stowe, felt that this was the right thing for a son of his, but Nick's temperament did not suit the experience and he was deeply unhappy for much of his time there.

On journeys back to school by car after holidays or weekends, he would be in tears, which Nicky and Grete reacted to by making consoling comments. He tried to get them to listen to his feelings, but they did not seem to understand that this was more than just an issue of settling in, so he gave up. The last few years there were more enjoyable, but he never forgot his early unhappiness and our parents' refusal to see it.

In later years, when he discussed this time with them, they were aghast at not having realised how unhappy he had been then, but at the time the subtle and not-so-subtle signs were not picked up, perhaps because they felt it would do him good in the long run and he would get through the difficulties.

Nicky does have a stubbornness that stands him in good stead when attempting to achieve a result, such as the Kindertransport or getting a job done for one of his charities, but it can also prevent him from recognising the point of view of someone who disagrees with him. In Nick's case, his obvious early unhappiness at Abingdon did not overcome Nicky's view that attending the school was important for his son's future life chances and that he would get over his distress as soon as he settled in. It was only looking back at it later, having listened to Nick's memories, that he considered that he may have been wrong in insisting it was for the best.

My schooling was a more straightforward affair. Having gone to the two local schools my parents had selected and moved house to achieve for me and Nick, I passed my eleven plus and went to the local girls' grammar school. Belatedly, at sixteen, my father thought perhaps I should also be given the same chance of a private education as Nick, half-heartedly suggesting Marlborough, which had just begun to take girls into the sixth form. My refusal to countenance it was met with no objections, so I happily continued my local education and social life.

As I reached sixteen or seventeen, my parents felt I was responsible enough to be left alone at home while they visited Europe as part of the Maidenhead Twinning Group or for a Rotary meeting in a twin town, and while Nick boarded thirty miles away. I don't remember being lectured to about parties, boys or generally behaving. I think I was trusted to be responsible, as no doubt their parents had trusted them. Of course as soon as their car had disappeared down the drive, I was on the phone to my friends signalling an empty house and all that might lead to. Whatever mischief I got up to was tidied up, so that as their car returned back down the drive, the final clear up had been done and friends had hotfooted it, sometimes just in the nick of time! There was no suspicion or close questioning; their expectation was that we would behave as they would want us to and I certainly did not want to ruffle that and endanger my freedom.

Any trouble I did get into was talked over, usually with my mother rather than father. He was brought in only if her negotiations failed to achieve the desired result. He was much less involved in my life in general, being mostly busy at work or at one of his evening social or voluntary activities. It was my mother who looked after our day-to-day welfare. She knew who my friends were and what they got up to, and would ask about what was going on with them. Any contact Nicky had with my friends occurred only if they turned up at the house, when he would chat in general terms about hobbies or schooling. However, though both parents were quite conservative 'with a small c' about behaviour, manners and careers, they were never dismissive or judgmental of even my most hippy-like, long-haired friends, always looking for the best in everyone.

At one time I met a 6'4" African-American student with a massive Afro hairstyle who was living for six months at the UK campus of Stanford University, California. This was just up the road from Maidenhead at Cliveden, the grand mansion once owned by Lord Astor and famed for the Profumo scandal, which had occurred there in 1963. (Indeed only six years later we swam in the same pool at Cliveden where Christine Keeler met Defence

Secretary Profumo.) I brought him home for tea, having failed to describe him in any way, other than as an American student. Neither of my parents blinked. They were both unfailingly welcoming and treated him as they would any other visitor; I had not expected anything else.

Their only concern was to keep me away from those deemed to be a bad influence – drug-takers mainly, which, in the late '60s, was not easy for them. Having been forbidden contact with a boyfriend discovered to be a 'druggie', they soon discovered I would not play ball and we had a heated standoff. Rather than play the Victorian father, after a few days' silence between us Nicky backed down, saying it was more important that we remained talking than that he got his way. Their only firm request was that I abstained from taking drugs, which I promised to do. Further disappointments that I gave them were treated in a similar way. Opinions were given, but if I rejected them they were not enforced. I always knew his often-forthright views, but he would not allow our relationship to suffer if I wouldn't agree.

Luckily, at least Nick was less rebellious. At the age of twenty-one he became President of the newly set-up Maidenhead branch of Rotaract, the young person's version of Rotary, and did charity work with them for a few years. Nicky, as a committed Rotarian, was delighted to see his son following in his footsteps and has had the photo of Nick receiving the President's badge of office in his study ever since. Mostly though, whatever Nick or I got up to, we were given moral, and sometimes financial, support from our parents. Nicky would suggest what he considered we should best do in the situations that arose, but would always accept the choices that we made, even if he didn't understand them. He was always ready to be helpful in practical ways, rather than as a shoulder to cry on. Grete was there for that.

After Nick and I had left home in the early 1970s, Nicky and Grete carried on with their busy lives. They had frequent trips abroad on Rotary visits or holidays visiting friends in Europe or further afield. Nicky had retired in 1971 and he now had more time for charitable works, as well as his prolific vegetable garden and flower borders. He also found time to take up a new and surprising hobby: needlepoint, a type of embroidery. He produced beautiful, intricately patterned cushion covers and wall hangings based on middle-eastern carpet designs, which kept him occupied for days on end. Get-togethers with Nicky's siblings continued regularly and Nick and I would be urged to visit as often as possible and, with no exceptions, were expected to be there for Christmas, which was the main family occasion of the year.

Nicky was not sorry to retire from work at the early age of sixty-two. He had not had the satisfaction from his jobs in Maidenhead that he had gained from his earlier pre-and post-war work, and his efforts on the Kindertransport. However, at the time, he had thrown himself into each one with enthusiasm and a commitment to doing the best job he could for the company that employed him and to make a success of it as best he could. Though at this time of life his work no longer took centre-stage, it was still necessary and, of course, he always found something there to stimulate and challenge him.

# 12

## *Work Loses its Shine*

### *2001*

In September 2001, Nicky was again invited to Prague, this time to the premiere of Matej's completed documentary about the Czech Kindertransport, called *Nicholas Winton: The Power of Good*. Due to his excitement at finding a living rescuer willing and able to talk about this historical event, Matej had based the whole story on Nicky, with hardly any mention of the other valiant participants who made the rescue possible. This obviously was not a totally objective piece of historical documentation, but Matej believed that it captured the spirit of the enterprise. For many of the 'children' who had been interviewed for the film, now mostly in their seventies, it had been an emotional but valuable experience. Finally their years of suppressing this part of their history were at an end. It had been, for many of them, an opportunity to revisit their early life and give thanks to their heroic parents whose selfless action had saved their child's life and now this was being acknowledged in public at last.

Alongside many of the rescued children, some from overseas and some from the Czech Republic, our whole family had been invited to attend. After the formal events – a talk at the US Cultural Centre and meeting with the US Ambassador Craig Stapleton and a get-together with his Czech 'children' at the Swedish Embassy – we took some time to do a bit of sightseeing.

On the eleventh, we were visiting Wenceslas Square in the centre of Prague where Nicky showed us the Hotel Europa, his base from his Kindertransport days, when the taxi driver picking us up told us something had happened in New York. We went straight to Nicky's hotel, switched on the TV and witnessed the North and South Towers of the World Trade Centre collapsing – a shocking sight that dumbfounded us and brought an acute sense of unreality into the day. It was uncanny a few hours later, taking a short walk on the Charles Bridge with my daughter to get some air, to be surrounded by American tourists who were obviously unaware of what had just happened back home. (It was still early days for mobile phones and before the time of internet phones.)

A long drive to Bratislava in Slovakia for the film opening there coincided with extra security fences being put up outside diplomatic buildings, particularly the US Embassy, and long holdups at the border crossing. Our return to Prague and the Czech premiere was only a few days later. We were amazed to see the US Ambassador and his wife Debbie stroll in accompanied, not by a host of security guys, but just one friend. They admitted that it had been a terrible week and so they had been glad to get a break from it at a more positive event. It was the beginning of a friendship that developed between Nicky and the Stapletons, which saw him invited to Paris when Craig became Ambassador there in 2005. Nicky was relaxed mixing with his Czech 'children' who came from a range of social groups, as well as the ambassadors, politicians and businessmen who were also keen to meet him.

His whole life had seen him mix with a wide set of people, both pre-and post-war. He had learned to get on with everyone and to take people at face value. It was an aptitude which stood him in good stead now, but also in earlier life when he was starting from scratch in his life in Maidenhead, and his new work as Finance Director for a factory, recently taken over by his new boss Guy Lawrence.

## 1950–71

Lawrence was a fascinating character; as a youth he was a champion skier and had learnt to fly, which led him to join Bomber Command as a pilot at the outbreak of the Second World War. He flew over fifty missions into Germany and occupied territories, surviving against huge odds, as only ten per cent of those flying early on in the war survived. He was awarded the DSO (Distinguished Service Order) and DFC (Distinguished Flying Cross) and finally an OBE. After the war, he started an aircraft-engineering and freight-carrying business in Buckinghamshire, but sold it after four years and bought the Koola Fruta factory in Maidenhead, which became Glacier Foods. The company concentrated on making ice lollies, which was a new idea at the time, and among the range was Orange Maid, a lolly made of frozen orange juice, and the Mivvi – ice cream centre with fruit-flavoured lolly outer. We must have eaten more Mivvis than anyone, as our freezer was never empty of them. How popular were we with our friends!

There was no sense that Nicky felt his new post as a step backwards in his career, despite what others may have thought. Before then, after all, he had been Deputy at the Reparations section of the IRO in Geneva, then a fairly high-ranking employee at the International Bank in Paris. Now he was working for a very small ice cream business in a small middle-England town, albeit as Finance Director. His mind was not fixed on a developing career in any case. His priorities lay elsewhere. He wanted to enjoy a settled family life and the opportunity to become part of a community again for the first time since leaving his parents' home. His drive to do things towards the common good in the world, brought to the fore by the events of the war, had not disappeared, but in 1950 it was no longer at the top of his agenda. His main priority was to support his incipient family in a way that suited him reasonably well, in a small company where he was relatively independent.

The production line at Glacier Foods was run by a couple of key workers who Nicky felt to be skilled and principled men. They could be relied upon to sort things out or report if anything was out of kilter. When Nicky found a short work experience job on the production line for Mark Lovell, the sixteen-year-old son of his friend Maurice, he informed Mark that he should follow them in their behaviour and work. When Mark, who was staying with Nicky and Grete for this period, told him with some glee over dinner how the factory workers talked with each other during the lunch break, using a wide range of swear words towards each other, Nicky was shocked. 'I didn't realise they disliked each other so much!' he commented. Mark had to explain that it was just their natural mode of joking and repartee.

For Nicky and his friends, swearing was only done under extreme provocation and his familiarity with how working-class men lived was fairly limited. Despite his socialist views and his work in many different organisations in Europe, his experience of other social classes and ways of living was not great. His parents were middle class, his schooling private and his friends from similar backgrounds. He supported class equality but had no close working-class friends. As I grew up, I would notice his bafflement about ways of living or behaving that I found normal, based on my wider range of friends and acquaintances from the local school and town.

Not many years after Nicky was employed in this enterprise, Guy decided to sell Glacier Foods to Lyons. They were the largest ice cream manufacturer in the UK and were looking to increase their market share, so as to compete with Walls in America by gradually amalgamating smaller ice cream manufacturers throughout the UK. Lyons had originally resisted making ice lollies as these had been considered a poor man's alternative to ice cream.

However, when lollies proved to be popular and started selling in large quantities, Lyons changed its mind and decided that buying Glacier Foods would increase their stake in the lolly market. Despite the sale, the factory continued from its Maidenhead base as a subsidiary for a number of years, with Guy in charge and Nicky continuing to manage the finances. Then, around 1957, Lyons set up a major new factory near London and began transferring all manufacturing there. By about 1959 the Maidenhead factory was closed down. Guy Lawrence became a director of Lyons and Nicky was taken on in their Chiswick office in West London on the financial and administrative side.

# The Koola Fruta makers

Koola Fruta Lollie managers and supervisors from the Maidenhead, Berkshire, factory gather for the company's annual dinner celebrations in the early Fifties. The same factory produced the original Orange Maid and Mivvi iced lollies.

The factory was renamed Glacier Foods, and finally closed down in 1960, with staff transferring to Lyons Maid, Bridge Park, or to Doncaster. Thanks to Jack Bartlett, formerly of Lyons Maid, for the picture. Jack, of Lower Parkstone, Poole,

is shown standing, third from right.
Names Jack remembers in the picture are (standing, from left:) G Hill (5th), N Winton (6th), T Fuller (10th), W Izat (12th). (Sitting, from left:) M Pringle (1st), J Stewart (2nd).

Glacier Foods employees circa 1952, taken from Allied Lyons magazine, Nicky standing sixth from left

At around this time Nicky had also begun a separate venture. This was called Hirex, a company established to finance hire purchase agreements. He obviously hoped this business would become a good source of income to boost his stressed bank balance, but it was not to be. As he was fully employed first at Glacier Foods, then Lyons, his accountant agreed to run Hirex for him. Before long the company got into trouble and finally went bust, causing him huge stress and worry, partly as he felt that his accountant had not given it his proper attention and had let him down.

A sympathetic letter from his mother in November 1959 suggested that the failure was not Nicky's fault and it would not be a catastrophe; he would get by. She noted that many companies were listed as failing in her Sunday paper. She went on to say, 'My father lost all his money, your father lost a good bit of his . . . You must now . . . really try to get out of that "trough of despondency" you have been in for months. I noticed it every time I saw you lately but put it down solely to your disappointment and fatigue of having to work in London when you were just so nicely settled in Maidenhead.'

So Nicky was not to break the family mould of businesses going bust, with his first and last foray into entrepreneurship. Luckily it did not bankrupt him but it did put him off another try. All he had wanted was enough income to maintain their lifestyle, which was not excessively materialistic but included running a family car and taking an annual holiday, plus an occasional trip to see his friend Hans in Germany. Neither he nor my mother had any inclination for spending on high living, new gadgets or *haute couture*. The life they wanted was quite simple, but maintaining a family house and three growing children was expensive, especially as, in those days, it was expected that only the man of the house would work and his salary would cover all the bills.

His mother was right in her letter when she suggested that he was not happy in his new job. Not only did he now have to commute to London, around an hour or so each way, but having been fairly independent in his work at Glacier Foods and before in Paris and Geneva, he was now under a boss: the son-in-law of one of the company directors.

Nicky not only felt constrained by an interfering superior, but also considered him to be manipulative, keeping others in the dark about different dealings. On one occasion Nicky was sent to Munich to try to negotiate a franchise for Lyons. He found what he thought was a good deal, returned and wrote up a report for his boss to hand on to the Chief Executive. Nothing came of it and he only discovered later that his boss had not passed it on, having decided himself that the Chief would not like the deal negotiated.

For someone used to wielding some authority, having a fairly free hand and thinking through and making decisions which were then carried out, the role he now had was pretty uncomfortable and frustrating. He didn't like his opinions being dismissed, having made what he considered was the right decision. It wasn't long before he was looking around for something else. He had discovered that it was not satisfying to be a small cog in a big wheel, where he did not have a level of independence to make his own decisions. He had worked happily as part of a team before, but his work with the Kindertransport and for the IRO had given him a level of satisfaction that other jobs had not. He had been responsible for getting the things he saw were necessary, done. His efforts had led to results. Now his opinion did not seem to count for anything and work he undertook led nowhere. It was all deeply frustrating. However, he did not have the capital behind him to start another business, and his recent experience of having his own company was not one he wanted to repeat.

Luckily it was not long before he found something he thought would suit him: a relatively small company with an old friend at the head and with enough freedom in his role to suit him. A neighbour from our Altwood Bailey days, Mr Abrey, who ran a sheet metal company on the Slough Trading Estate, was looking for financial assistance at the time. He offered a job to Nicky, which he was glad to take. It was much nearer to Maidenhead than Chiswick and he had certainly had enough of large impersonal companies.

The Slough Trading Estate was an early business park, run privately with its own power station supplying all the companies on the site. It was home to large companies such as Mars, Citroën and Gillette, as well as numerous small ones such as Abrey and Gerratt. The estate grew enormously over the years, though was not universally welcomed. The expansion of its factories and offices over what were previously green fields is believed to have caused John Betjeman to write, 'Come friendly bombs and fall on Slough . . .'

Mr Abrey was an engineering genius, according to Nicky. He invented the first hover mower and was full of ideas for useful machines. Everyone on the Slough Trading Estate came to him for help and he was happy to dole out advice and practical assistance. However, he could not manage the financial side of business and needed help. Nicky was happy to again be part of a smaller outfit, but he soon found a different set of problems assailing him.

Abrey had made a street cleaner at the request of the local council and when it was completed and officers from the council came to view it, they agreed it was a lovely machine. Nicky, as finance director, worked out the economic price at which it should be offered to them. Abrey's response was, 'I can't possibly charge them that, it's much too much.' Despite these customers already being very impressed by the new cleaner, Abrey proposed a very uneconomic price for it, adding, as icing on the cake, 'I wouldn't buy it now as there are modifications I can do to make it better.' How could Nicky do his job to keep the company solvent when incidents like that occurred? He became frustrated that Abrey wouldn't run the business in a way that could make a profit.

When things got bad and they were borrowing money at the rate of sixteen per cent, it began to be unviable. Nicky found it increasingly stressful to work there, as Abrey would ignore all his advice on pricing and undercharge his customers. Eventually the business could no longer function as it had been, and was struggling to survive. It needed to restructure to save costs. Nicky was asked to resign and, realising that another job would not easily come his way at his age, he stepped into an early retirement aged sixty-two. His letter of resignation was written in October 1971 and a letter from Mr Abrey, thanking him for his work which 'played a large part in stabilising the company and is very much appreciated', was sent to him the same month.

How he hoped to survive with no income at that point, he has long since forgotten. He was making occasional forays into the stock market around then, buying and selling carefully selected shares, but nothing on any scale that would compare to a wage. Nick was at university and I was just applying. Nicky and Grete were keen that we should have the opportunity to go, as neither of them had, and lack of finances was not to prevent it. Luckily things were not as they are now. Then grants were given to students from low-and mid-income families and no tuition fees were charged courtesy of the government, but there were still costs. And running a house wasn't free either. However, somehow they managed it.

It is ironic that in articles written about Nicky in recent years, he is often described as a successful businessman and ex-stockbroker who could afford to take early retirement, thus suggesting this was due to his profitable ventures. The truth is rather that he followed in his family's tradition of losing money, but lived well by being unmaterialistic and uninterested in extravagant spending, preferring to enjoy the simpler things in life, doing his charity work, socialising at home with friends and growing fruit and veg in the garden. Not forgetting that he was prepared to borrow money from his wealthier friends when in a tight spot.

I do not remember him ever buying a new or even newish car, for example, though we did once have a fabulous old Citroën (Traction Avant, Light 15) with wide running boards and doors that opened backwards. This late replacement for his much-loved Paris car was apparently built on the Slough Trading Estate and had many admirers, though was not new when we bought it. Most cars we had were less glamorous.

So, at the age of sixty-two, with plenty of energy and drive but having retired, Nicky was able to give at last his full attention to what he had enjoyed doing most since the 1950s: his charitable work.

# 13

## *'My Real Work'*

### *2003*

By the end of 2002, Nicky was getting used to his new single life. He invited friends or Bobby and Heather for Sunday lunches which he cooked, sometimes with help, sometimes without. He was becoming more confident in the kitchen, which had previously always been Grete's area of expertise, though he had never been averse to helping her when necessary. His life was also full of the charitable activities he still engaged with and his weekly Rotary lunches, as well as games of bridge organised with like-minded friends. Christmas was spent with my family down in rural Herefordshire as usual, with the normal eating, drinking and game playing.

We were caught unawares when we heard on the 31 December that Nicky had been awarded a knighthood in the Queen's New Year's Honours List. He had managed to keep it a complete surprise, as requested in the preceding letter he had received asking if he would accept such an award! He gave no inkling. He did as ordered and kept the news to himself. As usual, he had followed protocol and behaved honourably.

So, with Nicky ninety-three years old, and fifteen years after it had become public knowledge, the story of the Czech Kindertransport had at last reached the ears of the Prime Minister. We later discovered it had occurred through the channels of an adviser in the European Secretariat of the Cabinet Office at

Number 10, Alison Kerr. She had seen Matej's documentary, *Power of Good*, which was about to be shown in a season of European films at the Barbican centre in London, and shown it to her Secretariat colleagues. They had agreed that it was high time the British honoured Nicky for his 1939 deeds and encouraged the head of their department, Sir Stephen Wall, to show it to the then PM Tony Blair. However he went about it, the honour was settled.

Much media interest was generated by the announcement and many articles written about the rescue story. Since its original telling in 1988, which led to the discovery for many of the rescued children about how they came to England in 1939 and then to Nicky's honouring in Czechoslovakia, not much had been written about it in the British press and he was hardly known about here. The knighthood was to change that, and the publicity following it led to old lost friends and colleagues suddenly rediscovering him, as well as more general recognition by the public.

Nicky himself had mixed feelings about it all. He still felt his role in the rescue was overblown, in relation to others', such as Trevor Chadwick and Doreen Warriner who managed the Czech end of the operation or did more dangerous work in Prague assisting wanted fugitives. At least Doreen's Czech work had been recognised with an OBE in 1941. However, he recognised that the focus on him was because he was still alive while they were not. He also got exasperated by the same recurrent questions from journalists about this ancient history, especially as they asked him for details they could easily find the answers to themselves if they made a bit of an effort. The repetition of incorrect facts in some of the articles, despite his attempts to correct them, also irritated him. However, living alone with more time on his hands than he would like, he found a bit of excitement was always welcome and the visits from friends or journalists and requests from schools and groups to go and speak to them all helped to fill his time.

The actual investiture took place in March 2003, with me driving Nicky up to Buckingham Palace, collecting Nick and Bobby at Hyde Park Corner. It was a moving moment, hearing the Lord Steward announce his award – for Services to Humanity – then him kneeling in front of the Queen while she laid a sword on each shoulder. We followed the occasion with a family lunch at a nearby restaurant and it was a lovely happy day, though we were all aware of the poignancy of my mother's absence from the occasion. Many of her friends pointed out how much she would have hated becoming Lady Winton! It was not her style to want attention, whereas Nicky, though not using the Sir himself, was not so discomfited when others used it to address him, as long as his friends didn't. After all, he soon found that a title could come in useful when he wanted to get something done for one of his charitable schemes in a way plain 'Mr' could not.

Receiving a knighthood from Queen
Elizabeth II, 11 March 2003

## *1953–2013*

Nicky and Grete had possessed a common interest in the wider world. And so, despite the difficulties and joys of bringing up a family and earning a living, they kept up many of their previous interests in politics, European issues and helping those around them. Though Nicky, living in Maidenhead in the 1950s and with a growing family to support, had less contact with the London political scene, he had not given up on his political ideas and his affiliation with the Labour Party.

He decided to become active locally and, by 1953, had become Chairman of the local Labour Party and stood in the local municipal elections that year and the year following. However, Maidenhead was most definitely a Conservative area: a growing town surrounded by leafy quiet neighbourhoods, yet at a commuting distance from London.

Consequently his attempts to get elected came to nothing, though he obtained a respectable 41.3 per cent share of the vote. His letter to the local paper after his defeat is illuminating.

*Dear Citizens,*

*I should like to take the opportunity to thank those of you who voted for me last Thursday. At the same time it would not be honest for me to omit to reprimand those Labour sympathisers who did not take their civic duties sufficiently seriously to record their votes. The result of this apathy has been that a Conservative was returned with the support of only twenty-four per cent of the total ward electorate. Unless, at the next election, the privilege which you possess to elect your representative to the Council is taken far more seriously, then undoubtedly once more a Conservative will be returned with the backing of only a small minority of the total electorate. Finally, I must thank those who assisted me so ably in my campaign, a band which, albeit eager and enthusiastic, is small. If this letter is taken at all seriously maybe this band will soon grow in numbers and therefore in strength.*

*Yours sincerely,*

*Nicholas G Winton*

His election leaflet for the following year makes further interesting reading. As well as his exhortation to voters, his personal details list his work 'evacuating 600 refugee children from Chechoslovakia' (sic) – an example of how the media's repetition of the fabrication that he kept his pre-war efforts secret from everyone for fifty years was obviously nonsense!

That 1954 council election was his last attempt to enter local politics and his interest thereafter was only as a Maidenhead Labour Party member, helping the town residents with issues that concerned them, rather than as a candidate. He must have realised that he was not likely to succeed in getting elected and was not prepared to continue flogging a dead horse. He decided to put his civic efforts into more productive enterprises, where there was more chance of getting results.

An encounter soon after their arrival in Maidenhead, which Nicky ascribes to being one of the most important to his future life, was with Victor Moll. It was he who nominated Nicky to join the Maidenhead Rotary Club, sometime during the 1950s. It's possible they met due to Victor being Managing Director of the then Maidenhead Building Society and Nicky approaching him for a mortgage, though he can't remember if this was the case.

Ever since then, Nicky has remained a member of Rotary, with a short break on retirement, and the group has been the foundation of his social life and charity work. For Nicky, Rotary is a shining example of community spirit at work and if he had not been a member, he feels his life would have been significantly less rewarding.

Rotary clubs exist all over the world, having started in Chicago in 1905. Their stated purpose is to bring together business and professional people to provide humanitarian service, encourage high ethical standards in all vocations, and help build goodwill and peace in the world. It is open to all persons regardless of race, colour, creed or political preference, though remarkably only in 1989 was its membership opened to women. Members' weekly meetings, over a breakfast, lunch or dinner, are social events as well as a time to organise work on their service goals. To join Rotary, however, you have to be nominated by a current member, and members should represent a range of professions, with only a small percentage allowed from the same field.

Victor, as a current member in the 1950s, obviously considered that Nicky was a good candidate and nominated him to join. Before long, he and his wife Anita had become close friends with Nicky and Grete. They were a similar age and as well as Nicky and Victor being members of Rotary, both Grete and Anita became involved in the European Women's Movement, both of them being founder members of the Maidenhead Branch. Victor and Anita had lived in Maidenhead since soon after the war and Victor had become Managing Director of Maidenhead Building Society at the tender age of thirty-four. He and Nicky were both serious men with an ingrained sense of fairness, and though they were not of the same political colour, they both believed in service to the community.

Though Nicky left Rotary for a time on retiring, he rejoined shortly after and from then until now Rotary has been the bedrock of Nicky's life in the local community. He still attends their weekly lunches and many current members remain his close friends. His ventures into other charity work sometimes started via a Rotary member's request for assistance and he himself would often request aid from fellow Rotarians for one of his chosen ventures. The weekly lunches were also opportunities to talk to other

# Maidenhead Borough Council Elections
## Thursday, May 13th, 1954

## ST. MARY'S WARD

Dear Elector,

Once again I am asking you to support my candidature as your representative on the Maidenhead Borough Council for St. Mary's Ward.

In thanking those of you who voted for me last year, I would ask all who sympathise with the progressive aims of the Labour Party, to make a special effort this year to record their votes. The Borough Council here is still manned by Conservatives, which surely must have the effect of making discussion on any subject one-sided.

Please help the Labour Party to help you ; by recording your vote for me on May 13th.

Yours sincerely,

## NICHOLAS GEORGE WINTON

Personal Details :

*Resident in Maidenhead. Married with two children. Director of " Glacier Foods Ltd." Chairman of the Maidenhead Local Labour Party. Member of the Executive of the Divisional Labour Party. Associated with the Labour Movement for 20 years through the Fabian Society. Banker in London until the War. After Munich evacuated 600 refugee children from Chechoslovakia. Served with the R.A.F. Honorary Secretary of the Southern Section of the Amateur Fencing Association. Member of the Federation of Social Services.*

1954 election card

professional men about their work and lives and Nicky was always keen to discuss issues that interested him with knowledgeable people.

Another Rotarian in those early days, David Peterson, a police officer who later became Chief Superintendent of Thames Valley Police, says the subject of the Kindertransport was not one that ever came up, despite having serious discussions with Nicky across many topics over numerous lunches. David was forced to leave Rotary when his new post in Slough involved meetings that clashed with the weekly lunch. Nicky, being Nicky, was keen to intervene with the Chief Superintendent on David's behalf so as to allow his continued attendance. However, considering it unwise for his career, David turned down his offer and reluctantly left the club.

Other Rotarians considered Nicky a willing volunteer in their fundraising or community-supporting activities. In meetings he could seem reserved at times and would only speak if he felt strongly about a particular issue, but when he did contribute, it was with an air of authority. If he felt something needed doing, he would make it difficult for others to refuse to help him in the endeavour, by persisting and not readily taking 'no' for an answer. This method was not always popular and some people could find him insensitive to their perspective. It has been said that not everyone found him a pleasure to be around.

His first major charitable venture started in reaction to his own personal experience. Having found no support or help from any authorities or organisation to deal with all the issues that arose after Robin's diagnosis of Down's syndrome, Nicky and Grete felt there should be someone offering advice and support to all the families like theirs in the area. So it was, in the late '50s, a few years after Robin was born, that Nicky became instrumental in starting a Maidenhead branch of what is now called Mencap. The national organisation, in its infancy at the time, having started as a parent group in 1946, could only offer support from afar. This did not seem enough to help families struggling with the problems, both practical and emotional, that caring for a Down's syndrome child could induce, and so Nicky set out to bring to life a local society. He had heard through the grapevine that a house – Highview, just off Castle Hill, which had been converted into a centre for disabled people – was now vacant as that organisation had moved into new purpose-built premises. Mr Schwab, a German refugee who had made a good business in property, and was already known to Nicky, having leased Guy Lawrence the factory for Glacier Foods, had bought and done up Highview and donated it to the trust running the charity.

Schwab and his solicitor Cliff Hillman, a trustee of the charity, had been unable to find suitable tenants for their old building and were about to attempt to change its use to offices, using the rent obtained to fund their charity, The Maidenhead Centre for the Disabled. This was fraught with problems, as it was possible that the Charity Commission might not allow this. However, they had just decided to go ahead anyway. It was at this point that Nicky made a call to Cliff to ask about taking over Highview for their fledgling local group.

Cliff told me about their discussion at the time, saying he had explained to Nicky about his proposal to let the property as offices and pay the income to their charity. Nicky had replied, 'You are a man after my own heart as I do not believe in following red tape as long as you are achieving the aims intended.' It was the start of a long relationship, made closer after Cliff eventually joined Rotary in 2000 after retiring from full-time work.

However, with Nicky now on the scene suggesting his new group take over the property, this new proposition fitted the Trust's remit much better, as the house would still be used for those with disabilities. Highview therefore became the Maidenhead Mencap HQ and ever since then has been the central hub for all their local activities – meeting place, day centre, admin centre – and all due to the generosity of Mr Schwab and his charity trustees.

Despite Robin's early death, Nicky remained closely involved, acting as Chairman for many years as well as serving for some time on the Mencap national committee. Only fairly recently has his involvement become less active. His latest role is as President, a post he still holds at 104 years old. His skills as an organiser were always useful on the administrative side, but he also maintained close contact with the families at Highview. Friends who visited there with him over the years attested to the rapturous reception given him by the children when he arrived and he returned their love with enthusiasm. Having built such a close relationship with Robin, it was not hard for him to relate to other Down's children and several who attended Highview came with their parents to learn to swim in our pool, to join whoever else had dropped in for a dip during the summer.

In 1972, the year after he retired, Nicky started yet another voluntary post working for the Samaritans, which he continued from 1972 until the late 1980s. He no longer remembers what brought him to join them as a volunteer listener. Perhaps a friend had mentioned it to him as worthwhile work. No doubt being retired had meant he was on the lookout for yet more satisfying community service he could commit to. He did not want to spend all his free time gardening and he did not want to take up golf or similar pursuits that other retirees filled their time with.

Now those who knew Nicky well would have been surprised to imagine him in this field, but as volunteers do not speak of their involvement, it remained undisclosed. As it says on the Samaritans website: 'Samaritans volunteers listen in confidence to anyone in any type of emotional distress, without judging or telling people what to do.' Nicky is still visited by friends who talk to him about their problems, but he is not known for listening without telling them what he thinks about the situation and what he thinks they should do and even actively changing things for them!

Of his considerable time there, he remembers only two people who he felt he had really helped and where his support led to real successful outcomes in his eyes. These were instances where he developed a long-term relationship with the client and actively involved himself in their lives and problems. These cases are from a long time ago with no identifying details in line with the confidentiality of the work.

In the first, an older lady rang the Samaritans saying all she wanted to do was die, despite seeming to have a comfortable life.

Nicky went and visited her a number of times in her luxurious home, discovering nothing that she wanted, just to die. One day he asked her, 'There must be something you would like to do.' Her reply was that she would like to visit her daughter in the USA. When asked why she didn't, she told him that she had talked to her doctor about it and he had replied that the journey would kill her, due to her weak heart. Nicky's response was, 'Well, that's great, that's just what you want.' It's hard to believe that's what he had been trained to say to someone like that, but it certainly fitted Nicky's character to be so blunt and straightforward. Thus galvanised, she went, had a wonderful time and thereafter flew there regularly, her mood greatly improved.

In the second, a self-employed tradesman phoned him saying he was suicidal. I shall call him John. Through illness and misfortune, John had run up debts, was overdue on his mortgage payments and he could see no other way out but suicide. Nicky visited John at his home and offered to look at his finances to see if there was a practical solution. Looking at lists of the business assets, debts and mortgage, Nicky's suggestion that he sell his house and buy a cheaper one brought an admission from John. He had done some illegal building in the loft without planning permission, which would come to light on selling. Nicky felt there was a way out, and

with John's permission, took all the particulars to the local authority, told them the story and asked them to make the loft work legal,
which they did without protest. John was then able to sell the
house, pay off his debts and buy a smaller house. What had seemed
to him an intractable problem was resolved.

In the 1970s, volunteers were able to meet and get more involved
in helping those who called them, but mostly help was given over
the phone by listening to and supporting those who called. Of the
many others that remained just voices on the phone, Nicky had no
idea if he helped them. When he was told that interventions such
as he had offered were no longer Samaritan policy, he felt less
useful and after some time he left. His natural urge to help was not
satisfied by being an anonymous listening ear, he really wanted to
DO SOMETHING – something practical.

Nicky's most intensive and lengthy charity venture started at
around the same time as he began at the Samaritans, but fulfilled
his practical urge more successfully and kept him interested and
involved right up until the present day. Unlike his Mencap work,
taken on as a response to personal experience, this new venture
came through his local contacts and from someone asking for
help, rather than as a specific cause he wanted to support. His
involvement came from a request for help from the regional secretary for Abbeyfield, who gave a talk at the Rotary club asking for
a volunteer chairman with management skills.

Nicky obviously liked the sound of it. He followed up the
request and became the first Chairman of Maidenhead and
Windsor Abbeyfield. Perhaps he saw this as a task which would
not only be a good challenge, but which would also use all his business and organisational skills more fully than his chairmanship at
Mencap or his listening support at the Samaritans could do. At the
time though, he was unlikely to have realised quite how much of
his time and skills the role would need, and that forty years later
he would still be involved.

The Abbeyfield Society is a charity set up in 1956 by Richard Carr-Gomm, to provide sheltered accommodation for elderly people that offered support and companionship at affordable rents, and functioning through local societies. Carr-Gomm, a Major in the Coldstream Guards, saw a need to prevent loneliness in elderly people and resigned his commission to become an unpaid housekeeper for the first two Abbeyfield residents. His work, with the help of other volunteers, led to a national, then international, organisation of local groups.

Nicky's first task was to set up the local society. Other Rotarians joined the committee, though some 'volunteered' due to Nicky's refusal to take no for an answer. When he decided that someone could be helpful to his cause, he approached them in such a way that they seemed to have no alternative. Even a local farmer's wife with young children to look after, Kirsty Findlay, found herself press-ganged into volunteering – thirty-five years later she is still involved. Her comment was that when Nicky wanted something done, he would always go to the person at the top. He obviously had no personal anxiety about speaking to those in authority after his years working in Europe with all manner and level of officials. It has already been mentioned that not everyone sees Nicky coming with delight. Knowing that he may be after them to help with something, they have to move quickly to escape. When he sees a job to be done, he has no compunction in asking people to help and finds it hard to understand why someone would not be keen to volunteer. He has worked out the best way to make it happen; how can anyone disagree?

As a Rotary and Abbeyfield colleague, David Cager, commented, 'Yes, he can be a pain to work with, but in reality this is sometimes the only way to get anything done. His view on life is "Don't Ever Give Up" and there is no such word as "Can't", with which I totally agree. There certainly must have been people over the years who have seen him coming and tried to disappear

– I just wasn't quick enough! It is virtually impossible to say "No" if he asks for something to be done because he doesn't actually ask in the manner of a question; it is more a statement of intent and you are left, not thinking about whether it can be done but how you are going to do it.'

David also shed light on Nicky's obdurate responses to people who he does not agree with, even despite his inbuilt politeness. 'We had a visitor to Maidenhead Rotary Club who was scheduled to give a talk about Iran. He was of Persian birth and had married an English lady, in Iran, and they had two girls who were also born there. This was the early Eighties after the Shah of Iran had been deposed and the Muslim Clerics, led by the Ayatollah Khomeini, took control and introduced Islamic practices, making all females wear the chador – no western clothes allowed. The gentleman's grouse was that his two children were not allowed British Citizenship because they had a Persian father and had been born in Iran. He then spent quite a long time ranting about the appalling way we treated women in the UK which, bearing in mind what had just happened in Iran, really defied belief. Nicky had been asked, before the meeting, if he would do the Vote of Thanks (at the end of the talk). He stood up and looked long and hard at the gentleman speaker. He then said, "I am going to find this vote of thanks very difficult, as I disagree with everything you have said"!'

This gentleman, along with many others, discovered that Nicky, though polite, will generally speak his mind when he feels strongly about an issue. Despite his sometimes reticent façade, he will, when the occasion arises, say what he thinks without being rude, but with an inner certainty that he is right. Another method he uses is humour to soften the rebuke, so that the other person is laughing before he realises he is being chastised. Not everyone takes his brusqueness well, though, and undoubtedly he has hurt and offended quite a few people over the years.

Back to Abbeyfield and the nascent Maidenhead branch. Local groups are run fairly autonomously and do their own independent fundraising and service provision, without any financial aid from the national office. Maidenhead Abbeyfield Society was formed in 1973 and was closely followed by the building of the first Maidenhead Abbeyfield home, Hardwick House, in 1974. This was not achieved without difficulty, but it provided an early chance for Nicky to try out his powers of persuasion on the local authority.

The plan started when a local man, Major Brian Dixon, offered the society a cottage with land to build a home for eight residents and a housekeeper. This was a tremendous start to getting their plan for a local home for elderly people underway, and Nicky and his committee members were delighted to think a plot was being donated to their venture. However, it was not to be that easy as a local councillor and the site's neighbours objected to a new housing development in the area. Nicky and a fellow committee member, Griff Morris, were not to be put off and together they worked on a plan to get building consent. At a meeting with Maidenhead Council, Nicky suggested a local public enquiry into the matter, which was agreed by all parties. He then convinced the rest of the Abbeyfield committee to let him go alone to the enquiry, knowing that the room would be filled with people all of whom would be opposing the plan. He attended the meeting and sure enough, one side of the room was full of people who all made exactly the same objection, one after another. Nicky, alone on his side, used all his powers of persuasion to make his case for the home. He was betting on the 'opposition' overstating their case, and felt his cause to be just and right. The enquiry agreed with him and granted permission to build.

His method of getting things done, involving persuasion with a touch of cunning, was used over the years to get people on his side and overcome opposition. It could sometimes involve riding rough-shod over the wishes of others, but that would not stop him. Sparing others' feelings was not his priority. He had total belief in his own vision, and his overriding purpose would be to achieve his objective with the assistance of others or, if necessary, by himself. If he failed to get agreement, he could be furious.

Nicky, being Chairman of both the Maidenhead branch and the Hardwick House committee, soon got involved with the national committee. He became a member and attended meetings at their head office in St Albans. One of the ideas he put forward to them was the case for Abbeyfield to move into providing 'extra care' homes as well as their regular sheltered accommodation, so that those who had moved beyond caring for themselves could remain within the Abbeyfield family.

Around this time Nicky wrote an article on running small societies, having been asked to do so by, possibly, the national organisation – anyway it was written on Maidenhead Abbeyfield notepaper. This short piece gives substance to his preferred way of working and his humour. He suggests a new society needs to be initiated by one motivated person who should take the lead and form '*his committee*'. The make-up of the committee is important to the degree that it would be better to run it solo than with the wrong people, specifying particularly that people who 'make suggestions . . . but who never wish to take on a specific job themselves, are useless'. He states that experts are useful and their advice should be heeded, though 'amateur' comments can also prove useful. His final comment is that it may be difficult to get rid of a member of the committee (all being volunteers), 'but I am hoping someone else will write on how to get rid of the chairman'.

Another member of Rotary who became a great and life-long friend was Ric Fontaine. He admired Nicky's ability to 'get people to do things' that he thought needed doing, by offering them no alternative. Ric's wife Sheila has also found herself on the receiving end of this. She discovered that anyone showing any slight interest in what he was doing would lead Nicky to co-opt them to help him, her view being, 'He is a dangerous person to know; he can get you to do things and you can't say no.'

In their local club, when Nicky took his turn as President, Ric was the International President, and together they organised a meeting of the four European towns twinned with Maidenhead: Saint-Cloud (France), Bad Godesberg (Germany), Courtrai (Belgium) and Frascati (Italy). They were also keen to start a youth camp, and in the early '70s young people from the four towns came every year to Maidenhead to enable them to mix together and get to know each other. Nicky's original idea was that disadvantaged youth from these communities would come and stay with local families as an exchange which could continue. When, over time, those attending were more likely to be the sons and daughters of more middle-class families from the towns, Nicky handed it over to others to organise; it was not what he had envisioned and so he was not interested anymore.

In 1983, Stanley Platt, another Rotarian, and Ric decided to nominate Nicky for an MBE in recognition of all the charity work he had undertaken over the past twenty or more years. The award came as a great surprise to Nicky and Grete. It was announced while Nicky was abroad touring Denmark, Holland and Belgium as part of a group for Abbeyfield along with BUPA representatives to study care for the elderly in those countries. Grete was quoted in an article about his award in the local paper, which also mentioned his pre-war work on the Kindertransport. Her comment was: 'He's very thrilled. He has done voluntary work all his life and he had never expected anyone to take any notice of him.'

We went *en famille* to Buckingham Palace when he received his award from the Queen and he was pleased as punch. Who could have imagined then that, twenty years later, he would be back to receive a knighthood for work undertaken so long before.

\*　　\*　　\*

Having built Hardwick House in the 1970s, by the mid-1980s, Maidenhead Abbeyfield was ready for another venture and Nicky's next big challenge began. Having become enthused with the idea that they should be providing care for those no longer able to live independently alongside their normal sheltered accommodation, he had got his committee to agree that their next venture should be such a place. This idea led to the building of an extra-care home on a site they had discovered in Windsor. His involvement did not stop at the fundraising and building plans, but also comprised the selection and employment of the manager who would run it.

He had met Wendy Wheatley while they were both volunteering at the Samaritans and he discovered she ran a nursing agency. He was impressed with her manner and experience and asked her if she would consider running their new extra-care home if they got all their funding. As others had already discovered, it was impossible to refuse him and she found herself agreeing to give up her agency to run what became Winton House, in Windsor.

Nicky's view that when he set his mind to something it was always something that was undeniably necessary and important meant that he was often frustrated and even baffled by others' lack of enthusiasm or support. This happened with the British government in relation to the Kindertransport, but also with the local council when they did not readily support his charitable schemes. A major example occurred when Nicky and the Abbeyfield committee planned to build another extra-care home, this time in Maidenhead in the first years of the twenty-first century.

It happened this way. In recent years old-fashioned sheltered housing was becoming less viable as older people needed better facilities than were often offered by the older-style properties Abbeyfield owned. This meant that the numbers of residents in these properties diminished and they became unviable and the local society running them could no longer function successfully.

According to David Cager, by now Chairman of Maidenhead Abbeyfield Society, 'Nicky, surprise, surprise, saw this as an opportunity for the Maidenhead Society to obtain some funds! Basically, if any society ceased trading and sold their property/s, the proceeds would go back to what was then the Housing Corporation and/or the Charity Commissioners. Nicky hit upon the idea that it would be better for us to take them over – strictly not a takeover but a merger. We could then sell the freehold/s and build up a fund to finance a new project. This started in perhaps 2004 and between then and 2009, the Laleham, Shepperton, Slough, Egham and Burnham Societies all closed following a merger with Maidenhead.' The plan Nicky drew up was to guarantee a place in one of Maidenhead's current houses to any residents still living in one of these unviable properties. This system worked well and enabled Maidenhead Abbeyfield to accumulate quite a lot of money, which they wanted to use to build the new extra-care home.

Nicky thought that the local council would be thrilled for this to happen as the borough would get a new care home without having to fund it. Their housing association met with him and was shown Winton House as an example of what Abbeyfield would build and manage. He hoped that the council would help by providing a piece of ground in Maidenhead for the project. They agreed to help, but after ten months' wait they came to him and said, 'It's all organised and you don't even have to pay for it.' They showed him plans of the property that was destined for Abbeyfield to run and it was an affordable housing complex, not an extra-care nursing home. Nicky was furious and felt completely let down. Maidenhead needed this facility, but would not help him with the Abbeyfield enterprise, which would have been built and run without council finance.

Nicky, David and the rest of Maidenhead Abbeyfield were incensed that the council had wasted this opportunity. It was a constant refrain from Nicky and he used every occasion he could to vent his frustration. In 2006 he received a letter from US President George W. Bush thanking him for his work on the Kindertransport, which received some local publicity with an article in the *Maidenhead Advertiser*, the local weekly paper. Nicky seized the moment to criticise the council for their stance on the Abbeyfield issue, so that the article was headed, 'Note of Thanks from George W: President's letter but still no old people's home.' The article, with Nicky's complaint about the local council's intransigence within it, was accompanied by a photo of a curmudgeonly looking Nicky holding the President's letter. At the end was a comment from the embattled Borough Director of Care about why it was not possible for them to accept Abbeyfield's offer. I suspect he was not best pleased to be picked up in this way and given such negative publicity, but Nicky would not have been put off by the discomfort he had caused. His aim was to get an extra-care home built in Maidenhead. The embarrassment of council officials was not of great concern to him, when he felt his cause was exemplary and their hurt feelings were not in his thoughts.

Nicky continued to grumble, suggesting he should get himself prosecuted for some minor misdemeanour which would allow him to stand up in court to lambast the council. Luckily he is, in fact, too law-abiding to have really gone for that! As far as I know, his only brush with the law was a speeding fine, driving at 38mph in a 30 zone. He was ninety-eight at the time!

In the event, Maidenhead Abbeyfield found a site a few miles outside the Borough of Maidenhead and Windsor in Burnham and spent some years getting their latest extra-care home built, to house thirty residents, including those with dementia. As David described it to me, 'During these latter years I have constantly been reminded by Nicky that "If things take any longer I won't be here to see the completed home", to which I always replied that the matter was entirely in his hands and that I expected him to do his best. Well, he did his bit and we did ours, because Nicholas House opened last week ... (December 2011). Nicky, as we know, was 102 on the 19 May 2011 and his main object in life seems to be avoiding becoming a resident at either Winton or Nicholas House – nice as they are, he is absolutely right.'

Nicky officially opened the home, named after him, in May 2012, one week before his 103rd birthday. He was still seething about the council's folly as, 'since then the council have built two nursing homes themselves but had to borrow the money to do it'.

The US President's letter to Nicky in 2006, and used by Nicky for his own local agenda with the council, had come about through the lobbying of Peter Rafaeli, the Honorary Consul of the Czech Republic in Philadelphia, USA, himself a Holocaust survivor. Peter had discovered the story of the Czech Kindertransport on a visit to Prague in 2005 and decided that America had not given enough recognition to Nicky for his role in saving all those Czech children, many of them now US citizens.

Many people had read the copies of the letters, pasted in the famous scrapbook, written to Nicky in 1939 in response to his urgent requests for assistance from the US President, Franklin D. Roosevelt and New York's Jewish community. These replies had come from the US Embassy in London, the American Jewish Congress, the US Senate and the Governor of New York, all saying the USA couldn't take any endangered children at that time. Having had at least 5,000 endangered children on their lists in Prague, Nicky and his organisation realised that Britain alone couldn't take them all and looked to America to help bear the load, but to no avail.

Having seen that their government had not helped in that time of need, some Americans felt that they should now give credit to those who had. Peter, through his contacts in Washington, obtained this belated but high-level response. He followed it up the next year by convincing Congressman Ron Klein to put a

Resolution through the US Congress: 'Recognizing the remarkable example of Sir Nicholas Winton who organized the rescue of 669 Jewish Czechoslovakian children from Nazi death camps prior to the outbreak of World War II.'

Nicky had acted back then as he continued to do later in life when he wanted to achieve something: he wrote to the person in charge. In 1939, it was the President of the USA. In his more recent labours, he would still go to the person at the top, but then it would be the leader of the council or the most important person he could think of who he might influence to agree to his scheme.

Articles continued to be written from time to time about him in the local and national papers, which touched on his continued dedication to charitable works and the altruism that he so obviously demonstrated thereby. Whatever others thought, Nicky's feelings as to why he continued with his voluntary work differed from those noble motives.

In a speech he made to his own Rotary club some years ago, he explains his motivation:

Doing work of a humanitarian or charitable nature does not mean you deserve the title of being good or that you are in any way a better person than someone who takes no interest in this kind of work. On the contrary, I do such work as it gives me pleasure and because of this I could be called self-indulgent and certainly selfish. This I am saying because I do not feel I should be thanked in any way for the work I do. I am now retired for some years and without these charity jobs, I really can't imagine how I should have survived.

The type of charity I have gotten myself into has always come to me fortuitously. It has never been of my direct choosing. The refugee work I got into in 1938 was because a friend of mine, a master at Westminster, asked me to join him in Prague where he was being sent by the British Committee for Refugees

**THE WHITE HOUSE**

WASHINGTON

July 3, 2006

Sir Nicholas Winton
Maidenhead Berks
United Kingdom

Dear Sir Nicholas:

Your heroism during World War II saved the lives of more than 600 Czech children and brought hope to many more in the midst of the hatred and persecution of the Holocaust. Because of your remarkable actions, these men and women and their descendents live in freedom today.

I am grateful for your courage and compassion in the face of such cruelty and injustice. Your story of bravery and sacrifice continues to inspire people around the world and reminds us of the power of good to overcome evil.

Best wishes, and may God bless you.

Sincerely,

George W. Bush

Letter from President George W. Bush

from Czechoslovakia after the German occupation of
Sudetenland. The work with the mentally handicapped I got
into when Grete and I had a son with Down's syndrome and we
found out that the authorities just did not want to know. Work
with the old people I got into when the Registered Secretary of
Abbeyfield came to one of our Rotary members and asked for
a volunteer to chair a committee in Maidenhead.

Nicky has often said that most people do not make many real decisions in their life. Things happen and they react. His belief is that
his charitable work falls into that category, though again others
might interpret this differently in that he takes pleasure from helping others, rather than from purely helping himself. Nicky's belief
is that most people would get great satisfaction from helping
others and only need to be given the opportunity to do the same as
he has done. It is that belief which led him to presume others
would enthusiastically agree to join in whichever of his ventures he
asked them to. Just as he had responded positively to others'
appeals himself.

As he stated in his speech to Rotary, Nicky couldn't imagine
how he would have survived without the charity work he filled his
days with after retirement. It was this continuing community
involvement, as well as the increasing contacts coming from the
burgeoning interest in his historical Kindertransport activity, that
helped him fill his days in the years after Grete died.

## 14

## *Recognition Brings New Adventures*
### *2003–13*

Media interest in the story of the Czech Kindertransport multiplied as a result of Nicky's knighthood. Early January 2003 had brought a flurry of journalists to his door looking for an interesting article or angle. An enquiry of a slightly different nature came to me at the same time. The BBC TV programme *This Is Your Life* wanted to do an episode on Nicky, and as it is always a surprise to the subject themselves, the producers had to make their approach to a family member.

*This Is Your Life* was a British TV institution for nearly fifty years. In the show, the host surprised a special guest, before taking them through their life with the assistance of the 'big red book' and with people from different aspects of their life coming on to talk about them. They asked if Nick and I thought he would enjoy it. We were concerned about the effect of the surprise, but overall in favour, as there is nothing Nicky loves more than a party and spending time with old friends. This seemed to tick both those boxes. We agreed that we should have a go and it was a role reversal for us; now it was Nick and I keeping a secret from Nicky, whereas just a month before he had kept his knighthood from us.

I met with the producer and made a list of people who were significant in his life. So many of his friends were no longer with us, but there were still plenty to consider. We had a hectic few weeks while it was planned and the date was set for 21 February. A coach was to collect his Maidenhead friends and our family, with others brought in from further afield. Budget constraints restricted the involvement of more far-flung friends, the producers selecting just a couple to fit their agenda.

It was arranged that Nicky would be ambushed at the Winton House extra-care home anniversary tea party where, being President of the local Abbeyfield Society, he was invited to attend and cut the cake. Being concerned about the shock the surprise might give to my ninety-three-year-old father, I arranged to turn up, supposedly on my way past from a meeting, and go with Nicky to the Abbeyfield party, so as to be on hand to support him. I was so excited I couldn't believe he didn't notice something was up, but it went like clockwork. He didn't even react to the cameras already set up in the room when he arrived, just accepting that it was the local paper recording the event! Do they do that for a care home party? I don't think so!

As he was cutting the cake, Michael Aspel, the host of *This Is Your Life*, walked in and announced himself. Nicky dealt with the surprise like water off a duck's back – so much for our anxieties – and the programme itself was enormous fun. So many of his friends and family were there, as well as quite a few of his 'children' and their children, and additionally Elisabeth Maxwell, the person responsible for the story of the rescue becoming known. A group of fencers came to represent that aspect of his life; two pilots he had served with during the war, one being Airlie Holden-Hindley, his old friend and my godfather; also the daughter and granddaughter of his best friend Stanley Murdoch, both being Nicky's goddaughters.

There were some film clips of those sending good wishes, including his local MP Theresa May, Esther Rantzen and Judy Leden, world champion hang-glider and a microlight pilot who was the daughter of one of his rescued children, now deceased. In it she promised to take him up for a microlight flight for his ninety-fourth birthday three months later. The programme ended with a group of children appearing on the stage, all descendants of those he had rescued sixty-four years earlier. There was a lovely party afterwards and there's no doubt that Nicky thoroughly enjoyed himself.

His own birthday later that year was the occasion for the promised microlight flight, which took place at White Waltham, a local airfield. The site was inundated with people coming to wish him well, watch his flight and, for quite a few, to also go for a spin in Judy's microlight, which she generously offered in return for a donation to Abbeyfield.

The birthday parties have continued every year in one form or another – mostly informal affairs in Nicky's garden – but for his 100th birthday in 2009, as well as a big party at home for friends

Birthday microlight flight with Judy Leden

100th birthday party at the Czech Embassy
surrounded by his 'children'
(Courtesy Czech Embassy)

and family, the Borough of Windsor and Maidenhead threw a
bash for him at the Guildhall in Windsor attended by his Rotary
colleagues and other local friends. On top of those, party number
three was the biggest, hosted by the Czech Embassy, with many of
his 'children' and their families in attendance, having flown in
from around the world for the occasion.

Last year, when I half-heartedly suggested that perhaps having
a party every year was a bit too much, his reply was that, as he
didn't know when the last one would be, he intended to keep
having them.

Occasional trips abroad continued as a result of invitations to
attend an event or for a film showing of the documentary. In
October 2007, Nicky was invited by Václav Havel to an event close
to his heart: the Forum 2000 conference in Prague. He had met
President Havel of the Czech Republic several times and admired

his position of taking an ethical path in public life and politics. He was supportive of the aims of the Forum 2000 Foundation, which Havel had initiated and continued to run with colleagues and other similar minded people. It was founded to 'support the values of democracy and respect for human rights, assist the development of civil society, and encourage religious, cultural and ethnic tolerance. It provides a platform for global leaders, as well as thinkers and courageous individuals from every field of endeavour, to openly debate and share these critical issues.'

He was the guest of honour and invited to make a speech at an evening event during the conference. It was a very busy few days as, knowing Nicky was in town, many others wanted to see him and invite him to meetings. He never actually made it to witness any of the Forum debates, but was ferried around Prague, to dinners with his 'children' and to the Ministry of Defence, where he inspected the guard with the Minister, Vlasta Parkanová, a lovely red-haired ex-singer who presented him with the highest award she could bestow: the Cross of Merit.

A couple of days later, having become tireder and tireder, he was taken ill and rushed to hospital, where he remained for ten days, suffering from a chest infection, which affected his already weak heart. The Czech media, which had written reams about Nicky over the past eighteen years, were soon onto it and the hospital had to lock the ward to prevent journalists sneaking in. His room was soon filled with flowers from well-wishers, and Mrs Parkanová – convinced that his standing in the cold to review the troops was the cause of his illness – offered a plane to fly him home. He recovered gradually and the following year Mrs Parkanová invited him back as a kind gesture so that he could enjoy a private trip to do whatever he wanted.

The most unusual honour he had been given was by the directors of the Klet' Observatory in South Bohemia in 2001. Jana Tichá and Miloš Tichý, a husband and wife team, had discovered a minor planet, otherwise known as an asteroid, in 1998 and named it Winton, in honour of Nicky. Ever since he was given a plaque about 'his' planet, he had spoken to Stephen, his son-in-law (my husband) who teaches astronomy in schools with a mobile planetarium, about the possibility one day of visiting the observatory together. This invitation by the Czech Minister of Defence was the chance to carry out that wish and another that had been brewing for the same length of time.

With Minister of Defence of Czech Republic, Vlasta Parkanová after receiving Cross of Merit, October 2007
(Courtesy Z. Mináčová)

A request by a Czech school in 2001 to be allowed to name their school after him had led to a continuing relationship between their pupils and Nicky. The school in Kunžak, also in South Bohemia, now named the Basic School of Sir Nicholas Winton, had sent Nicky letters and photos and, of course, with a trip to South Bohemia on the cards, he now wanted to call on the school as well.

It was a wonderful trip, with not only myself and Steve in tow, but also our son Laurence, then a physics student at Cambridge, and so also keen to see the observatory. We were taken by helicopter from Prague and landed on the Kunžak school playing fields to visit the excited pupils before taking to the air again and swooping over the beautiful medieval town of Český Krumlov, en route to a mountain field near the observatory. With Mrs Parkanová, we looked through the giant telescope and were shown the work done there by the directors. We returned to England from that unforgettable trip having fulfilled Nicky's two wishes without mishap.

How could anything top that? Well, the next year there was another surprise in store. The Queen was due to make a state visit to Slovakia and those organising it thought that the Kindertransport story and the effect it had had on local schoolchildren in the capital, Bratislava, would be an interesting part of her visit.

Matej Mináč, the Slovak film director who had made the documentary *Power of Good*, had discovered that children of all ages reacted with excitement and enthusiasm after seeing the film. It seemed to make them feel that they could emulate those historical people who had helped others and make a difference themselves. All kinds of projects were started by schools where the film had been shown, comprising charitable works locally or internationally. Matej had told others of this effect and it had snowballed into a plan for the Queen's visit, to bring together Nicky, some of his 'children' who had come originally from Slovakia and current schoolchildren working on charitable projects inspired by seeing the documentary.

Nicky was all for the trip; it was a bit of an adventure, and some excitement which he didn't often have, since his mobility got less and he could no longer drive. He liked nothing more than a good discussion about current world affairs and politics out at some local pub with friends or a game of bridge, but for much of the time he was alone at home and he often complained of boredom. He was not, and had never been, a solitary person. His early life had been spent living with family and friends, followed by fifty years of a happily married existence.

So off he went, with me along as assistant. Bratislava, the capital of Slovakia, is a pretty town on the Danube and the few days we spent there went by in a whirl of activity. Joe Schlesinger, one of his 'children' originally from Bratislava, now living in Canada and a renowned CBC (Canadian Broadcasting Corporation) journalist, had been the presenter of the documentary that had brought so much attention to the story. He, along with several other 'children' was there with Nicky to meet the Queen and later attend the State Banquet in her honour. The trip was demanding on Nicky's energy; he was ninety-nine years old at the time, and so the diplomats involved went out of their way to try and make the travel as easy as possible. This led to an amazing offer: the Queen had invited Nicky and me to fly home to England on her own flight, a chartered British Airways plane.

We arrived at the airport and got Nicky up the long flight of steps into the plane, where we were seated with the Queen's attendants and looked after 'royally'. The last item on her itinerary in Slovakia was a trip to Poprad, a small town on the edge of the Tatra Mountains. While she and Prince Philip attended their local events, Nicky chatted with Tim Hewlett, a former RAF pilot and Director of Royal Travel, about their experiences of flying in different times. This led to Nicky being invited up to see the cockpit on the flight back, during which he had a short chat with the Queen as he passed her compartment. Leaving Poprad, we were treated to a complete circuit of the High Tatras appearing through the clouds. Special dispensation had apparently been given for the plane to pass into Polish airspace to allow the whole mountain range to be seen. I was told that the Duke of Edinburgh was interested in seeing the effects of acid rain on the trees covering the mountain flanks, perhaps something that had been discussed earlier in their visit. It was certainly an amazing end to the adventure.

The seventieth anniversary of the start of the Second World War took place in 2009, the year Nicky reached his own centenary.

As 1 September was the date the final Kindertransport train from Prague was cancelled, Czech Railways decided to mark it with a commemorative re-enactment of the journey the children had taken from Prague to London seventy years before. It was magnificently organised and twenty-two of the original children travelled with their families along their previous route, in trains from that era. It was a journey filled with emotion – sadness and yet also joy – because this time their loved ones were with them – families who existed because their parent had escaped the fate so many others had not. After four days crossing Europe on a series of steam trains, they arrived at Liverpool Street station to be greeted by Nicky and a huge waiting crowd. This time, unlike seventy years before when he had been at the station to meet their arrival, they knew who he was. It was an unforgettable experience for everyone involved.

The most recent trip abroad for Nicky was to Prague again in 2011, to the premiere of Matej's latest and – perhaps – final film about Nicky and the Czech Kindertransport. This time there was much less strain for Nicky. He did not have the energy for rushing around and so he met friends, schoolchildren and his 'children' at his hotel next door to the Congress Centre where the film was to be shown. The highlight, apart from meeting his Czech 'children', was a private discussion with ex-President Václav Havel who had been invited by Matej to the premiere, and who sauntered in to see

Nicky, early and without fanfare or attendants. His health now failing, he looked frail but cheerful, and he and Nicky had half an hour where they sat, drank wine and talked. Listening to two modest and unassuming men discussing issues close to their hearts was wonderful, and for Nicky, it was a treat to be able to talk to this man he really admired, without pomp or journalists. Havel's death at the end of that year was a great sadness for Nicky. He truly felt that Havel was one of the very few modern-day politicians who tried to bring an ethical perspective to the fore in his undertakings.

Nicky with ex-President Václav Havel, January 2011
(Courtesy Z. Mináčová)

Since that trip in 2011, outings have been restricted to Britain as Nicky's famous energy began to let him down, making big events too much of a strain. He still loves the idea of a good evening out and manages with the help of friends to visit a pub or cinema, but he acknowledges with great frustration his new limitations. Keeping in touch with family and friends far and near is his main joy, as well as the opportunity for a good discussion about current affairs.

He still, at 104, attends Music Society evenings and the occasional Poetry Society get-together where, if asked, he will read from his copy of *The Merry Tales of Hans Sachs*, a favourite book from childhood and much funnier than those usually covered. His memory has weakened, but he is able to recall his childhood poetry, which he can still recite, bringing out an apposite quote in response to a particular situation. A repetitive unwelcome task will often lead to:

> Yonder see the morning blink:
> The sun is up, and up must I,
> To wash and dress and eat and drink
> And look at things and talk and think
> And work, and God knows why.
> Oh often have I washed and dressed
> And what's to show for all my pain?
> Let me lie abed and rest:
> Ten thousand times I've done my best
> And all's to do again. (A. E. Housman)

And 'There are more things in heaven and earth, Horatio, Than are dreamt of in your philosophy' (*Hamlet*) will roll out whenever the conversation reaches an unknown region. There are many more . . .

Other outings include making an appearance at the annual Maidenhead Abbeyfield AGM, or meetings of other local groups that he supports, from which he may well come home grumbling about the lack of progress on one project or another and the intransigence of those in power over us.

Opera remains an ongoing pleasure that sustains him in old age; this love affair started when he was in Hamburg doing his banking training and attending lots of operas with a friend, while playing their game of getting nearest to the stage. He became familiar with different composers this way and over time grew to love a wide range of styles. A highlight in his life came in 2002 when a musical acquaintance with influence in that sphere offered him a trip to Bayreuth, home of Wagnerian opera. Nicky loves the drama of Wagner's operas, separating with no problem the man and his links to Naziism and anti-Semitism from his music. So he was delighted to go on such a long trip for a chance to sit on the hard benches of Bayreuth to hear *Tannhaüser*, followed by *Das Rheingold*. Two years later he went back for *Parsifal*. He has had even more recent trips to Covent Garden, taken by friends or even one or other of his 'children' who also love the medium. For someone who does not demonstrate emotion easily, he is deeply moved by great emotional arias and he will talk at length with enthusiasm about any number of different operas and hum their well-known highlights to all and sundry.

Another life-long hobby that gives him stimulation in his later years is playing bridge, which he learnt from his mother as a child. He still plays now as often as possible and it is both a social and intellectual activity. Grete wasn't interested in bridge, so he didn't play so much during their married life, but after her death in 1999 it became a regular event, playing with two different groups of friends: his 'ladies' group and his 'men's' group. Until very recently his men's group met at his house every week, drinking a bottle or two of wine, eating some sandwiches and playing all evening.

Talking about the issues of the day will enliven him much more than repeated questions about history. He is very fond of quoting Hegel, in his own paraphrased words: 'The only thing we ever

learn from history is that we never learn anything from history.'
Though he recognises that people are interested in his rescue story,
he doesn't feel that it can teach people to behave well themselves,
even though educational projects using just this story have been
taught successfully in schools in the USA, UK, Czech Republic and
Slovakia and have led children to write moving letters to him about
how his story has inspired them to help others.

He remains close to a number of his 'children' who made
contact following the initial unveiling of the story in 1988, as they
came to discover his role in their lives and wanted to see and thank
him. For many 'children', one meeting was enough to help them
understand that previously unknown part of their history. For
others though, meeting Nicky has led to a long and close
friendship.

One such was Vera Gissing, the first person introduced to him
in the *That's Life!* studio, making that intensely emotional piece of
TV when she put her arms around him and said 'Thank you', both
of them ending up in tears. Having discovered that she had been
living only a ten-minute drive from Nicky and Grete for many
years without either's knowledge, she was soon a regular visitor.
She helped them with the enormous correspondence that soon
built up about the Kindertransport and was co-author of the first
book written about Nicky and the rescued children. Their close
relationship continues to this day. Though Vera is no longer able to
help him due to her own poor health, their mutual affection
remains intact.

Another local 'child', Ruth Drahota, who first met Nicky at the
Freedom of the Borough ceremony in Windsor in 1999, was soon
visiting regularly with her husband Jaroslav and continues to do
so still. Others come from further afield to take him out to a theatre, an opera or a local pub for lunch, while some who are not so
healthy in their old age make do with regular phone calls to check
up on him and share family news.

Some keep in touch from across the world, such as Joe Schlesinger, the distinguished CBC journalist who narrated both of Matej's documentaries about the Czech Kindertransport. Joe's experience as a foster child with his uncle and aunt in England during the war was not a happy one. They did not really want him and his brother, sending them away to school for most of the war years and back to Prague as soon as it was all over. His feeling of being unloved was strengthened on his return to Czechoslovakia. His parents having been murdered in some unknown camp, he felt himself a burden on a country overwhelmed by parentless youngsters, abandoned and rootless. Despite this unpromising start, he ended up in Canada with 'a wonderful family, a job I loved and altogether a great life'.

Describing his discovery of his rescue and his relationship with Nicky, 'Then Nicky and the story of how he had saved my life and that of so many others surfaced. Something in me clicked. Here, finally, there was a father figure, someone who obviously cared deeply for others, a man one could be proud of, a role model to emulate. As I got to know him better, that feeling of respect and love has increased, particularly because in a way it was reciprocated. He seemed to have found in what I had done with my life, an empathetic resonance to his own youthful wanderings. In short, Nicky Winton is and always will be a surrogate for the father I lost in the Holocaust.'

Many others, whose names are listed on those pages taped into the back of the scrapbook, have expressed similar sentiments. Matej, having interviewed so many of them for his two documentaries, did not hesitate to call the last film *Nicky's Family*, because that is what many of them feel themselves to be.

They visit with their own husbands or wives and children, and even grandchildren, and give back to Nicky some of the love and attention that he lost when his darling Grete died. He is always happy to chat, to laugh and to listen to their thoughts, much as he does when his old friends and neighbours drop in.

Visitors who discuss with him their own enterprises or problems will find he is always looking for solutions and encouraging them not to give up, continuing to believe in his old adage: 'If it's not impossible, there must be a way to do it.'

With Joe Schlesinger
(Courtesy Czech Embassy)

# 15

## *Who is Nicholas Winton?*

People often ask Nicky about the secret to his long life. He generally selects from two answers depending on his mood and who's
asking.

The first is: 'Choose the right parents.' I think the science of
genetics would agree with him here.

The second is: 'Keep active.'

He cites an Abbeyfield medical colleague from the 1970s, Dr
Berwick-Wright, who he asked once about health and exercise. He
was told, 'When you are gardening and feel tired and think you
have had enough, do another half an hour.' When he met Berwick-
Wright again, well into his eighties, he reminded the doctor of his
advice and asked him if it remained the same. The answer this
time was, 'Now you are in your eighties, I suggest when you are
gardening and feel tired, you should do only another fifteen
minutes.' Nicky has followed this advice for as long as he could.
Having given up gardening in his late nineties, he still tries to do
just a bit more exercise than he feels able to.

However, I feel there is a third secret to his long life, which was
demonstrated very recently when he fell at the age of 103 and
broke his hip. He was in hospital, in some pain, and the surgeon
and anaesthetist arrived to discuss the operation he needed that
day to replace the hip joint, which had broken. They told me they
would need to ask the usual question regarding resuscitation if his

heart should not outlast the operation. I listened as they solicitously asked him whether, if the worst should happen, he would like them to 'let him slip away peacefully' or whether he wanted them to attempt resuscitation. He looked at them incredulously and retorted, 'Resuscitate me, of course; I want to live!'

There is not now, and never has been, any doubting Nicky's zest for life and urge to go on living whatever his health throws up now, in old age, or during the emotional challenges occurring at intervals through his life. His agnosticism also leads him to consider that now is all he has, with no sense that he will continue in any form of afterlife. This love of life propels him along and leads to complaints if he sees his body letting him down. His health throughout his life has been remarkable, and his first hospital stay that I know of was for his first hip replacement at the age of ninety. Since then, as his health has declined, the complaining has commenced – no stoic acceptance here. He really cannot understand why it can't all just be fixed; there must be a solution to any problem, even physical. This is, of course, the same mindset which led him to run the Czech Kindertransport and more recently the charity work he undertook. He refuses to accept that there is no solution to his final challenge: old age.

I have tried with this biography to record the events of Nicky's life as accurately as possible in order that they will help to answer the questions that many people have asked about him over the years since the Kindertransport story entered the media. The initial questions include: What impelled a twenty-nine-year-old stockbroker to help get children out of Czechoslovakia when others did not? What made him think they were in danger when the government believed there would not be a war?

I hoped that, by looking in detail at his family history and young life, questions of why he was motivated to help and how he had the skills to get the job done would become clear. Early chapters have described how his family background and adolescence gave him a taste for enquiry, a refusal to accept the common view and an acute awareness of the threat from the Nazis. His early experiences also engendered in him the sense of being European rather than parochially English alongside an empathy for the underdog. His schooling encouraged him to follow his own interests and convictions and to believe in himself as well as augmenting his moral impetus to help others in need. His banking and stock exchange career developed his confidence in his own abilities despite demonstrating that his motivations and ethics did not always chime with those in authority over him. Stockbroking also forged his aptitude for organisation and management of fast-moving situations, while keeping a cool head.

His burgeoning social conscience led him into left-wing politics where he was dazzled by passionate and committed men and women dedicating their lives to causes they believed in. This alliance cultivated and deepened his insight into the political transformations occurring across Europe to the degree that he felt he understood the dangers of Hitler's ambition more than his own government did, and made him unable to swallow the reassurances of the British government that there would be 'peace in our time'.

A third question asked over and over in all the articles written on the Kindertransport is: Why did he keep this act a secret for fifty years afterwards? Many attempt to answer it by suggesting it was down to modesty and a refusal to boast about his deeds.

This question itself can be shown to be untrue. The rescue operation is listed in his *curriculum vitae* at various times, he talked about it occasionally to like-minded friends, and his view that his scrapbook of the rescue must hold some interest for some organisation or another led to him attempting, over many years, to find it a home before it finally came to fruition through Elizabeth Maxwell. As with many others who lived through those dark years, he was intent on looking forward, not back, and facing the challenges of the present. His frequent paraphrasing of Hegel's quote – 'We learn from history that we do not learn from history' – is in response to people constantly telling him that the past must be studied so mistakes are not repeated. His more blunt comments have been given many times; one such was, 'People are always talking about the past, the past. But the past doesn't mean a thing to me.'

I think this is probably an exaggeration of his true feelings that is given in response to those who urge him to review his pre-war history over and over. There's no doubt, though, that he certainly prefers to look forward, to discuss current issues, both on a world and a personal scale, and worry about what is happening now, not what happened previously.

What is true is that neither he, nor the rest of us who were shown the scrapbook in the years before 1988, recognised the magnitude of what was contained in the book and the rescue itself. It took the meetings with those directly involved – the children themselves – to demonstrate the enormous impact the historical deed had made on so many lives. No one had foreseen the impact on those, now adult, rescued 'children' of discovering finally, after so long, how exactly they had escaped their family's fate and who was responsible. For many it was a complete shock and brought out a tidal wave of suppressed emotions.

Dave Lux, a rescued 'child' now living in California, struggled to describe his reaction in Matej's film, *Nicky's Family*: 'A lady asked my name, and I said Pinkasovic. When I saw my name and my brother's name printed in this (list) . . . the biggest shock of my life . . . I couldn't speak, I couldn't breathe, I had goosebumps all up my arms. All these years . . . fifty years . . .' and he tails off, overcome with his recollection.

Vera Gissing, interviewed in the same film, said, 'Nobody knew who had masterminded our rescue. Then I was asked to take part in a TV show, *That's Life!*, where to my joy and such fulfilment, I came face to face with the man who saved my life.'

It was hearing these responses over and over that made clear how this relatively short, though intense, episode in Nicky's life was without doubt the most effective and significant deed undertaken in a life full of charitable action.

My second reason for writing this biography was to show the whole person and not just the myth described in articles about his bravery, heroism and humility. Hopefully by describing Nicky's family and work life's ups and downs, it can be seen that though he is obviously a warm-hearted, determined and enthusiastic figure, he is not free from some negative traits. His ability to elicit love and devotion in friends and those he helps can sometimes be matched by a capacity to induce discomfort, irritation and even dislike in those who may not support the same goals, and who he may trample over in order to get his schemes accomplished. His focus on his own schemes can also lead to others feeling that their views and lives are of less interest to him than his own.

The idea that he retired early due to his business successes is overturned with the realisation that most of his married life was spent rather short of money, rather than comfortable, at times borrowing money from friends to keep afloat. He is described by some as unassuming, a quiet modest person, while at the same time others attest to his sharp wit and love of jokes. Both facets are there in his behaviour, depending on the circumstances he finds himself in. Being a child of the post-Victorian era, he learnt to behave modestly when necessary and to respect authority.

Other friends and colleagues have told anecdotes that demonstrate his wilful refusal to do what is expected and sometimes even to break the rules. Sometimes this is for noble causes, as in the Kindertransport, but it can equally be out of a sense of mischief for which he is well known or that he just doesn't feel the rule is sensible.

His law-abiding nature and respect for authority one instant will, the next minute, be overturned by other pressing motives.

Despite his slowing memory and abilities, he can still catch people unaware with a snappy quip. His quick-fire retorts have caused much hilarity all his life and he is still able to produce them out of thin air. His latest, on discussing whether they should wear evening dress to an opera he was attending with his friend Richard, being, 'My only evening dress these days is pyjamas.'

When I recently asked Nicky what he would like the biography to say (I am sure this breaks the first rule of biography writing, but what the heck!), he said, 'I think it should show my history with religion – from Jewish to Christian to agnostic, and the fact that I came to believe through my life that what is important is that we live by the common ethics of all religions – kindness, decency, love, respect and honour for others – and not worry about the aspects within religion that divide us.' This is the message that he likes to drive home whenever he is asked for his opinion about anything these days.

His parents, though Jewish by race, were not in any way religious and they did not teach their children any Jewish rules or rituals, despite socialising with many German-Jewish families in London. Their social group seemed to be bound together by shared history and class, rather than for religious reasons. I suspect that having their children baptised was not a religious act, as much as a social statement of conforming to the British way of life. There is no objective evidence that his parents themselves became Christian or attended church. They supported his wish to be confirmed at school, but again there is no sense that this was from their own religious belief.

Though religion left his life as war began, his love of people and his impulse to help those he met who were in need did not diminish and remained a major motivation throughout his life. The dialogue he had with Hugo Marom regarding Hugo's attempt to have Nicky recognised by Yad Vashem as a 'Righteous Gentile' in 1990 demonstrates his uneasiness about the attempts to be labelled one thing or another. 'I very much appreciate your efforts with Yad Vashem on my behalf. What you are asking them is something I really neither want nor think I deserve. Many more did more than I and it is really only by chance that after this lapse of over fifty years that my name has become known in connection with the children. May I also say what I already told you in Tel Aviv – that I set out to rescue CHILDREN. Under the conditions at the time there were naturally a preponderance of Jewish children, but nevertheless ten per cent [it was actually fifteen per cent] of the children on my transports were in danger from the Nazis but were not Jews.

'On top of all this is my own position about which I wrote you some time ago. Having been brought up as a Christian, I know next to nothing of the Jewish Religion. Obviously I myself had no say whatsoever in being baptised as a baby. However, most or maybe all the Jews might well consider me Jewish – Hitler would have done. This puts you all in a difficult position vis-à-vis me, as this is difficult territory even for the Jews! Even if Yad Vashem thought me in every way entitled to the honour you suggest, they might well stumble over this point and if they did not stumble they might well be criticised by others for not stumbling.

'Well, we . . . can discuss this in greater detail. May I say, this feeling of falling between two stools is one I've had on numerous occasions in my life, but all this exposure because of the "children" has brought it very much to the front and I can't say that I find it comfortable.'

This letter indicates again the confusion of identity Nicky has always felt. He had left behind the German, Jewish, Christian labels he had been bound to in his childhood. As he grew up and for most of his life, he felt himself to be truly English, agnostic and socialist. With questions thrust on him after 1988, about his motivations and the place his family background had in his later actions, he began to wonder himself who he truly was. However, it has never been his nature to go in for deep psychological analysis; he is, after all, a practical man rather than a philosopher. He may consider these issues when the subject is raised, but they will never stop him sleeping at night. I think that the right place to leave my exploration of my delightful, determined, self-centred and exasperating father is to accept his own labels for himself – an Englishman and an agnostic – and add one given him by others: a humanitarian.

Nicky and me on his 103rd birthday

# Acknowledgements

This book could not have been written without the support and assistance of many people. First of all, I need to thank my father, Nicholas Winton, for patiently allowing me to interview him repeatedly, over a prolonged period of time, and for letting me pillage his study to examine the diaries, letters, documents and photographs that he has kept throughout his life. Secondly, much gratitude is due to my family: Stephen, Laurence and Holly Watson for their support, encouragement and feedback, which kept me going when I faltered. Thanks also to Magda Šebestová and Mike Levy for spurring me on and helping to get this book across the final hurdles, to Joe Bidder and Hilary Porter for reading the manuscript and giving the constructive feedback I needed to finish, and to Christine Lawson and Sam Llewellyn for their early encouragement and advice.

In the course of my research, I spoke to many people from my father's life who co-operated generously with their memories and anecdotes. I hope I have remembered them all and apologies to anyone I may have left out. Thanks go to family near and far: Nick Winton, Andrew Winton, Anne Hollings, John Wortham, Mandy Curry, Karin Carruth; to friends: Sheila Fontaine, David Cager, Esther Rantzen, Airlie Holden-Hindley, Cliff Hillman, Valerie Bosley, Kirsty Findlay, Beth Powell, Matilda Bradley, Ann Lovell, Babs Armstrong, Nick Abrey, Richard Baker, Mark Lovell, Michael Roberts, Rudi Sheldon, David Peterson, Randell Moll, Dirk Ippen,

Jac Skelt; and to Nicky's 'children': Ruth Drahota, Vera Gissing, Joe Schlesinger, Milena Grenfell-Baines, Susanne Medas, Ruth Federmann, Judith Hawkins and Alf Dubs.

Other information, help and photos were kindly given by Matej Mináč, Zuzana Mináčová, Peter Needham, Charles Chadwick, Henry Warriner and Dan Hawkins. Some information regarding the Czech Kindertransport was derived from, or double-checked, using the following sources: William Chadwick's *The Rescue of the Prague Refugees 1938–39*, Doreen Warriner's memoir *Winter In Prague*, Karen Gershon's *We Came as Children*, Muriel Emanuel and Vera Gissing's *Nicholas Winton and the Rescued Generation* and Barry Turner's *And The Policeman Smiled*.

Family picture 1998 L–R: standing Nick, Barbara, Stephen, seated Laurence, Grete, Nicky, Holly (Courtesy S. Fontaine)